Volume Tw

MW01691375

Sadlier Math

Catherine D. LeTourneau

Allan E. Bellman, Ph.D.

Jill A. Perry, Ph.D.

Sadlier School

The Publisher of *Progress in Mathematics*

Program Reviewers

The publisher wishes to thank for their comments and suggestions the following teachers and administrators, who read portions of the series prior to publication.

Marcia J. Phillips
Curriculum Director/Assistant Principal
Happy Valley School-Peoria
Peoria, Arizona

Lynn M. LeTourneau
Principal
Our Lady of Charity
Cicero, Illinois

Esther Park
Teacher, Grade 4
Saint Columbkille Partnership School
Brighton, Massachusetts

Lisa A. Nelson, Ph.D.
Assistant Principal
St. Vincent de Paul School
Omaha, Nebraska

Kimberly N. Stevenson
Principal
Holy Trinity Catholic School
McKees Rocks, Pennsylvania

Elizabeth Snow
Principal
Sacred Heart Cathedral School
Pensacola, Florida

Jane Carrillo
Teacher, Kindergarten
St. Leo School
Versailles, Kentucky

Molly Schwaiger
Academic Director
Partnership Academy
Richfield, Minnesota

Barbara Jones
Mathematics Department Chair
Rumson Country Day School
Rumson, New Jersey

Jodie L. Dawe
Teacher, Grade 3
Christopher Elementary School
Christopher, Illinois

Judy Helton
Teacher, Grade 2
St. Leo School
Versailles, Kentucky

Dr. Jeanne Gearon
Principal
Our Lady of Lourdes Catholic School
Saint Louis, Missouri

Theresa Hurst
Teacher, Grade 2
St. Martin de Porres Marianist School
Uniondale, New York

Chad Riley, Ph.D.
Principal
St. Joseph Catholic School
Arlington, Texas

Cover Series Design: Silver Linings Studios

Photo Credits

Cover: Fotolia.com/Scanrail: *bottom*; Getty Images/Fred Smith: *top*.

Interior: Alamy Stock Photo/Sergey Borisov: 561, 562; Iulia Timchenko: 577, 579; JG Photography: 375, 376; Value: 591, 592. Dreamstime.com/ Floralena: 405, 406; Olga Kostenko: 330 *background*, 376 *background*, 406 *background*, 452 *background*, 482 *background*, 532 *background*, 562 *background*, 592 *background*. Getty Images/AzmanL: 373; Panoramic Images: 481, 482; phototropic: 531, 532. iStockphoto.com/carterdayne: 451, 452. Shutterstock.com/Susan Leggett: 589; Lludmyla Soloviova: 329, 330. United States coin images from the United States Mint.

Illustrators

Bob Holt, Scott Borroughs, Sarah Beise, Nathan Jarvis, Jose Ramos, Joseph Taylor. Shutterstock.com/Agor2012, incredible_movements, miniaria, whanwhan.ai, Zmiter.

® is a registered trademark of William H. Sadlier, Inc.

Printed in the United States of America.
ISBN: 978-1-4217-8991-0
4 5 6 7 8 9 10 WEBC 25 24 23 22 21

For additional online resources, go to SadlierConnect.com.

Welcome to Sadlier Math

Dear First Grader,

Do you know why math is important? Well, we all use math every day. We use it when we:

- cook
- read a clock
- plant a garden
- describe objects
- take a survey
- and much more!

Throughout this book are special signs and symbols. When you see them, be sure to stop and look.

Objective This is what you will be studying in the lesson.

Math Words Look at these words. They are important words for the lesson.

Problem Solving Get ready to use math in the real world.

Write About It This is a question or idea for you to write about.

PRACTICE These are exercises for you to show what you know.

MORE PRACTICE These are exercises to help you better understand the math you are learning.

HOMEWORK These are exercises for you to do at home.

We wrote this book just for you!

The Authors

Contents

Volume One Chapters 1–8

Volume Two Chapters 9–16

Chapter 1 Addition Facts and Strategies Within 10

The upper part of your book's front cover shows an old steam-powered train. The first steam train was built by Richard Trevithick of Great Britain. It made its first journey in 1804.

Chapter 2 More Addition Within 10

Chapter 3 Subtraction Facts and Strategies Within 10

Chapter 4 Addition and Subtraction Relationships Within 10

Chapter 5 Measurement: Length

Steam trains were common in the United States until the mid-1900s. The fastest steam train could travel 126 miles per hour, but most steam trains were much slower.

Chapter 6 Place Value to 100

Chapter 7 Place Value to 120

Chapter 8 Addition Facts Within 20

Chapter 9 Subtraction Facts Within 20

Chapter 10 Data and Graphical Displays

Steam trains were later replaced by trains powered by diesel fuel or electricity. The bottom part of your front cover shows a modern high-speed electric train.

Chapter 11 Addition: Two-Digit Numbers

Chapter 12 Subtraction: Two-Digit Numbers

Electric trains can travel much faster than steam trains. Some electric trains can reach speeds of over 200 miles per hour. Electric trains also don't pollute the air.

Chapter 13 Geometry

Chapter 14 Equal Shares

Chapter 15 Time

The fastest train in the world is currently the Shanghai Maglev in China. It has a top speed of almost 270 miles per hour. Instead of wheels, the Shanghai Maglev uses magnets to float above the tracks without touching them.

Chapter 16 Money

Subtraction Facts Within 20

CHAPTER 9

Bicycling is a way that people can travel. Bicycling instead of driving can help keep the air clean. It can also reduce traffic. Bicycling is a healthy way to exercise.

By the Numbers

- Bicycle sizes are 13 inches to 23 inches.
- Most people who ride bicycles can go about 10 miles in an hour.

What You Can Do

- Go on a bicycle ride with family or friends.
- Always obey safe bicycling rules.
- Ride your bicycle to get exercise.

Dear Family,

In this chapter, we will be learning about subtraction facts within 20.

Here are the Key **Math Words** for this chapter:

add	**equal sign**
subtract	**true**
fact family	**false**

You can use the glossary to check out the definition of each word and help your child make flash cards to study each day we work on the lessons for this chapter.

During the Chapter Opener and Performance Assessment, we will also be making STEAM connections about the benefits of bicycling. Read the opening to the chapter together and discuss the **By the Numbers** and **What You Can Do** statements.

Keep Your Skills Sharp

Here is a **Keep Your Skills Sharp** activity to do at home to prepare for this chapter.

Ask your child to tell a story that involves subtraction within 20. Provide prompts to help your child get started. Have your child draw a picture to model the story. Talk about ways we use subtraction in everyday situations.

Name ____________________

Objective

- Make 10 to subtract from numbers greater than 10.

Math Word

subtract

Make 10 to Subtract

Annie has 14 pennies. She uses 6 pennies. How many pennies does Annie have left?

You can make a 10 to subtract.

Subtract 14 − 6.

Start with 14. Break apart 6.

14 − 6 = ?

14 − 4 − 2 = ?

Subtract 4 to make 10.

14 − 4 − 2 = ?

10 − 2 = ?

Then subtract 2 more.

10 − 2 = 8

Annie has 8 pennies left.

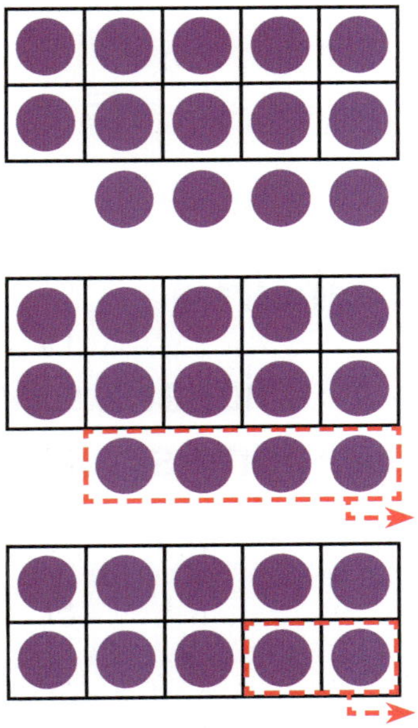

PRACTICE

Make a 10 and then subtract.
Use a ten-frame and counters to help.

1. 17 − 8 = ?

17 − __7__ − __1__ = ?

10 − __1__ = __9__

So, 17 − 8 = __9__.

2. 16 − 9 = ?

16 − ____ − ____ = ?

10 − ____ = ____

So, 16 − 9 = ____.

PRACTICE

Make a 10 and then subtract.
Use a ten-frame and counters to help.

3. $15 - 6 = ?$

15 – 5 – 1 = 9

4. $17 - 9 = ?$

17 – ____ – ____ = ____

5. $13 - 5 = ?$

____ – ____ – ____ = ____

6. $14 - 8 = ?$

____ – ____ – ____ = ____

Problem Solving

7. Ellen has 15 stickers. She gives 7 stickers away. How many stickers does she have left? Draw a picture to show how you know.

Ellen has ____ stickers left.

Write About It

8. If you had to tell a friend how to break apart numbers to make a 10 and solve 13 – 7, what would you say? Use words or pictures.

____

____

Name ______________________________

Make 10 to Subtract

You can make a 10 and then subtract.

Subtract 14 − 6.

Start with 14. Break apart 6.

14 − 6 = ?

14 − 4 − 2 = ?

Subtract 4 to make 10.

14 − 4 − 2 = ?

10 − 2 = ?

Then subtract 2 more.

10 − 2 = 8

So, 14 − 6 = 8.

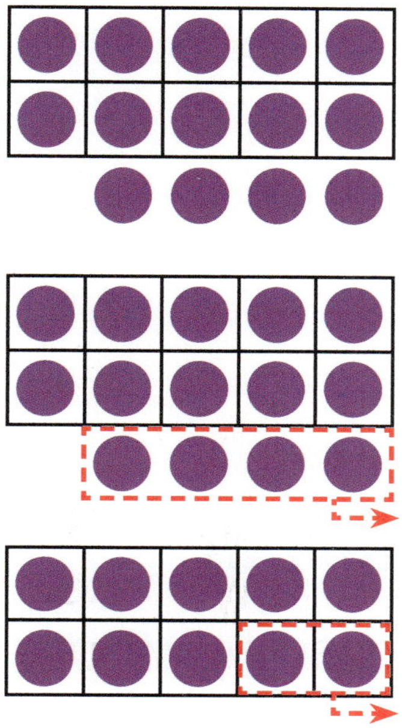

MORE PRACTICE

Make a 10 and then subtract.
Use a ten-frame and counters to help.

1. 16 − 7 = ?

16 − 6 − 1 = ?

10 − 1 = 9

So, 16 − 7 = 9.

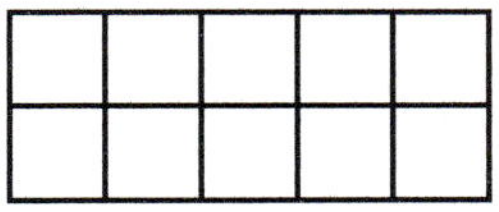

2. 13 − 8 = ?

13 − _____ − _____ = ?

10 − _____ = _____

So, 13 − 8 = _____.

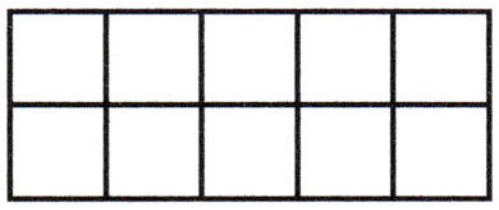

HOMEWORK

Make a 10 and then subtract.
Draw a ten-frame and counters to help.

1. $14 - 6 = ?$

$14 - \underline{4} - \underline{2} = ?$

$10 - \underline{2} = \underline{8}$

So, $14 - 6 = \underline{8}$.

2. $12 - 7 = ?$

$12 - \_\_\_ - \_\_\_ = ?$

$10 - \_\_\_ = \_\_\_$

So, $12 - 7 = \_\_\_$.

Problem Solving

3. Circle the answer with the Make 10 strategy.

Evan:

$13 - 7 = ?$

$13 - 2 - 5 = ?$

$11 - 5 = 6$

So, $13 - 7 = 6$.

Gene:

$13 - 7 = ?$

$13 - 3 - 4 = ?$

$10 - 4 = 6$

So, $13 - 7 = 6$.

Write About It

4. Explain why you cannot make 10 to subtract $18 - 2$.

____

____

Name ______________________________

Subtract from 11 and 12

Objective

- Use subtraction facts to subtract from 11 and 12.

Math Words

subtraction fact
difference

Devon has 11 marbles.
He gives 5 marbles away.

Albert has 12 marbles.
He gives 5 marbles away.

How many marbles does each friend have left?

You can use other subtraction facts to help you find differences.

Devon's Marbles

$11 - 5 = ?$

$10 - 5 = 5$

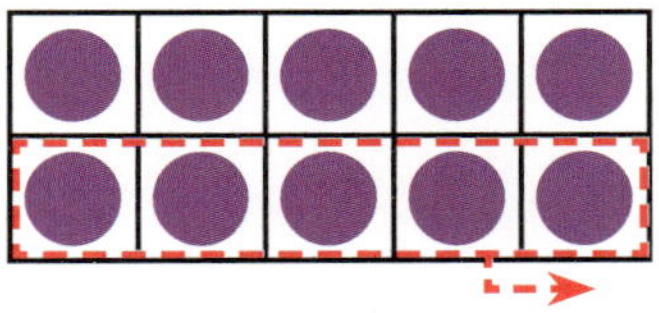

11 is 1 more than 10.

$11 - 5$ is 1 more than $10 - 5$.

So, $11 - 5 = 6$.

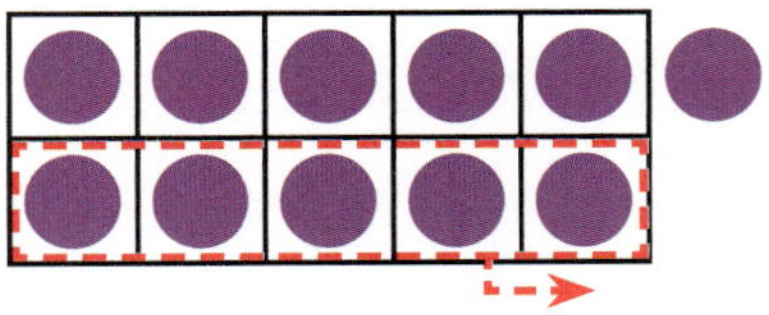

Devon has 6 marbles left.

Albert's Marbles

$12 - 5 = ?$

$10 - 5 = 5$

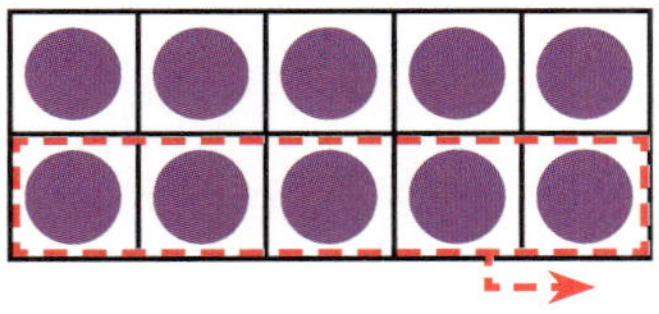

12 is 2 more than 10.

$12 - 5$ is 2 more than $10 - 5$.

So, $12 - 5 = 7$.

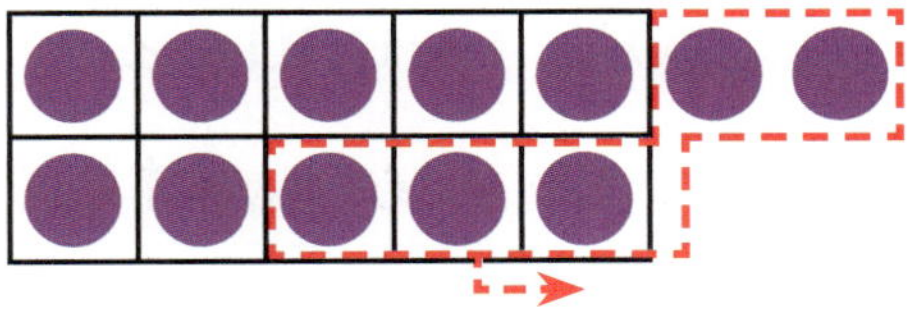

Albert has 7 marbles left.

PRACTICE

Write the difference.

1. 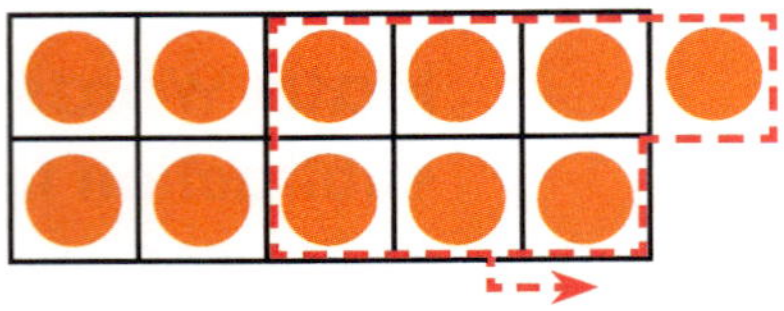

11 − 7 = 4

2. 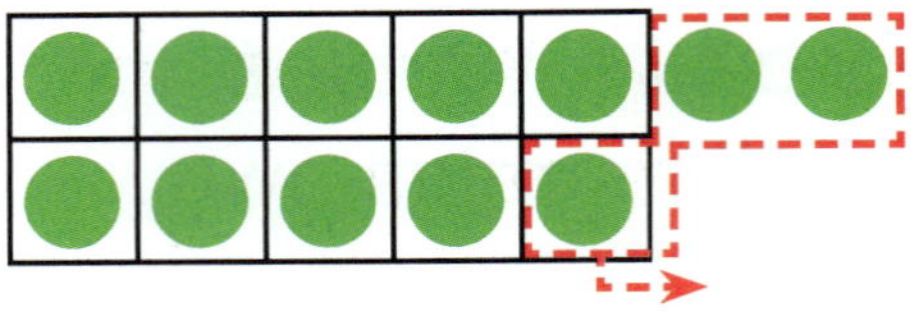

12 − 3 = ____

Problem Solving

Use a strategy to find the difference.

3. Claire has 11 grapes. She gives 9 grapes to her friend. How many grapes does Claire have left? Draw a picture to show the strategy you used.

Claire has ____ grapes left.

Write About It

4. Explain how using a 10 strategy can help you subtract from 11 and 12.

____

____

____

Name ______________________________

Subtract from 11 and 12

You can use other subtraction facts to help you find differences.

11 − 5 = ?

10 − 5 = 5

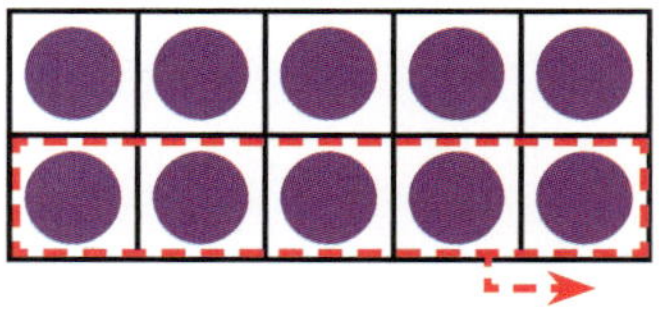

11 is 1 more than 10.

11 − 5 is 1 more than 10 − 5.

So, 11 − 5 = 6.

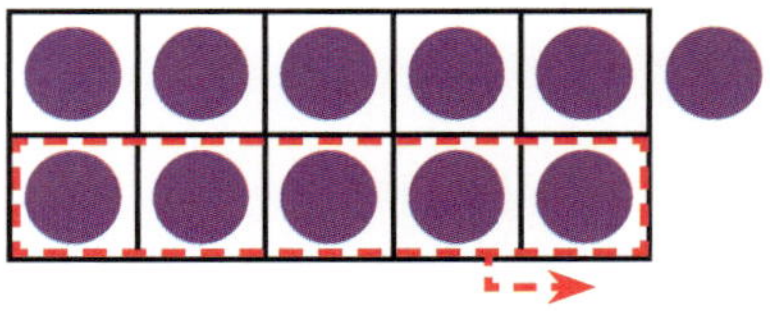

12 − 5 = ?

10 − 5 = 5

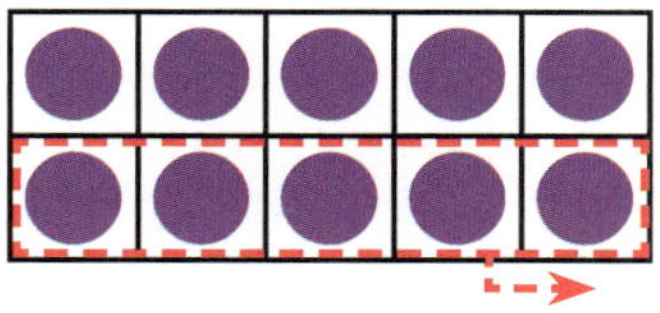

12 is 2 more than 10.

12 − 5 is 2 more than 10 − 5.

So, 12 − 5 = 7.

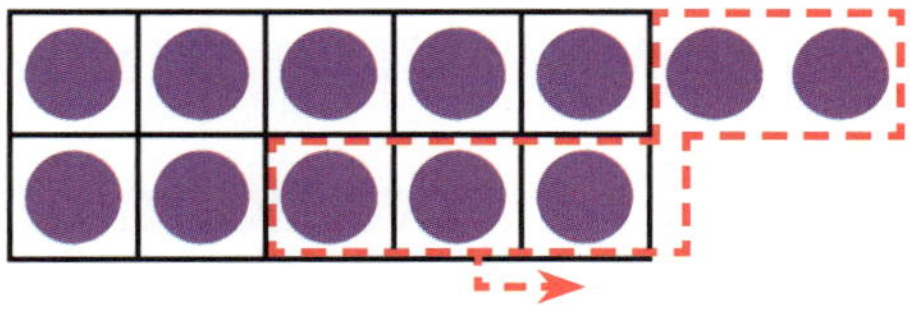

MORE PRACTICE

Write the difference.

1. 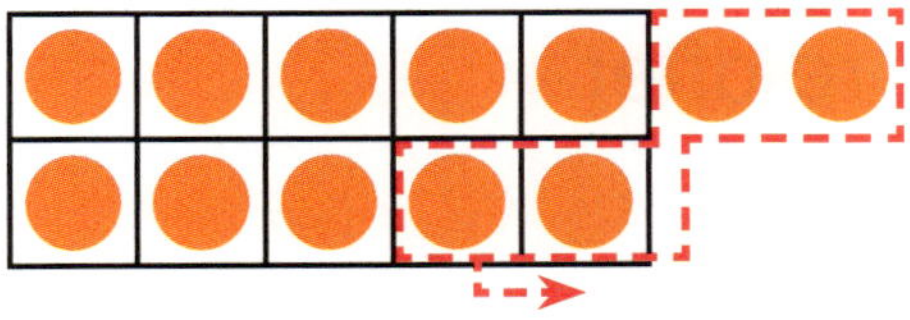

12 − 4 = ____

2. 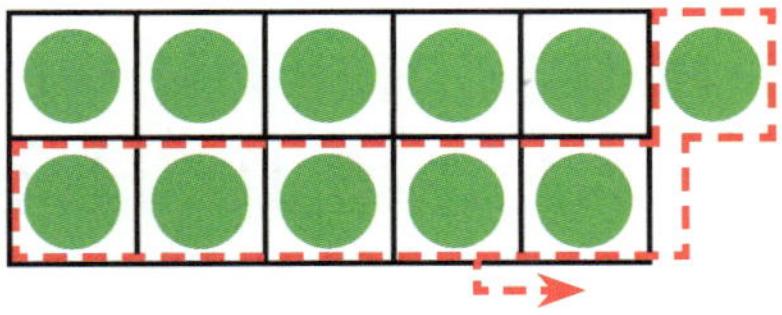

11 − 6 = ____

HOMEWORK

Write the difference.

1.

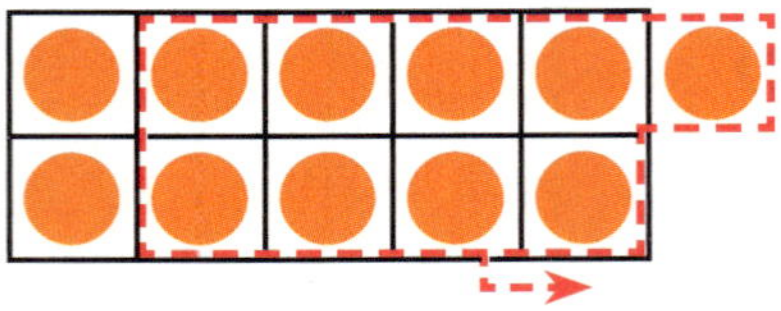

$$\begin{array}{r} 11 \\ -\ 9 \\ \hline \end{array}$$

2.

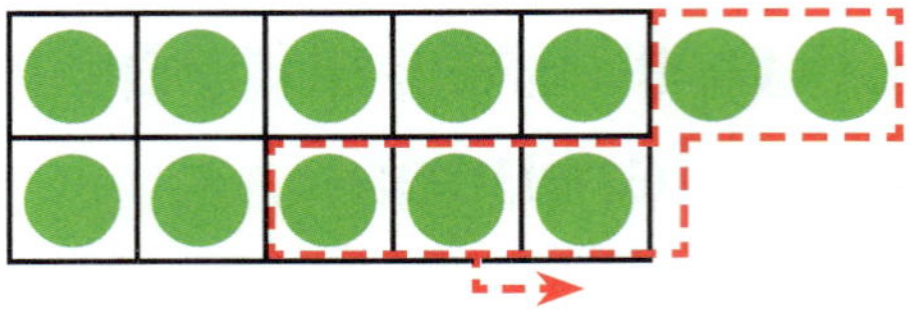

$$\begin{array}{r} 12 \\ -\ 5 \\ \hline \end{array}$$

Problem Solving

Use a strategy to find the difference.

3. Amelia has 11 crackers. Her sister eats 4 of them. How many crackers are left? Draw a picture to show what strategy you used.

   There are ____ crackers left.

Write About It

4. For "1 more than 10," you add 1 more after subtracting from 10. How is the strategy "2 more than 10" different?

   ____

   ____

Name ______________________________

Objective
- Subtract from 13 and 14.

Math Words
whole
part
subtract

Subtract from 13 and 14

Tegan has 14 shirts. 7 shirts are white.
How many shirts are not white?

Subtract:
whole − part = part

14 − 7 = ?

14 − 7 = 7

Add to check:
part + part = whole

7 + 7 = 14

7 shirts are not white.

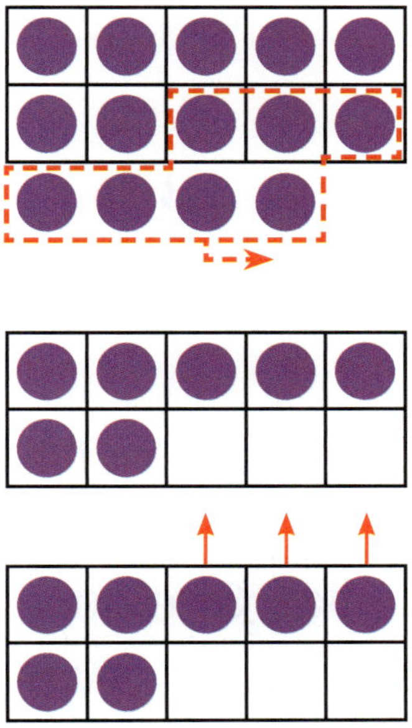

Think
What is the whole?
What is the known part?

PRACTICE

Subtract. Add to check.

1.

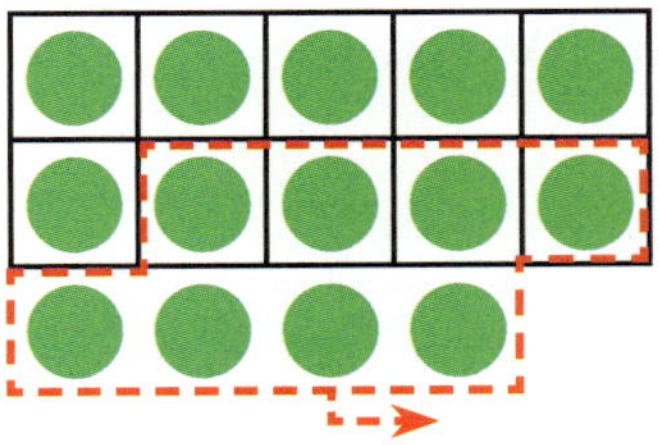

14 − 8 = 6

6 + 8 = 14

2.

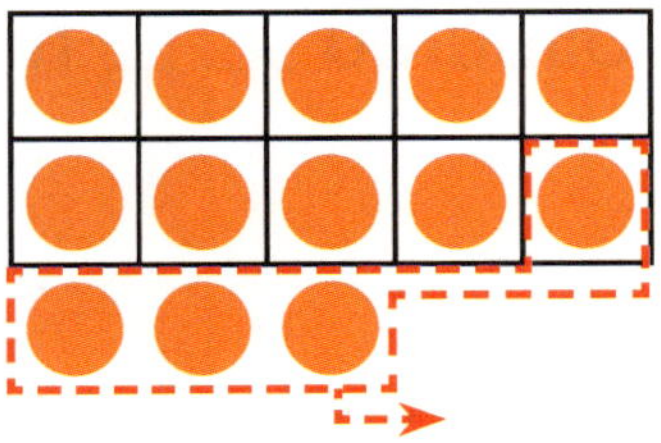

$$\begin{array}{r} 13 \\ -\ 4 \\ \hline \end{array} \qquad \underline{+\quad\quad}$$

PRACTICE

Subtract. Add to check.
Use ten-frames and counters to help.

3. $14 - 6 =$ ____

____ + ____ = ____

4. $13 - 7 =$ ____

____ + ____ = ____

5. $14 - 9 =$ ____

____ + ____ = ____

6. $\begin{array}{r} 14 \\ -\ 5 \\ \hline \end{array}$ $\quad + \underline{\quad}$

7. $\begin{array}{r} 13 \\ -\ 8 \\ \hline \end{array}$ $\quad + \underline{\quad}$

8. $\begin{array}{r} 13 \\ -\ 6 \\ \hline \end{array}$ $\quad + \underline{\quad}$

Problem Solving

9. Rachel went on a hike. She collected 14 stones and 9 leaves. How many more stones did she collect than leaves?
Use the strategy Make 10 to subtract.

____ − ____ − ____ = ?

____ − ____ = ____

Rachel collected ____ more stones than leaves.

Write About It

10. Write a math story about subtracting from 13 or 14. Show how you can add to check the answer.

____

____

Name ______________________

LESSON 9-3

Subtract from 13 and 14

First, subtract from the whole.
Then add the parts to check.

Subtract:
whole − part = part

14 − 7 = ?

14 − 7 = 7

Add to check:
part + part = whole

7 + 7 = 14

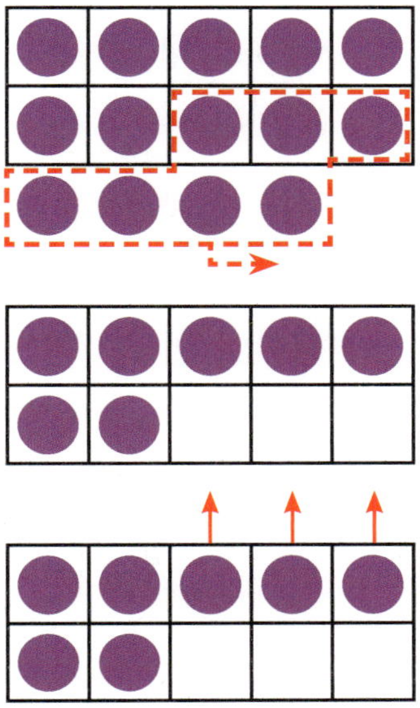

Think
What is the whole?
What is the known part?

MORE PRACTICE

Subtract. Add to check.

1.

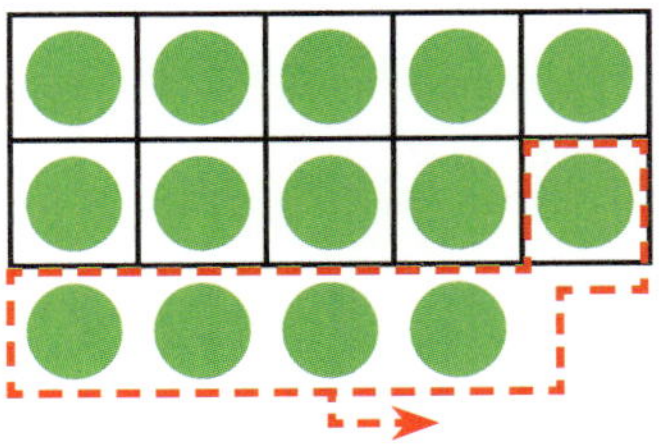

14 − 5 = 9

9 + 5 = 14

2.

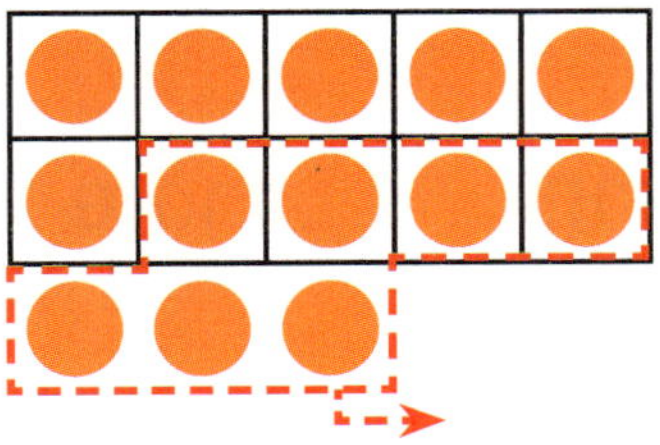

$$\begin{array}{r} 13 \\ -\ \ 7 \\ \hline \end{array} \qquad \begin{array}{r} \\ + \quad \\ \hline \end{array}$$

3.

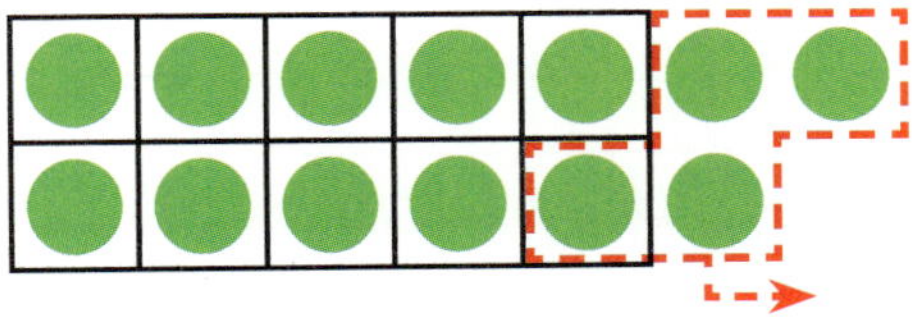

13 − 4 = ____

____ + ____ = ____

HOMEWORK

Find the difference. Add to check.

1.
$$\begin{array}{r} 14 \\ -\ \ 6 \\ \hline 8 \end{array} \qquad \begin{array}{r} \boxed{8} \\ +\ \boxed{6} \\ \hline 14 \end{array}$$

2.
$$\begin{array}{r} 13 \\ -\ \ 9 \\ \hline \end{array} \qquad \begin{array}{r} \boxed{} \\ +\ \boxed{} \\ \hline \end{array}$$

3.
$$\begin{array}{r} 14 \\ -\ \ 7 \\ \hline \end{array} \qquad \begin{array}{r} \boxed{} \\ +\ \boxed{} \\ \hline \end{array}$$

4. 13 − 7 = ____

____ + ____ = ____

5. 13 − 5 = ____

____ + ____ = ____

Problem Solving

6. Jake paints 13 birdhouses red. He paints 7 yellow. How many more does he paint red than yellow? Use the strategy Make 10 to subtract.

13 − ____ − ____ = ____

10 − ____ = ____

Jake paints ____ more red birdhouses.

Write About It

7. Subtract 9 from 14. Tell how to use a whole and parts to subtract and then check your answer.

____

____

CHAPTER 9
Check Your Progress

Name ____________________

Find the correct answer.

1. Make a 10 to solve.

   $15 - 6 = ?$

   $15 -$ ____ $=$ ____

   $10 -$ ____ $=$ ____

   So, $15 - 6 =$ ____.

2. Make a 10 to solve.

   $17 - 9 = ?$

   $17 -$ ____ $=$ ____

   $10 -$ ____ $=$ ____

   So, $17 - 9 =$ ____.

3. Subtract. You can use the ten-frame and draw counters to help.

   $11 - 8 = ?$

   A. 2
   B. 3
   C. 4
   D. 5

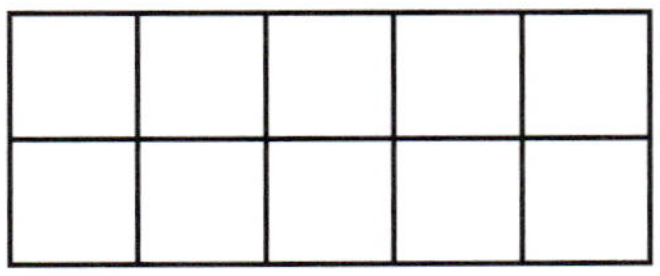

4. Subtract. You can use the ten-frame and draw counters to help.

   $12 - 6 = ?$

   A. 4
   B. 5
   C. 6
   D. 7

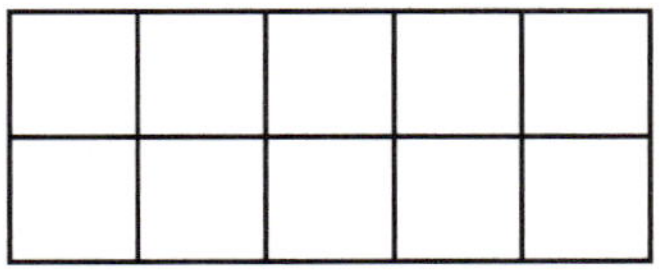

5. Subtract.

   $11 - 4 =$ ____

6. Subtract.

   $12 - 5 =$ ____

Find the correct answer.

7. Make a 10 to solve.

$14 - 5 = ?$

$14 -$ ____ $=$ ____

$10 -$ ____ $=$ ____

So, $14 - 5 =$ ____.

8. Make a 10 to solve.

$12 - 3 = ?$

$12 -$ ____ $=$ ____

$10 -$ ____ $=$ ____

So, $12 - 3 =$ ____.

9. Subtract. You can use the ten-frame and draw counters to help.

$14 - 3 = ?$

A. 10
B. 11
C. 12
D. 13

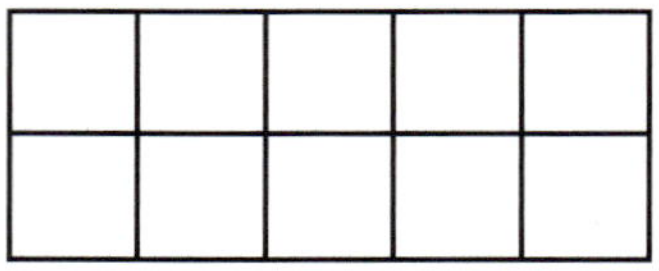

10. Subtract. You can use the ten-frame and draw counters to help.

$13 - 6 = ?$

A. 5
B. 6
C. 7
D. 9

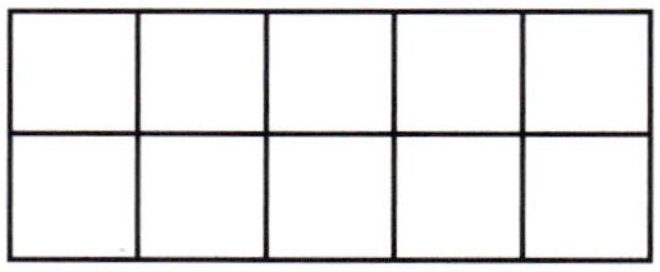

11. Subtract. You can use the ten-frame and draw counters to help.

$12 - 4 =$ ____

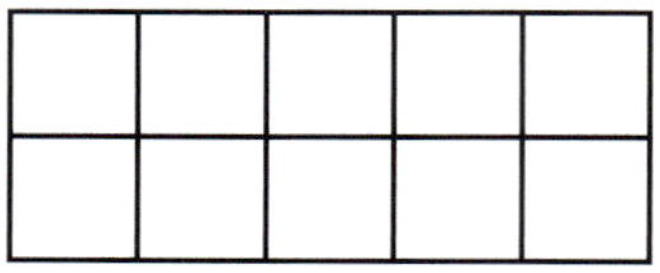

12. Subtract. You can use the ten-frame and draw counters to help.

$14 - 7 =$ ____

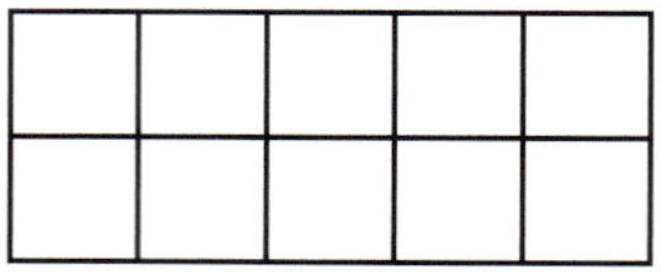

Name ______________________________

LESSON 9-4

Objective

- Subtract from 16 or less.

Math Words

whole

part

Subtract from 16 or Less

Sadie has 16 beads.
She uses 9 beads to make a bracelet.
How many beads does she have left?

Subtract:
whole − part = part

16 − 9 = ?

16 − 9 = 7

Add to check:
part + part = whole

7 + 9 = 16

Circle the part taken away.

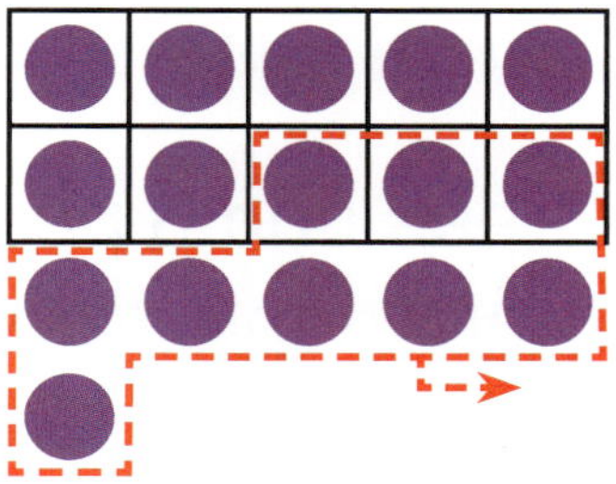

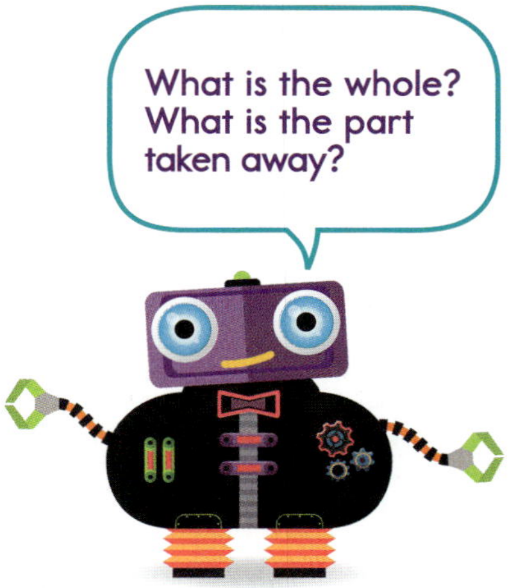

Sadie has 7 beads left.

PRACTICE

Draw counters for the whole.
Circle the part taken away. Subtract.

1. $\begin{array}{r} 16 \\ -\ 7 \\ \hline 9 \end{array}$

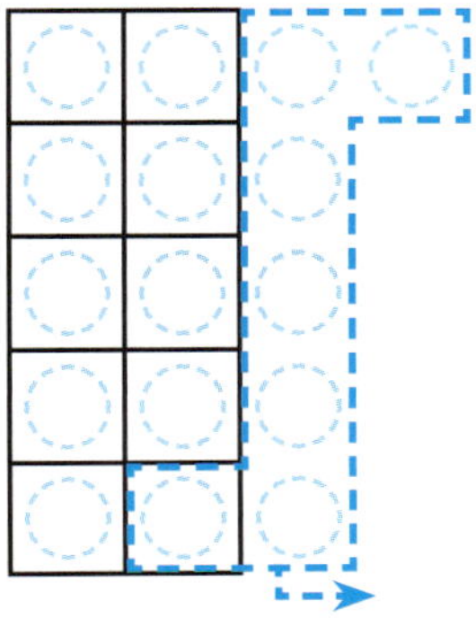

2. 15 − 6 = ____

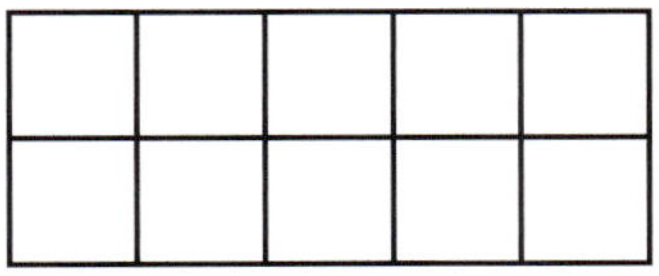

PRACTICE

Subtract. Use a ten-frame and counters to help.

3. 15 − 9 = ____

4. 13 − 5 = ____

5.
```
  16
−  9
----
```

6.
```
  15
−  6
----
```

7.
```
  13
−  9
----
```

Problem Solving

8. There are 15 apple trees and 8 peach trees on a farm. How many more apple trees are there? First, circle the part taken away to subtract. Then check using Make 10.

Subtract ____ and then subtract ____ more:

15 − 5 − ____ = ____

There are ____ more apple trees.

Write About It

9. Write a math story about subtracting from 16. Tell how you take away a part from the whole.

____

____

____

Name ____________________

Subtract from 16 or Less

What is the whole? What is the part taken away?

Subtract:

whole − part = part

16 − 9 = ?

16 − 9 = 7

Circle the part taken away.

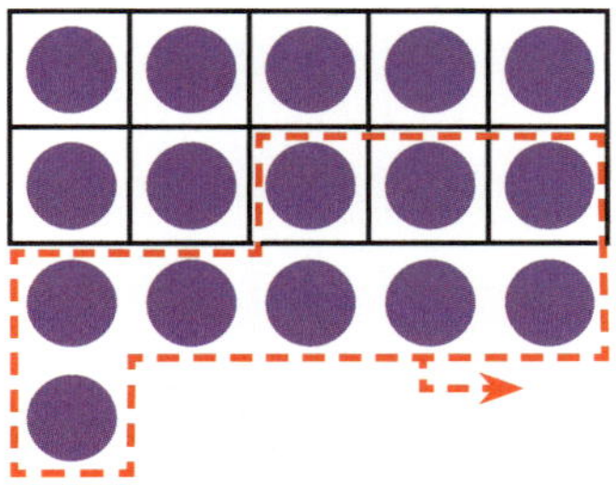

MORE PRACTICE

Draw counters for the whole.
Circle the part taken away. Subtract.

1. $\begin{array}{r} 15 \\ -\ 6 \\ \hline \end{array}$

2. $\begin{array}{r} 16 \\ -\ 9 \\ \hline \end{array}$

3. 14 − 8 = ____

4. 16 − 7 = ____

HOMEWORK

Draw counters for the whole.
Circle the part taken away. Subtract.

1. 14 − 7 = ____

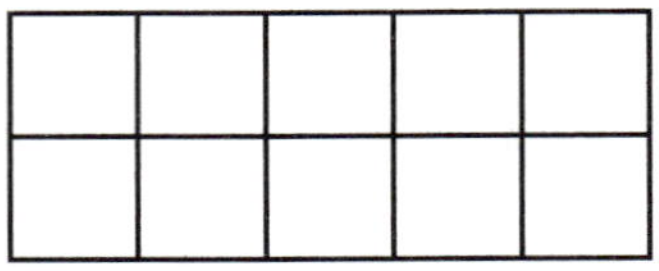

2. 13 − 8 = ____

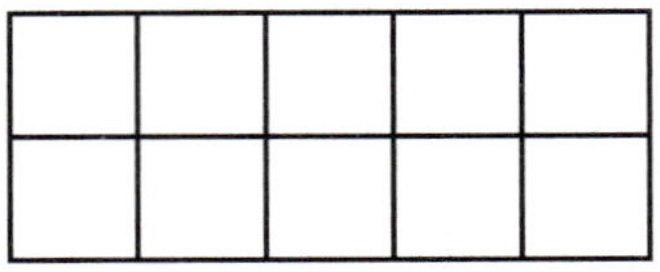

Problem Solving

3. Zoe has 15 blocks. Beth has 7 blocks.
How many more blocks does Zoe have?
Use the strategy Make 10 to subtract.

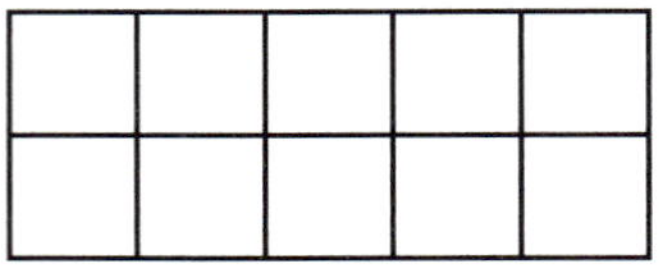

Subtract ____ and then subtract ____ more:

15 − 5 − ____ = ____

Zoe has ____ more blocks than Beth.

Write About It

4. Write a subtraction story for 16 − 8 = 8.
Show how you take away a part to find the answer.

___

___

Name ____________________

Subtract from 20 or Less

LESSON 9-5

Objective
- Subtract from 20 or less.

Math Word
subtract

Kent makes 18 pans of rolls and sells 9 pans. How many pans are left?

Subtract:
whole − part = part

$18 - 9 = ?$

$18 - 9 = 9$

Make 10 to check.

$9 + 9 = ?$

$9 + 1 + 8 = ?$

$10 + 8 = 18$

Circle the part taken away.

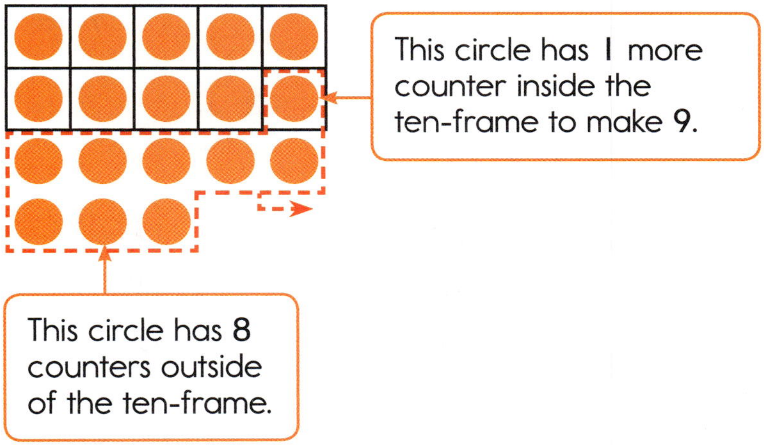

There are 9 pans of rolls left.

PRACTICE

Draw counters and subtract. Circle the part taken away. Make 10 to check.

1. $16 - 8 = 8$

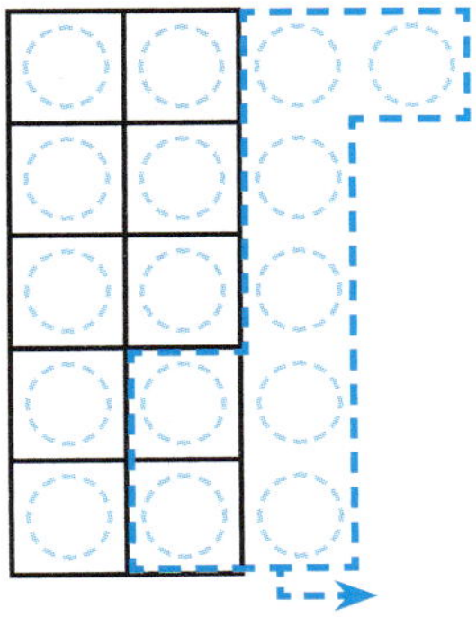

$8 + \underline{2} + \underline{6} = \underline{16}$

2. $19 - 10 = \_\_\_$

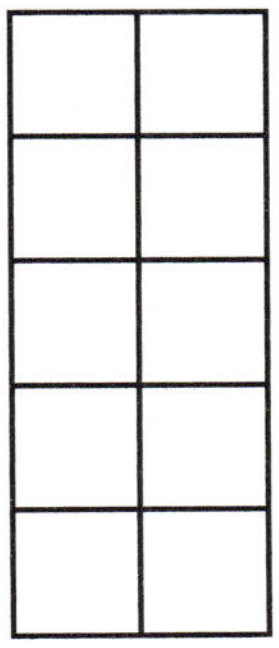

$10 + \_\_\_ = \_\_\_$

PRACTICE

Subtract. Use a ten-frame and counters to help. Make 10 to check.

3. $\begin{array}{r} 19 \\ -\ 7 \\ \hline \end{array}$

____ + 7 = ?

10 + ____ + ____ = ____

4. $\begin{array}{r} 15 \\ -\ 7 \\ \hline \end{array}$

____ + 7 = ?

8 + ____ + ____ = ____

5. 17 − 6 = ____

____ + 6 = ?

10 + ____ + ____ = ____

Problem Solving

6. Elaine has 17 pennies and 9 dimes. How many more pennies than dimes does she have? Use the strategy Make 10 to subtract.

17 − ____ − ____ = ____

Elaine has ____ more pennies than dimes.

Write About It

7. How can you use a doubles fact to help you subtract 18 − 9?

Think about the parts and the whole.

____

____

____

Name ____________________

Subtract from 20 or Less

Subtract:
whole − part = part

18 − 9 = ?

18 − 9 = 9

Make 10 to check.

9 + 9 = ?

9 + 1 + 8 = ?

10 + 8 = 18

So, 9 + 9 = 18.

Circle the part taken away.

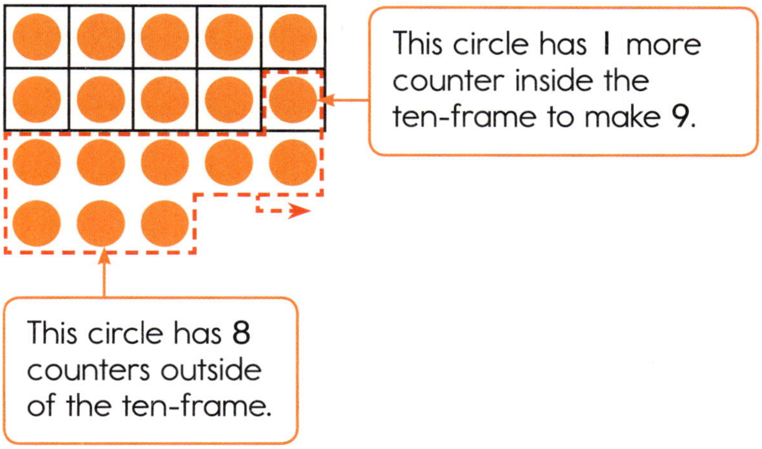

MORE PRACTICE

Draw counters and subtract. Circle the part taken away. Make 10 to check.

1. 17 − 6

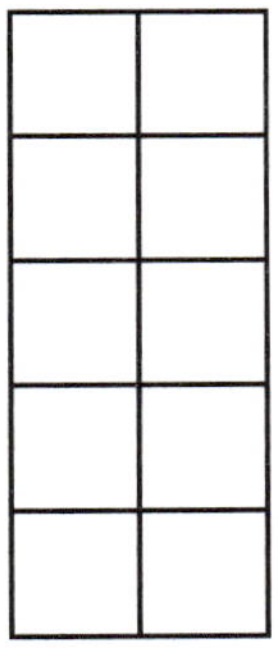

____ + 6 = ?

10 + 1 + 6 = 17

2. 18 − 6

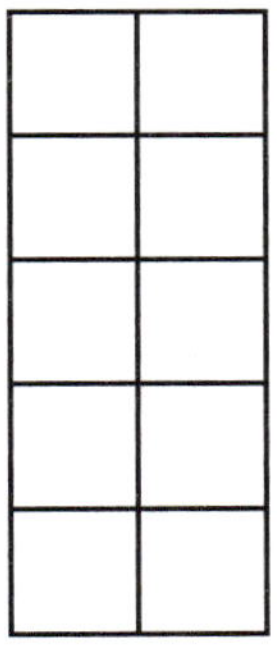

____ + 6 = ?

10 + ____ + ____ = ____

HOMEWORK

Draw counters and subtract. Circle the part taken away. Make 10 to check.

1. $\begin{array}{r} 18 \\ -\ \ 8 \\ \hline \end{array}$

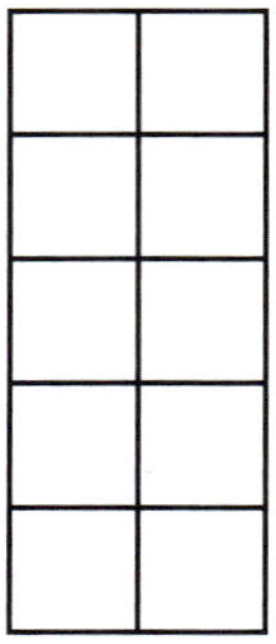

_____ + 8 = ?

10 + _____ = _____

2. $\begin{array}{r} 18 \\ -\ \ 7 \\ \hline \end{array}$

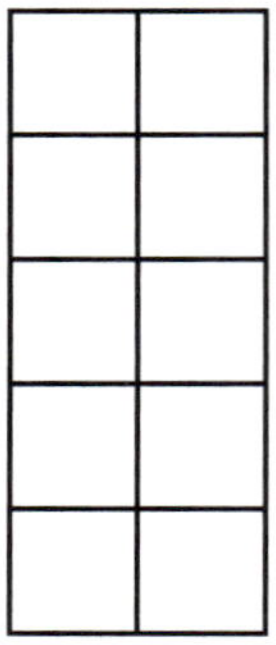

_____ + 7 = ?

10 + _____ + _____ = _____

Problem Solving

3. Andrea buys 18 pears. She buys 9 apples. How many more pears than apples does she buy? Use a doubles fact to help you subtract.

Doubles fact: 9 + _____ = _____

18 – _____ = _____

Andrea buys _____ more pears than apples.

Write About It

4. Lexy subtracts 17 – 6. Can she use a Make 10 strategy to subtract? Tell how you know.

____

____

Name ______________________________

Objective

- Write a fact family for a given set of numbers.

Math Words

fact family
related facts

Fact Families Through 20

Ms. Rolan asks her class to use the numbers 7, 9, and 16 to make four number sentences. The number sentences can show addition or subtraction.

The numbers 7, 9, and 16 make a fact family.

A fact family shows all the related facts.

Addition	Subtraction
$7 + 9 = 16$	$16 - 9 = 7$
$9 + 7 = 16$	$16 - 7 = 9$

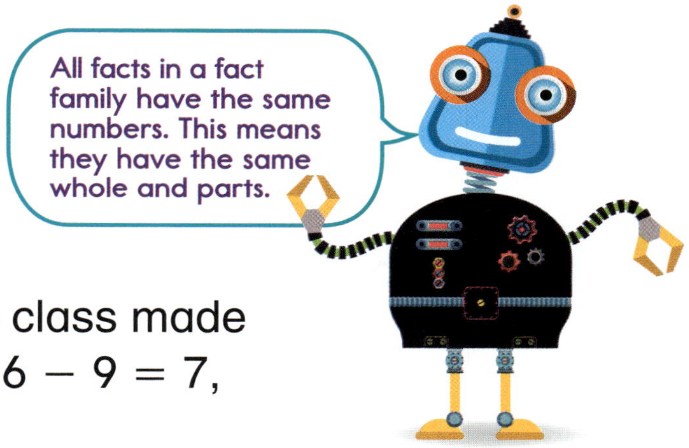

The four number sentences the class made are $7 + 9 = 16$, $9 + 7 = 16$, $16 - 9 = 7$, and $16 - 7 = 9$.

PRACTICE

Use the number sentence. Write the fact family.

1. $5 + 7 = 12$

7 + 5 = 12
12 − 5 = 7
12 − 7 = 5

2. $8 + 6 = 14$

____ + ____ = ____
____ − ____ = ____
____ − ____ = ____

PRACTICE

Use the numbers to write the fact family.

3. 8, 7, 15

$$\begin{array}{r} 8 \\ + 7 \\ \hline \end{array} \quad \bigcirc \square \quad \bigcirc \square \quad \bigcirc \square$$

4. 4, 7, 11

$$\begin{array}{r} 7 \\ + 4 \\ \hline \end{array} \quad \bigcirc \square \quad \bigcirc \square \quad \bigcirc \square$$

Problem Solving

5. Jon used the numbers 8, 2, 3, and 11 to make a fact family. One number does not belong. Which number is it? Tell how you know.

The number ____ does not belong.

____

____

Write About It

6. Ben says he can write three more equations because he knows 6 + 13 = 19. Is he right or wrong? Tell how you know.

____

____

____

Name ______________________________

Fact Families Through 20

The numbers 7, 9, and 16 make a fact family.

Addition	Subtraction
7 + 9 = 16	16 − 9 = 7
9 + 7 = 16	16 − 7 = 9

All facts in a fact family have the same numbers.
This means they have the same whole and parts.

So, a fact family shows all the related facts.

MORE PRACTICE

Use the numbers to write the fact family.

1. 2, 9, 11

2 + 9 = 11
9 + 2 = 11
11 − 9 = 2
11 − 2 = 9

2. 8, 5, 13

____ + ____ = ____
____ + ____ = ____
____ − ____ = ____
____ − ____ = ____

3. 4, 12, 16

____ + ____ = ____
____ + ____ = ____
____ − ____ = ____
____ − ____ = ____

HOMEWORK

Use the numbers to write the fact family.

1. 19, 9, 10

□ + □ = □   □ ○ □ = □   □ ○ □ = □   □ ○ □ = □

2. 17, 6, 11

□ + □ = □   □ ○ □ = □   □ ○ □ = □   □ ○ □ = □

Problem Solving

3. Mya wrote a fact family for 5, 6, and 11.

$6 + 5 = 11$ $5 + 6 = 11$ $6 - 5 = 11$ $11 - 5 = 6$

Are all of the facts in the fact family correct? Tell how you know.

____

____

____

Write About It

4. Sean knows that $7 + 8 = 15$. Tell how he can solve three more addition or subtraction equations.

____

____

____

Name ________________________________

Problem Solving

Read › Plan › Solve › Check

Use a Number Sentence

Objective

- Use a number sentence to solve subtraction word problems.

Math Words

difference
whole

Dave has 18 baseball cards.
He gives 3 to James.
Then he gives 4 to Harry.

How many baseball cards does Dave have now?

Sometimes a math story has more than one part. Ask questions about the story to find what you need to know. Then solve using a number sentence.

FIRST: What do you know?	Dave has 18 baseball cards. He gives 3 to James.
What do you need to know?	How many baseball cards does Dave have now?
Subtract.	$18 - 3 = 15$
SECOND: What else do you know?	Dave gives Harry 4 baseball cards.
What do you need to know?	How many baseball cards does Dave have now?
Subtract again.	$15 - 4 = 11$

Dave has 11 baseball cards now.

PRACTICE

Answer the questions. Write number sentences to solve the problem.

1. Olivia has a bowl of 17 cherries. She eats 4 cherries at breakfast. Later she eats 9 cherries. How many cherries are left in the bowl now?

FIRST: What do you know?	Olivia has _____ cherries. She eats _____ cherries at breakfast.
What do you need to know?	How many cherries does she have now?
Subtract.	_____ − _____ = _____
SECOND: What else do you know?	Olivia eats _____ cherries later.
What do you need to know?	How many cherries are left?
Subtract again.	_____ − _____ = _____

There are _____ cherries left in the bowl now.

Write About It

2. Why is it important to answer the first part of a subtraction problem before solving the rest?

____

____

Name ______________________

Problem Solving
Use a Number Sentence

There are 15 books on a shelf.
Missy takes 4 books.
Then her sister takes 2 more books.

How many books are left on the shelf?

Answer the questions and use number sentences to solve a math story with more than one part.

FIRST: What do you know?	There are 15 books on a shelf. Missy takes 4 books.
What do you need to know?	How many books are left on the shelf?
Subtract.	$15 - 4 = 11$
SECOND: What else do you know?	Missy's sister takes 2 more books.
What do you need to know?	How many books are left now?
Subtract again.	$11 - 2 = 9$

Use the answer to the first part to solve the second part.

There are 9 books left on the shelf.

MORE PRACTICE

Answer the questions. Write number sentences to solve the problem.

1. Carl has 17 building blocks.
   He uses 5 blocks to build a tower.
   Then he uses 8 blocks to build a house.

   How many blocks are left?

FIRST: What do you know?	Carl has _____ building blocks. He uses _____ blocks to build a tower.
What do you need to know?	How many blocks are left?
Subtract.	_____ − _____ = _____
SECOND: What else do you know?	Carl uses _____ blocks to build a house.
What do you need to know?	How many blocks are left now?
Subtract again.	_____ − _____ = _____

There are _____ blocks left.

Name ______________________________

HOMEWORK

Answer the questions. Write number sentences to solve the problem.

1. Sara has 19 stamps.
   She gives 7 stamps to her sister.
   Then she gives 3 stamps to her friend.
   How many stamps does Sara have now?

FIRST: What do you know?	Sara has ____ stamps. She gives ____ stamps to her sister.
What do you need to know?	How many stamps does Sara have left?
Subtract.	____ − ____ = ____
SECOND: What else do you know?	Sara gives ____ stamps to her friend.
What do you need to know?	How many stamps does Sara have now?
Subtract again.	____ − ____ = ____

Sara has ____ stamps now.

HOMEWORK

2. Mr. Harris has 18 stickers. He gives 9 away one day. Then he gives 5 away the next day. How many stickers does Mr. Harris have left?

FIRST: What do you know?	Mr. Harris has ____ stickers. He gives away ____ stickers.
What do you need to know?	How many stickers does Mr. Harris have left?
Subtract.	____ − ____ = ____
SECOND: What else do you know?	Mr. Harris gives ____ more stickers away.
What do you need to know?	How many stickers does he have now?
Subtract again.	____ − ____ = ____

Mr. Harris has ____ stickers left.

Write About It

3. Xavier needs to solve a problem with more than one part. He says he can add first to find out how much to subtract in all. Do you agree with Xavier? Tell how you know.

____

____

____

LESSON 9-8

Name ______________________________

True and False Equations

Objective

- Understand the meaning of the equal sign and determine if an equation is true or false.

Math Words

true
false

Are the equations below true or false?

$14 - 4 = 10$ $\quad$ $11 + 6 = 16$

- An equation is true when both sides of the equal sign make the same number.
- An equation is false when both sides of the equal sign do not make the same number.

Is $14 - 4 = 10$ true or false?

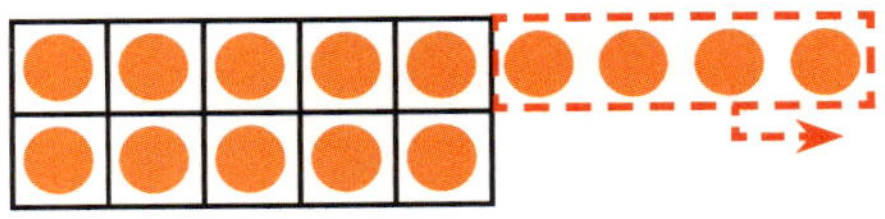

Subtract $14 - 4$ to check.

Does $10 = 10$? Yes.

So, $14 - 4 = 10$ is true.

Is $11 + 6 = 16$ true or false?

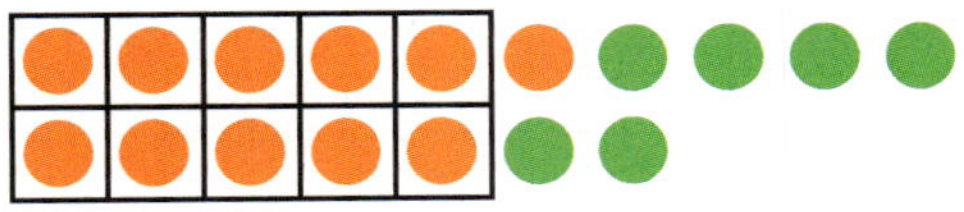

Add $11 + 6$ to check.

Does $17 = 16$? No.

So, $11 + 6 = 16$ is false.

PRACTICE

Circle the equations that are true. Cross out the equations that are false. Use ten-frames and counters to help.

1. $9 = 18 - 9$
2. $12 + 7 = 19$
3. $16 = 10 - 6$
4. $15 - 9 = 6$
5. $8 = 6 + 3$
6. $13 - 6 = 7$

PRACTICE

Circle the equations that are true. Cross out the equations that are false. Use ten-frames and counters to help.

7. $5 = 10 - 2$	8. $9 + 4 = 13$	9. $13 - 2 = 11$
10. $15 + 3 = 18$	11. $8 = 14 - 2$	12. $16 - 6 = 10$

Problem Solving

13. Lisa has 16 flowers. She has 7 pink flowers. The rest are yellow. How many are yellow? Write a true equation and solve.

____

Write About It

14. How do you know if the equation $13 - 7 = 10$ is true or false? Show how you check your answer.

____

____

____

____

Name ______________________________

True and False Equations

- An equation is **true** when both sides of the equal sign make the same number.
- An equation is **false** when both sides of the equal sign do not make the same number.

Is 14 − 4 = 10 true or false?

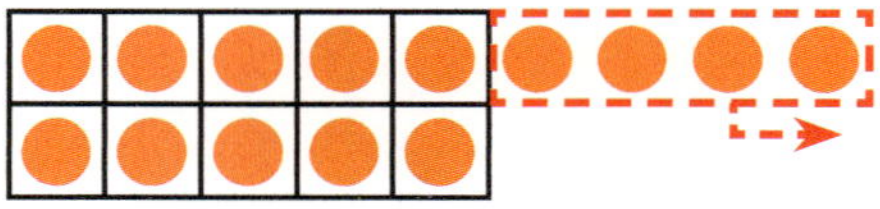

Subtract 14 − 4 to check.

Does 10 = 10? Yes.

So, 14 − 4 = 10 is true.

Is 11 + 6 = 16 true or false?

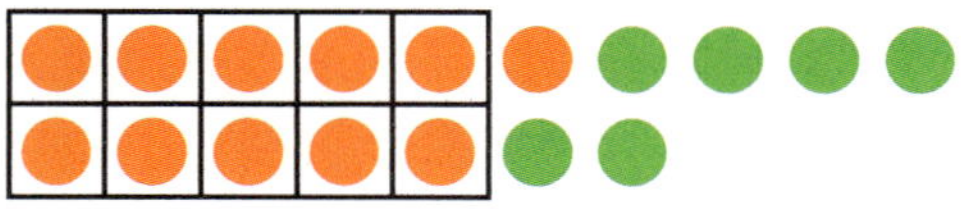

Add 11 + 6 to check.

Does 17 = 16? No.

So, 11 + 6 = 16 is false.

MORE PRACTICE

Circle the equations that are true. Cross out the equations that are false. Use ten-frames and draw counters to help.

1. ~~11 − 2 = 10~~

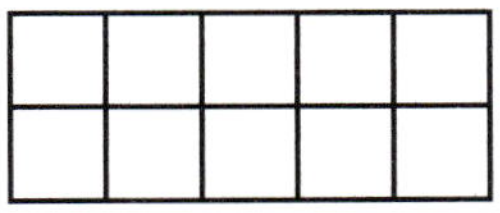

2. 15 − 4 = 11

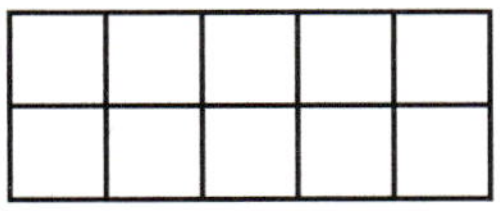

3. 14 = 8 + 6

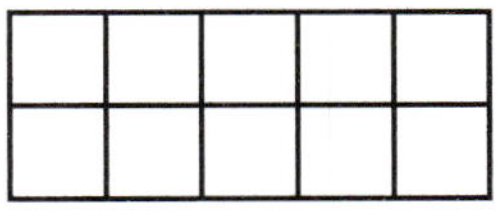

4. 17 − 7 = 10
5. 12 = 6 + 7
6. 19 − 6 = 13

HOMEWORK

Circle the equations that are true. Cross out the equations that are false. Use ten-frames and draw counters to help.

1. $6 = 10 - 3$

2. $11 + 1 = 12$

3. $6 - 1 = 5$

Problem Solving

4. Simon baked 18 muffins. Some muffins are blueberry. There are 9 banana muffins. How many muffins are blueberry? Write a true equation to solve.

____

Write About It

5. Bria and Anne looked at the equation $16 - 5 = 9$. Bria says the equation is true. Anne says the equation is false. Who is correct? Tell how you know.

____

____

____

____

Name ____________________

Objective

- Use addition or subtraction to find a missing part of an equation.

Math Word

equation

Missing Part of an Equation

Becky feeds 7 chickens and some ducks.
She feeds 11 animals in all.
How many ducks does Becky feed?

You can find the answer using the equation $7 + ? = 11$. How can you find the missing part?

You can count on.

$7 + ? = 11$

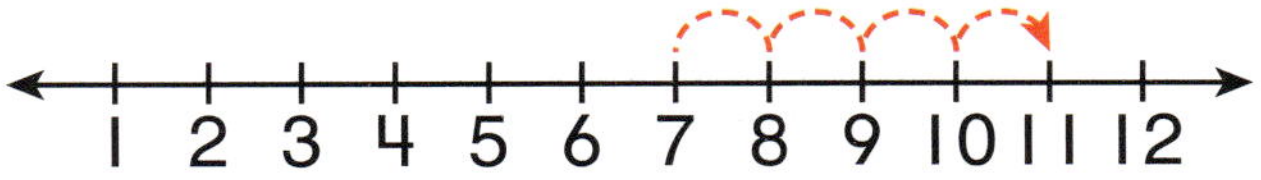

Count on from 7: 8, 9, 10, 11.

You counted on 4, so $7 + 4 = 11$.

You can use a subtraction fact.

$7 + ? = 11$

Start with the whole.
Subtract the known part.

$11 - 7 = 4$

Becky feeds 4 ducks.

PRACTICE

Find the missing number to make the equation true. Use cubes to help.

1. 17 − <u>2</u> = 15	**2.** <u>3</u> + 9 = 12	**3.** 15 − <u>3</u> = 12
4. 14 − ____ = 12	**5.** ____ + 1 = 10	**6.** 14 − ____ = 8
7. 9 + ____ = 18	**8.** 15 − ____ = 10	**9.** ____ + 12 = 14

PRACTICE

Find the missing number to make the equation true. Use to help.

10. ____ − 4 = 15

11. 5 + ____ = 13

12. ____ − 3 = 14

Problem Solving

13. Mario uses 6 red beads and some yellow beads. He uses 17 beads in all. How many yellow beads does Mario use? Write a subtraction equation to solve. Use addition and count on to check.

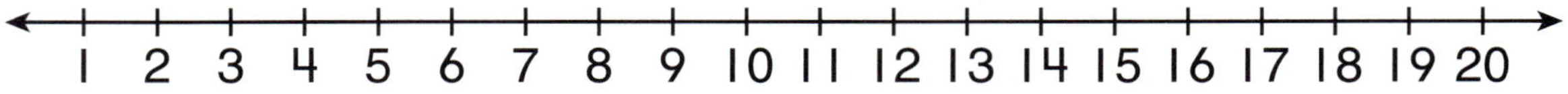

____

____

____

Write About It

14. How can you find the missing part in the equation 8 + ? = 10. Tell two ways.

____

____

____

Name ______________________________

Missing Part of an Equation

Find the missing part of the equation:

7 + ? = 11

You can count on.

7 + ? = 11

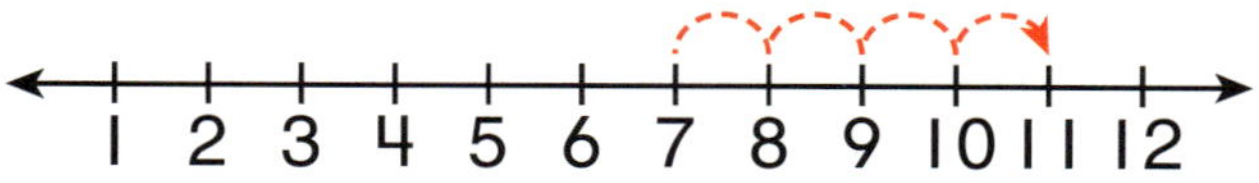

Count on from 7: 8, 9, 10, 11.

You counted on 4,
so 7 + 4 = 11.

You can use a subtraction fact.

7 + ? = 11

Start with the whole.
Subtract the known part.

11 − 7 = 4

MORE PRACTICE

Find the missing number to make the equation true. Draw counters or a number line to help add or subtract.

1. 17 − 2 = 15

2. 6 + ____ = 14

3. ____ − 3 = 14

4. ____ + 12 = 17

5. 13 − ____ = 11

6. 9 − ____ = 6

HOMEWORK

Find the missing number to make the equation true. Draw counters or a number line to help add or subtract.

1. 12 − ____ = 6

2. ____ − 4 = 11

3. ____ + 9 = 15

Problem Solving

4. There are 16 apples in a bag. Doug takes out 4 apples. How many apples are still in the bag? Write a subtraction equation to solve. Use addition and count on to check.

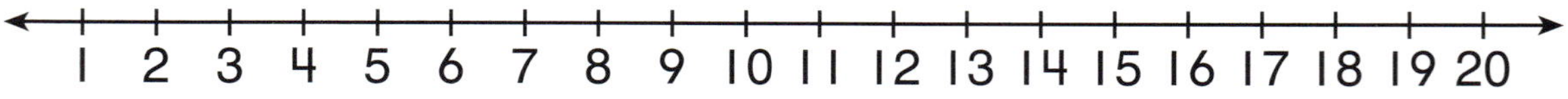

____

____

Write About It

5. Denise uses addition to find the missing number in the equation 9 + ? = 13. She gets 5 as the missing number. What did Denise do wrong? Find the missing number.

____

____

Name ____________________

Find the correct answer.

1. Subtract.

$16 - 7 = ?$

A. 6
B. 7
C. 9
D. 10

2. Subtract.

$12 - 8 = ?$

A. 4
B. 5
C. 6
D. 7

3. Subtract. You can use the ten-frame and draw counters to help.

$$\begin{array}{r} 16 \\ -\ \ 3 \\ \hline \end{array}$$

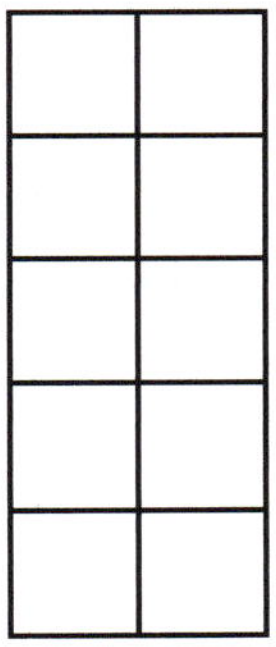

4. Subtract. You can use the ten-frame and draw counters to help.

$$\begin{array}{r} 14 \\ -\ \ 5 \\ \hline \end{array}$$

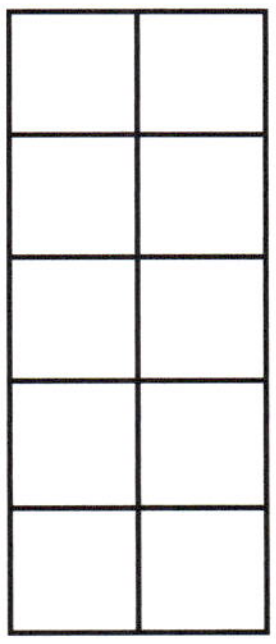

5. Subtract. You can use the ten-frame and draw counters to help.

$$\begin{array}{r} 17 \\ -\ \ 9 \\ \hline \end{array}$$

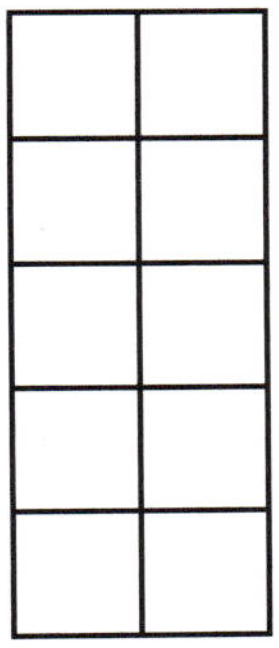

6. Subtract. You can use the ten-frame and draw counters to help.

$$\begin{array}{r} 18 \\ -\ \ 5 \\ \hline \end{array}$$

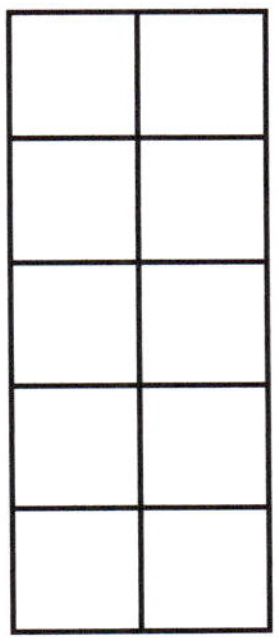

Find the correct answer.

7. Make a 10 to solve.

13 − 4 = ?

13 − ____ = ____

10 − ____ = ____

So, 13 − 4 = ____.

8. Write the rest of the fact family for the equation.

7 + 8 = 15

____ + ____ = ____

____ − ____ = ____

____ − ____ = ____

9. Which number makes the equation true?

? − 3 = 9

A. 11
B. 5
C. 6
D. 12

10. Which TWO equations are false?

A. 8 = 12 − 4
B. 5 = 17 − 2
C. 10 = 18 − 8
D. 5 = 19 − 4

11. Which equation is true?

A. 13 − 3 = 9
B. 10 − 7 = 3
C. 11 − 0 = 10
D. 9 − 1 = 7

12. Which equation is false?

A. 10 − 3 = 7
B. 9 − 3 = 6
C. 18 − 2 = 16
D. 12 − 1 = 10

Name ____________________

CHAPTER 9 Performance Assessment

Courtney, Lisa, and Jin each draw a map. The maps show a picture of a bicycling trail.

Courtney's map shows a trail that is 15 miles long.

Lisa's map shows a trail longer than Jin's, but shorter than Courtney's.

1. What are some of the distances Lisa and Jin's maps could show? Draw a picture to show each girl's maps.

____

____

____

2. Use the numbers from the maps you drew. How much longer is Courtney's trail than Lisa's trail? How much longer than Jin's trail?

____

____

____

CHAPTER 9
Fluency Practice

Name ______________________________

Find the correct answers.

1. Add.

$$\begin{array}{r} 9 \\ +9 \\ \hline \end{array}$$

A. 5
B. 8
C. 7
D. 18

2. Subtract.

$18 - 3 = ?$

A. 21
B. 19
C. 16
D. 15

3. Add.

$$\begin{array}{r} 3 \\ 2 \\ +7 \\ \hline \end{array}$$

4. Write the fact family.

$8 + 9 = 17$

____ + ____ = ____

____ − ____ = ____

____ − ____ = ____

5. Find the missing addend.

$15 + ? = 20$

A. 1
B. 6
C. 5
D. 2

6. Which equation is true?

A. $7 = 6$
B. $8 = 7 + 2$
C. $2 + 3 = 3 + 2$
D. $15 - 2 = 17$

Data and Graphical Displays

CHAPTER 10

There are different ways to get to school. Some children ride in a school bus. Some children ride in cars. Others walk or ride on a bike. In some places, children may even take a subway.

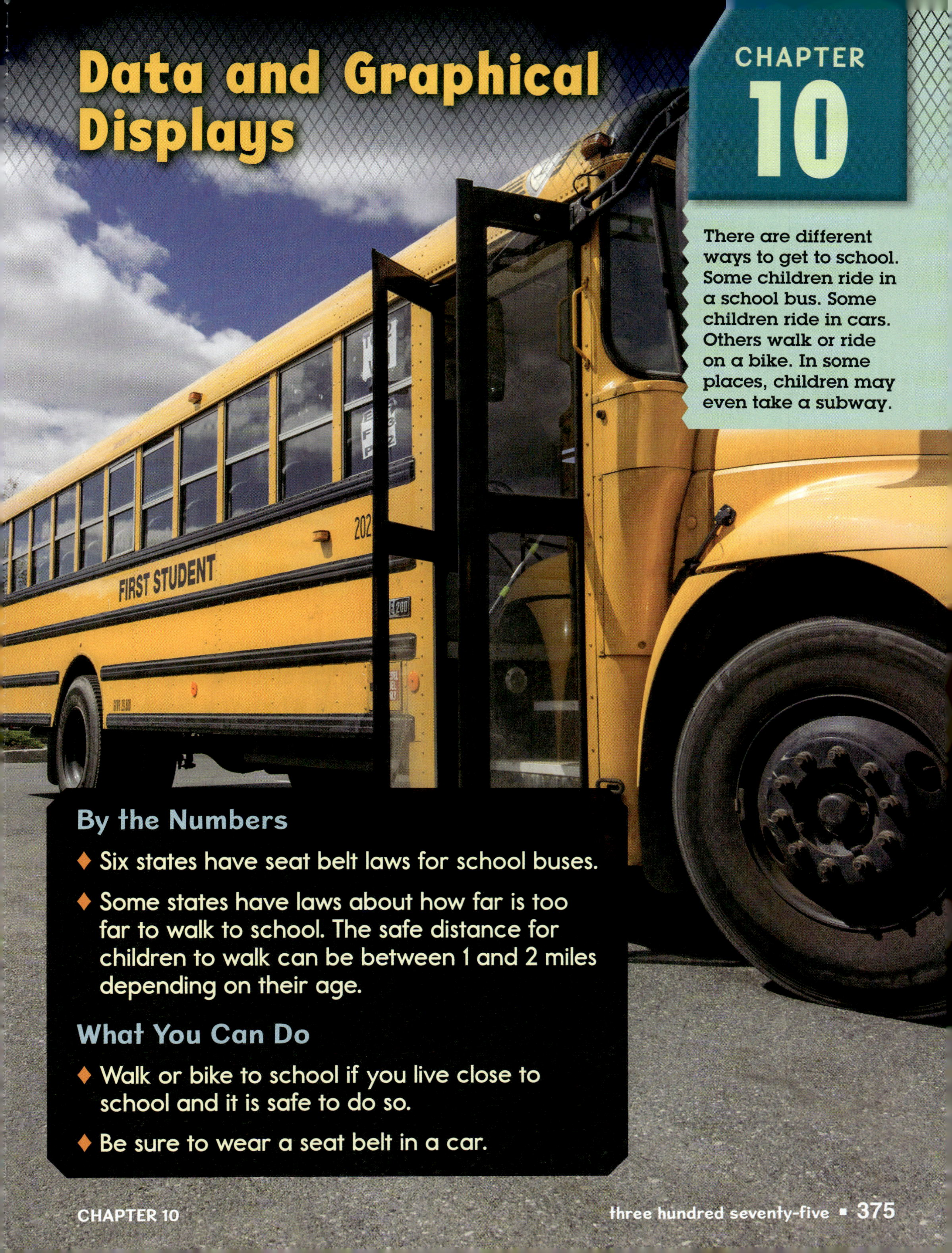

By the Numbers

- Six states have seat belt laws for school buses.
- Some states have laws about how far is too far to walk to school. The safe distance for children to walk can be between 1 and 2 miles depending on their age.

What You Can Do

- Walk or bike to school if you live close to school and it is safe to do so.
- Be sure to wear a seat belt in a car.

Dear Family,

In this chapter, we will be learning about data and graphical representations.

Here are the Key **Math Words** for this chapter:

tally chart	**data**
tally mark	**picture graph**

You can use the glossary to check out the definition of each word and help your child make flash cards to study each day we work in this chapter.

During the Chapter Opener and Performance Assessment, we will be making STEAM connections about transportation to school. Read the opening to the chapter together and discuss the **By the Numbers** and **What You Can Do** statements.

Keep Your Skills Sharp

Here is a **Keep Your Skills Sharp** activity to do at home to prepare for this chapter.

Collect a total of 12 coins using pennies, nickels, and dimes. Help your child make a table to show the number of each. Draw pictures for each number of pennies, nickels, and dimes. Then use tally marks and numbers to show how many of each. Alternatively, collect 12 buttons or dot stickers of different sizes and/or colors.

Name ______________________________

Objective

- Read tally charts.

Math Words

tally chart
tally mark
data

Read Tally Charts

Sadie writes her friends' favorite colors in a tally chart. How many more friends choose blue than choose green?

Favorite Colors		
Color	**Tally**	**Total**
Blue	卌 II	7
Green	卌	5
Red	III	3

This is a tally chart.

Each tally mark shows 1.

卌 stands for 5.

The line across stands for the 5th tally mark.

To find how many more friends choose blue, read the data in the tally chart and subtract.

7 friends choose blue. 5 friends choose green.

$7 - 5 = 2$

2 more friends choose blue than choose green.

PRACTICE

Use the tally chart above to answer the question.

1. How many friends like red the most?

There are __3__ friends who like red the most.

PRACTICE

Ryan writes the number of stickers he has in a tally chart.

Ryan's Stickers		
Sticker	**Tally**	**Total**
 Earth	卌	5
 Moon	||||	4
 Sun	卌 ||||	9

2. How many moon and sun stickers does Ryan have in all?

   _____ + _____ = _____

   Ryan has _____ moon and sun stickers.

Problem Solving

Mr. Jones writes his students' favorite drinks in a tally chart.

Favorite Drinks		
Drink	**Tally**	**Total**
 Juice	卌 |	6
Milk	卌 |||	8
 Water	卌 |	6

3. Which drink do students choose the most? How do you know?

   Most students choose _________.

   ____

   ____

   ____

Write About It

4. Why is using tally marks a good way to show how many?

   ____

   ____

Name ______________________________

Read Tally Charts

Sadie writes her friends' favorite colors in a tally chart.

Favorite Colors		
Color	**Tally**	**Total**
Blue	卌 II	7
Green	卌	5
Red	III	3

This is a tally chart.

Each tally mark shows 1.

卌 stands for 5.

The line across stands for the 5th tally mark.

MORE PRACTICE

Use the tally chart above to answer the questions.

1. How many friends choose blue?

   ______

2. How many more friends choose green than red?

   ______

3. How many friends in all picked red or blue?

   ______

HOMEWORK

Beth writes the number of sports balls in a tally chart. Use the tally chart to answer the question.

Sports Balls		
Ball	**Tally**	**Total**
 Basketball	III	3
 Soccer	卌 I	6
 Tennis	卌 III	8

1. How many more tennis balls than basketballs are there?

   There are ____ more tennis balls than basketballs.

Problem Solving

Miss Smith writes her students' favorite days in a tally chart.

Favorite Day		
Day	**Tally**	**Total**
Friday	卌	5
Saturday	卌 IIII	9
Sunday	卌 I	6

2. Which day do most students like? How do you know?

   Most students like ______________.

   ____

   ____

Write About It

3. Explain what each tally mark shows in a tally chart.

   ____

   ____

   ____

Name ______________________________

LESSON 10-2

Objective
- Make and use tally charts.

Math Words
tally chart
tally mark

Make Tally Charts

Don sees some animals at the zoo.
How many penguins, bears,
and seals does Don see?

You can record the number of animals in a tally chart.

Draw a tally mark for each animal you see.

Don sees 3 penguins.
Don sees 6 bears.
Don sees 7 seals.

Zoo Animals

Animal	Tally	Total
Penguin	|||	3
Bear	卌 |	6
Seal	卌 ||	7

PRACTICE

Use the tally chart above to answer the question.

1. Which tallies show 5 plus 2 more?

   The tallies for the ________ show 5 plus 2 more.

PRACTICE

Fill in the tally chart. Cross out each fruit as you tally it.

2.

Fruit		
Fruit	**Tally**	**Total**
Apple		
Lemon		
Berry		

Problem Solving

3. If Cara has 2 more beans, how many total beans will her tally chart show?

Cara's chart will show _____ tally marks and a total of _____ beans.

Cara's Garden		
Vegetable	**Tally**	**Total**
Bean	||	2
Pepper	卌 |||	8
Tomato	卌 |	6

Write About It

4. Tell how a tally chart can help you record answers.

____

____

Name ____________________

Make Tally Charts

You can record the number of animals in a tally chart by using 1 tally mark for each animal.

Zoo Animals		
Animal	**Tally**	**Total**
Penguin	|||	3
Bear	||||/ |	6
Seal	||||/ ||	7

MORE PRACTICE

Fill in the tally chart. Cross out each marble as you tally it.

	Marbles		
	Marble	**Tally**	**Total**
1.	Blue		
2.	Red		
3.	Yellow		

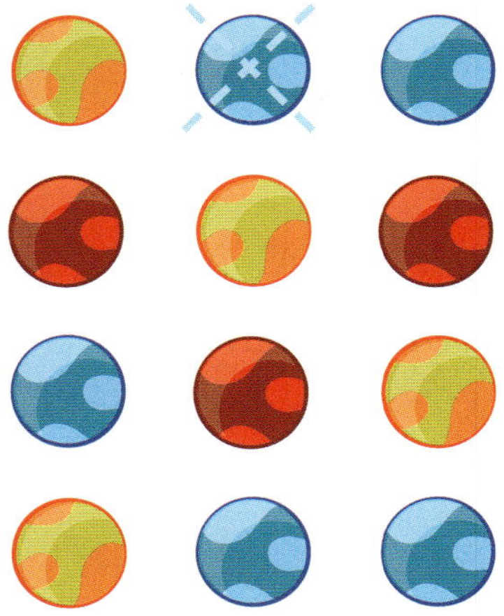

HOMEWORK

Fill in the tally chart. Cross out each toy as you tally it.

Toys			
	Toy	Tally	Total
1.	 Car		
2.	 Blocks		
3.	 Duck		

Problem Solving

4. Zoey counts 8 balls. She draws ~~IIII~~ IIII. Do her tallies show 8? Why or why not?

   Zoey's tallies ________ show 8.

   ____

Write About It

5. How are the tally column and total column in a tally chart the same or different?

   ____

   ____

   ____

Name ____________________

Find the correct answer.

1. Read the tally chart.

Favorite Colors		
Color	**Tally**	**Total**
	𝍸 II	7
	𝍸	5
	III	3

How many more blue are there than red?

A. 2
B. 4
C. 10

2. Read the tally chart.

Zoo Animals		
Animal	**Tally**	**Total**
	III	3
	𝍸 I	6
	𝍸 II	7

Which shows how many more seals there are than bears?

A. $7 - 6 = 1$
B. $7 - 3 = 4$
C. $6 - 3 = 3$

3. How many tally marks are shown?

𝍸

A. 1
B. 4
C. 5

4. Which shows 2 tally marks?

A. II
B. IIII
C. 𝍸 II

Find the correct answer.

5. Benjamin draws 4 tally marks to show the number of a kind of fruit. Which fruit did he tally?

A. apple
B. lemon
C. strawberry

6. Complete the tally chart.

Tech Tools

Technology	Tally	Total
	IIII	
	卌 III	
	卌 I	

How many are there in all?

______

7. How many tally marks should be used to show the number of blue marbles?

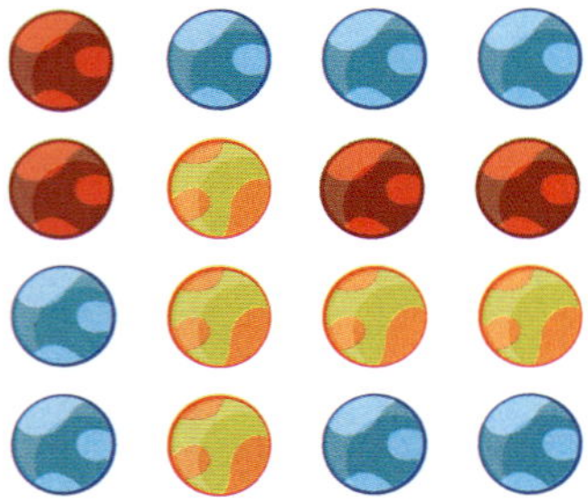

A. IIII
B. 卌
C. 卌 II

8. Which shows the tally chart for the fruit in problem 5?

A.

Kinds of Fruit

Fruit	Tally	Total
	II	2
	IIII	4
	卌 I	6

B.

Kinds of Fruit

Fruit	Tally	Total
	IIII	4
	II	2
	卌 I	6

Name ____________________

LESSON 10-3

Objective
- Use picture graphs to show data.

Math Word
picture graph

Read Picture Graphs

Abby goes to the beach. She records the animals that she sees.

How many more birds than fish does Abby see?

Animals Abby Sees		
Animal	**Tally**	**Total**
Bird	卌 III	8
Crab	II	2
Fish	卌	5

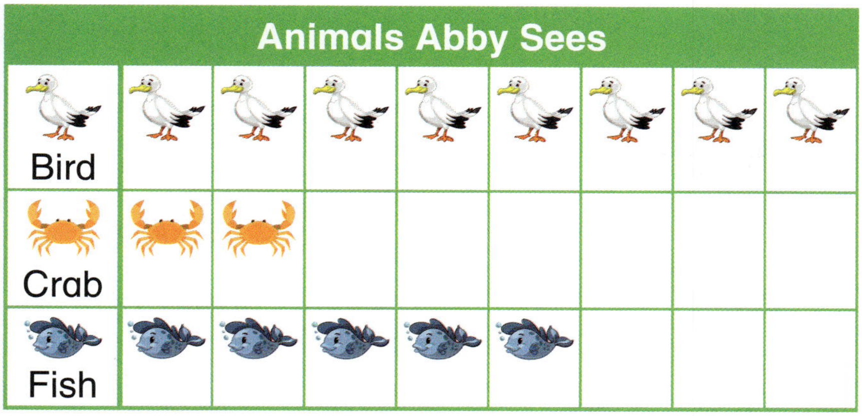

Abby puts pictures in a picture graph to show how many. There is 1 picture for each tally mark.

There are 3 more pictures of birds than pictures of fish.

Abby sees 3 more birds than fish.

PRACTICE

Use the picture graph above to answer the question.

1. How many animals does Abby see in all?

   Abby sees 15 animals in all.

PRACTICE

Read the picture graph, then answer the question.

Eli's Books		
Type	**Tally**	**Total**
Animal	|||	3
Comic	卌	5
Picture	||||	4

2. How many more comic books than picture books does Eli have?

Eli has _____ more comic book than picture books.

Problem Solving

Read the picture graph and answer the question.

3. Which color is chosen the least? How do you know?

________ is chosen the least.

I know because the graph shows _____ picture for ________.

Write About It

4. Explain how you can use a picture graph to tell how many more or less there are.

____

____

Name ______________________________

Read Picture Graphs

You can use a picture graph to show how many.
There is 1 picture for each tally mark.

Animals Abby Sees		
Animal	**Tally**	**Total**
Bird	𝍸 |||	8
Crab	||	2
Fish	𝍸	5

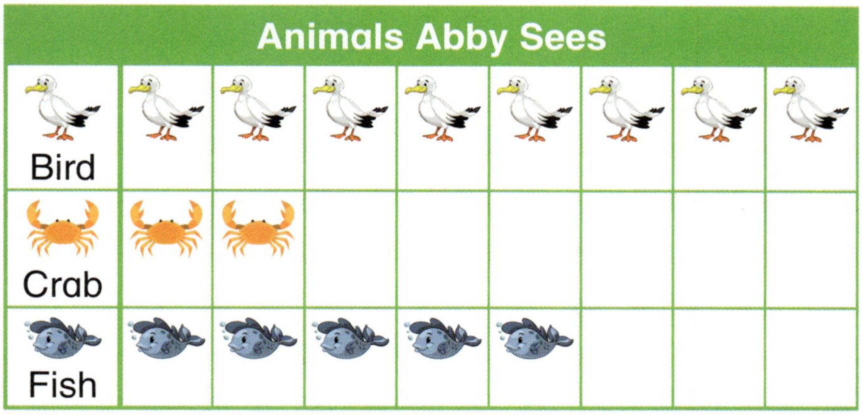

There are 8 pictures of birds, 2 pictures of crabs, and 5 pictures of fish.

MORE PRACTICE

Use the picture graph above to answer the questions.

1. How many more fish than crabs does Abby see?

   Abby sees _____ more fish than crabs.

2. Which animal does Abby see the fewest of?

   Abby sees the fewest number of _______.

3. How many fish and birds does Abby see in all?

   Abby sees _____ fish and birds.

HOMEWORK

Read the picture graph, then answer the question.

1. Which two colors are chosen the same number of times?

The colors ________ and ________ are chosen the same number of times.

Problem Solving

Read the picture graph and answer the question.

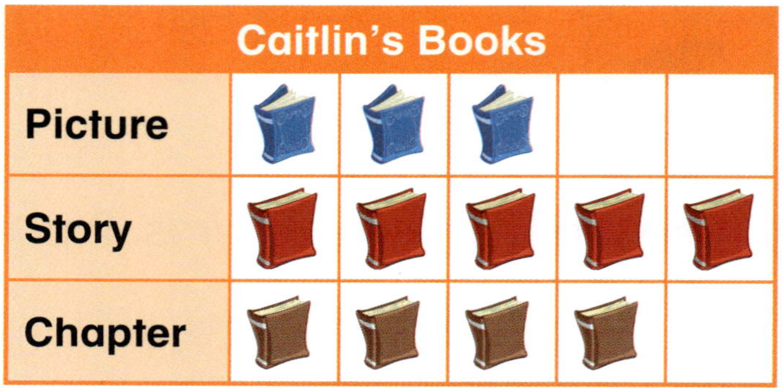

2. Brooke says Caitlin has 3 story books. What mistake did Brooke make?

____

____

Write About It

3. Carl makes a picture graph about favorite seasons. It shows that fewer people like winter than summer. How can he find out how many fewer without subtracting?

____

____

Name ___________________________

LESSON 10-4

Objective

- Make and use picture graphs.

Math Word

picture graph

Make Picture Graphs

Bryson made a tally chart. It shows the number of buttons he has collected. How can he use his chart to make a picture graph?

Buttons Collected

Color	Tally	Total
Blue	𝍸	5
Yellow	III	3
Green	I	1

Buttons Collected

Blue	●	●	●	●	●
Yellow	●	●	●		
Green	●				

Bryson can draw a picture of one button for each tally mark.

PRACTICE

Use the tally chart to make a picture graph.

Camila's Gemstones

1.	Red					
2.	Blue					
3.	Green					

Camila's Gemstones

Color	Tally	Total
Red	II	2
Blue	IIII	4
Green	𝍸	5

PRACTICE

Use the tally chart to make a picture graph.

Favorite Weather

4.	Rainy						
5.	Snowy						
6.	Sunny						

Favorite Weather

Type	Tally	Total
Rainy	|||	3
Snowy	卌 |	6
Sunny	卌	5

Problem Solving

Use your picture graph above to answer the question.

7. Which weather is the favorite? How do you know?

_______ is the favorite.

____

____

Write About It

8. Which would you rather use, a tally chart or a picture graph? Tell why.

____

____

Name ______________________________

Make Picture Graphs

To make a picture graph from a tally chart, draw one picture for each tally mark.

Buttons Collected

Color	Tally	Total
Blue	卌	5
Yellow	|||	3
Green			1

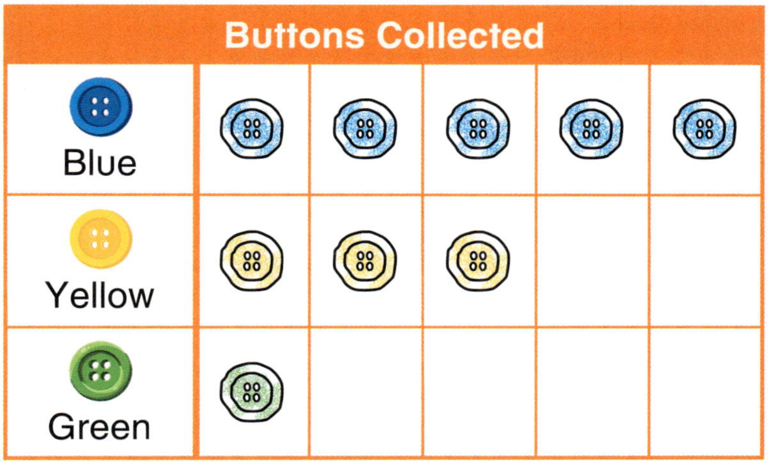

MORE PRACTICE

Use the tally chart to make a picture graph.

Tamika's Marbles

1.	Purple							
2.	Yellow							
3.	Green							

Tamika's Marbles

Color	Tally	Total
Purple	卌 ||	7
Yellow	卌	5
Green	|||	3

HOMEWORK

Use the tally chart to make a picture graph.

Ryan's Gemstones			
1. Red			
2. Blue			
3. Green			

Ryan's Gemstones		
Color	**Tally**	**Total**
Red	|	1
Blue	|||	3
Green	||	2

Problem Solving

Use your picture graph above to answer the question.

4. Ryan says he has 9 gemstones. Explain Ryan's error.

____

____

____

Write About It

5. When might it be better to use a tally chart instead of a picture graph? Tell why.

____

____

____

Objective
- Use a model to solve word problems.

Math Word
model

Name ____________________

Problem Solving
Read › Plan › Solve › Check

Use a Model

Molly asks her friends to name their favorite color. She makes a tally chart.

How many friends does Molly ask about their favorite color?

You can make a model using one connecting cube for each tally mark.

Favorite Color

Color	Tally	Total
Red	𝍸	5
Blue	𝍸	5
Green	III	3

Red: 5

Blue: 5

Green: 3

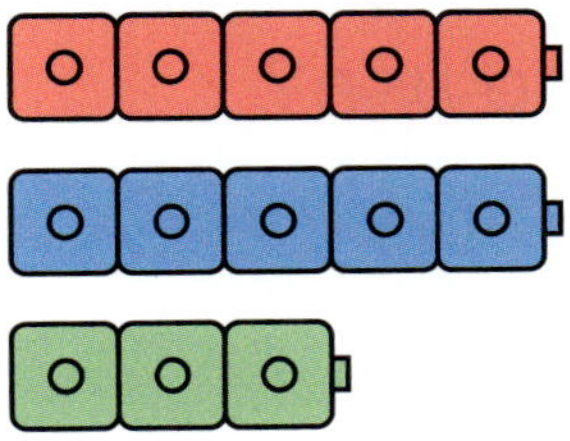

Add to find the answer.

$5 + 5 + 3 = ?$

$10 + 3 = 13$

There were 13 friends who were asked about their favorite color.

PRACTICE

Use the model and chart above to answer the questions.

1. Which colors show an equal number?

_________ and _________

2. Which color has the fewest cubes?

____

PRACTICE

The model shows the number of stickers in Dan's collection. Use the model and cubes to answer the questions.

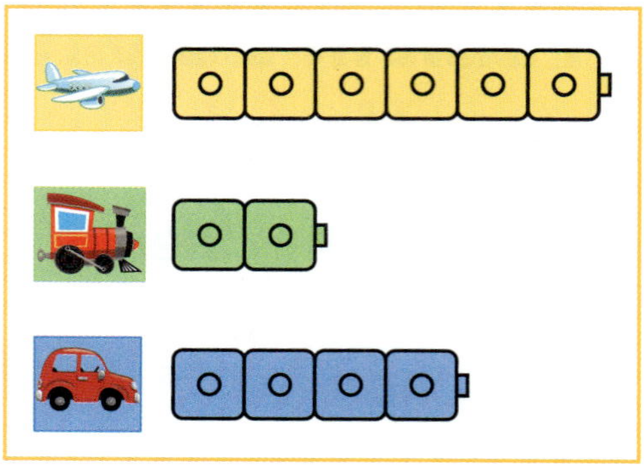

3. How many more airplane stickers than car stickers does Dan have?

   Dan has _____ more airplane stickers than car stickers.

4. Dan puts his stickers in a book. He puts 1 sticker on each page. How many pages will he use?

   He will use _____ pages.

5. How many more stickers does Dan need to have 20 stickers in all?

   He needs _____ more stickers.

Write About It

6. Explain how using connecting cubes is the same or different from using a picture graph.

   ____

   ____

   ____

Name ______________________________

Problem Solving
Use a Model

How many children were asked to name their favorite color?

You can make a model using one connecting cube for each tally mark.

Favorite Color		
Color	**Tally**	**Total**
Red	卌	5
Blue	卌	5
Green	|||	3

Red: 5

Blue: 5

Green: 3

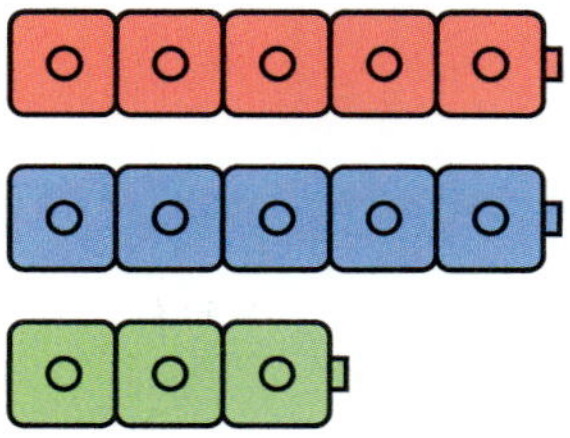

Add to find the answer.

$5 + 5 + 3 = ?$

$10 + 3 = 13$

There were 13 children who were asked about their favorite color.

MORE PRACTICE

Use the model above to answer the questions.

1. Molly chooses green as her favorite color and adds a tally to the chart. Now how many connecting cubes are needed for green?

   There are now _____ cubes for green.

2. Which colors were chosen by an equal number of children?

   An equal number of children chose _______ and _______ as their favorite color.

MORE PRACTICE

The model shows the number of sticks Marie has to make a stick bridge. Use the model and connecting cubes to answer the questions.

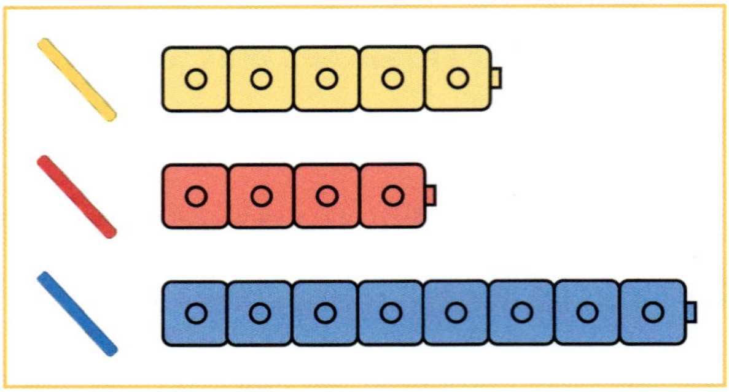

3. How many sticks does Marie have in all?

   She has _____ sticks in all.

4. Marie loses 1 of her blue sticks. How many connecting cubes should she use for blue?

   She should use _____ cubes for blue.

5. Marie needs 5 sticks in each color. Which color needs more?

   She needs more _____ sticks.

6. Marie makes a yellow-red-blue stick pattern. How many times can she make the pattern?

   She can make the pattern _____ times.

7. How many more yellow than red sticks does Marie have?

   She has _____ more yellow than red sticks.

Name ____________________

Problem Solving
Use a Model

HOMEWORK

Use the tally chart to answer the questions. You can draw connecting cubes to help.

<table>
<tr><th colspan="3">Favorite Musical Instrument</th></tr>
<tr><th>Instrument</th><th>Tally</th><th>Total</th></tr>
<tr><td>
Keyboard</td><td>||||</td><td>4</td></tr>
<tr><td>
Drum</td><td>卌 |||</td><td>8</td></tr>
<tr><td>
Guitar</td><td>卌 |</td><td>6</td></tr>
</table>

1. Dante wants to use connecting cubes to model the tally chart. How many cubes does he need?

   He needs _____ cubes.

2. How many cubes does he need for the guitar?

   He needs _____ cubes for guitar.

3. How many more cubes will Dante use for the drum than for the keyboard?

   He will use _____ more cubes.

4. If 2 people change their favorite from keyboard to guitar, which instruments will have the same number of votes?

   _______ and _______ will have the same number.

HOMEWORK

The model shows the number of stickers in Miguel's collection. Use the model to answer the questions.

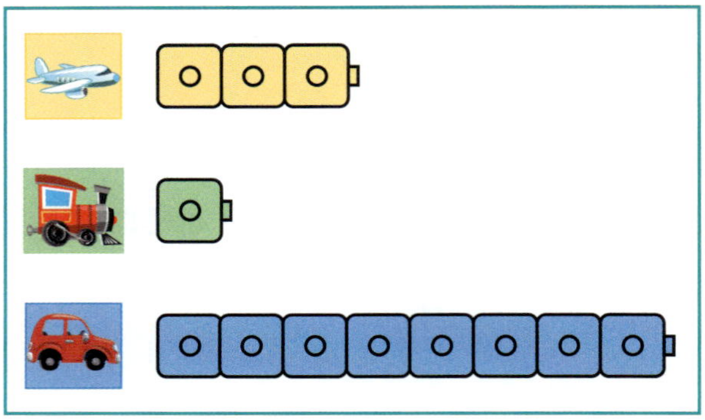

5. How many stickers does Miguel have in all?

   He has _____ stickers in all.

6. Miguel puts his stickers in a book. He puts 2 stickers on the first page. How many stickers does he have left?

   He has _____ stickers left.

7. Miguel loses 1 blue car sticker. How many connecting cubes will he use now for the blue car stickers?

   He will use _____ cubes.

Write About It

8. Explain how making a model using connecting cubes is the same as using a picture graph to solve problems.

____

____

____

Name ______________________________

CHAPTER 10 Review

Find the correct answer.

1. Read the tally chart.

Stickers Collected		
Sticker	**Tally**	**Total**
 Earth	𝍸	5
 Moon	IIII	4
 Sun	𝍸 IIII	9

How many stickers are there in all?

A. 9
B. 13
C. 14
D. 18

2. Complete the tally chart.

Zoo Animals		
Animal	**Tally**	**Total**
 Penguin	III	
 Bear	𝍸 I	
 Seal	𝍸 II	

Which shows how many in all?

A. $3 + 6 = 9$
B. $3 + 7 = 10$
C. $6 + 7 = 13$
D. $3 + 6 + 7 = 16$

3. How many tally marks are shown?

IIII

A. 1
B. 2
C. 4
D. 8

4. Which shows 7 tally marks?

A. II
B. IIII
C. 𝍸
D. 𝍸 II

5. If you use the tally chart to draw a picture graph, how many rainy and snowy pictures will you draw?

Favorite Weather		
Type	**Tally**	**Total**
Rainy	|||	3
Snowy	卌		6
Sunny	卌	5

A. 3
B. 6
C. 9

6. Erin uses the tally chart to make a picture graph.

Erin's Gemstones		
Color	**Tally**	**Total**
Red	||	2
Blue	||||	4
Green	|||	3

How many gemstones **in all** should Erin draw?

A. 2
B. 3
C. 4
D. 9

7. Read the picture graph.

Which color is chosen the most?

A. orange
B. red
C. yellow
D. They are all chosen the same amount.

8. Kenneth asks his friends about their favorite colors. He finds 4 like red, 6 like blue, and 2 like orange. How many more blue cubes than orange cubes should Kenneth use in a model?

A. 2
B. 4
C. 6

Name ______________________________

CHAPTER 10 Performance Assessment

The table shows how children in Ava's class get to school.

Method	Number
Bus	7
Car	5
Walk	2

1. Use the table to make a tally chart.

School Transportation		
Method	**Tally**	**Total**
Bus		
Car		
Walk		

2. How many more children ride in a bus than in a car?

   There are _____ more children who ride in a bus than in a car.

3. Ask 10 classmates how they get to school. Make a picture graph that shows your data.

School Transportation	
Bus	
Car	
Walk	

4. Look at your picture graph. How do most of your classmates come to school?

   ____

CHAPTER 10
Fluency Practice

Name ____________________

Circle the correct answer.

1. What number do the tally marks show?

A. 7
B. 6
C. 8
D. 5

2. How many more slides than swings are there?

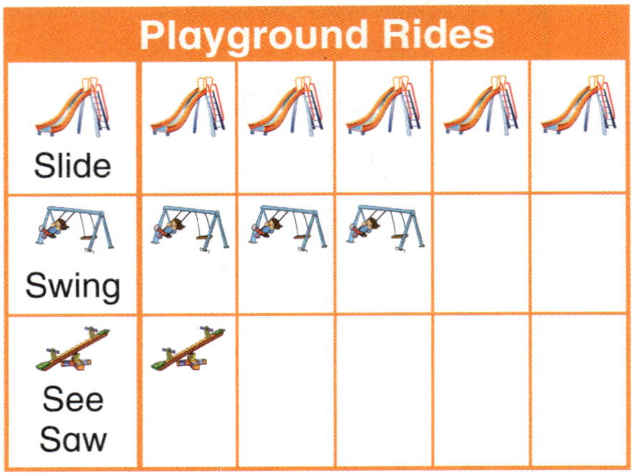

A. 6
B. 4
C. 2
D. 10

3. Subtract.

$7 - 3 = ?$

A. 3
B. 4
C. 7
D. 10

4. Add.

$10 + 7 = ?$

A. 10
B. 11
C. 17
D. 18

5. Subtract.

$16 - 8 = ?$

A. 8
B. 9
C. 10
D. 12

6. Add.

$5 + 3 + 4 = ?$

A. 8
B. 10
C. 12
D. 13

Addition: Two-Digit Numbers

CHAPTER 11

Some people grow plants in containers called flats. A flat has small cups. Each cup holds a seed that grows into a plant. The plant can then be put in a larger pot as it keeps growing.

By the Numbers

- Small flats may have as few as 4 cups.
- Large flats may have as many as 100 cups!
- You need several flats with 6 plants to start a garden.

What You Can Do

- Fill cups with soil and grow 10 plants.
- Arrange the cups to look like a flat.

Dear Family,

In this chapter, we will be learning about addition of two-digit numbers.

Here are the Key **Math Words** for this chapter:

addend	**ones**
bar model	**sum**
count on	**tens**
expanded form	

You can use the glossary to check out the definition of each word and help your child make flash cards to study each day we work on the lessons for this chapter.

During the Chapter Opener and Performance Assessment, we will be making STEAM connections about growing plants in flats. Read the opening to the chapter together and discuss the **By the Numbers** and **What You Can Do** statements.

Keep Your Skills Sharp

Here is a **Keep Your Skills Sharp** activity to do at home to prepare for this chapter.

Prepare a bowl filled with countable objects, like dried beans or beads. You and your child take a handful of objects. Count your objects, sorting by tens and ones. When finished, try to add your totals together. Discuss strategies to help you count.

Name ______________________________

Mental Math: Find 10 More

Objective
- Use place value to find 10 more than a two-digit number.

Math Word
ten

Marci reads 15 pages of a book.
Rachel reads 10 more pages than Marci.
How many pages does Rachel read?

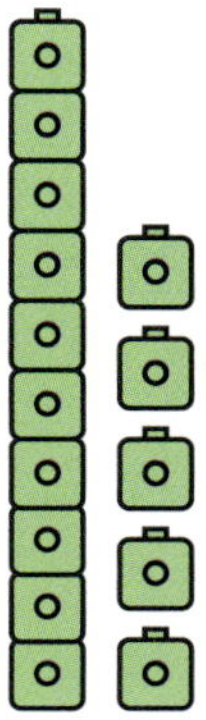

1 ten 5 ones

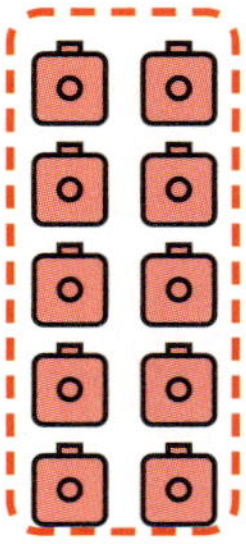

10 ones

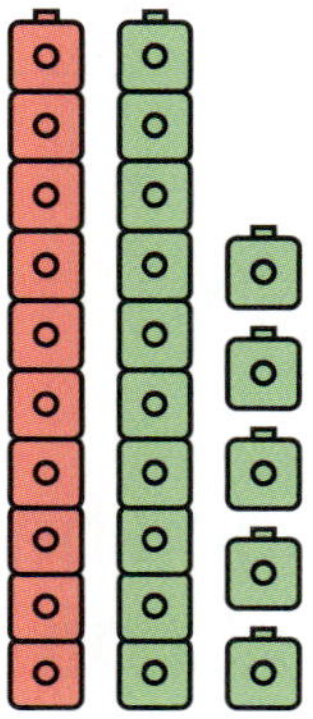

2 tens 5 ones = 25

15 and 10 more make 25.

Count on by tens to check. 5 15 25 35

Rachel reads 25 pages.

PRACTICE

Look at the model. Write the number that is 10 more.

1. 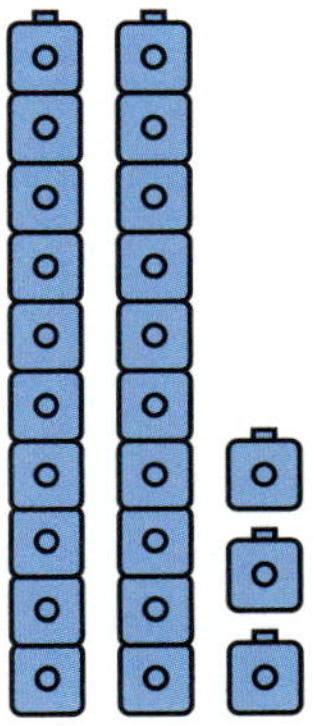

23 33

2. 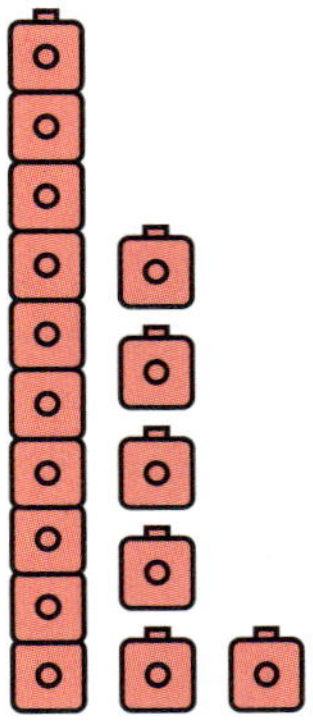

16 ______

3. 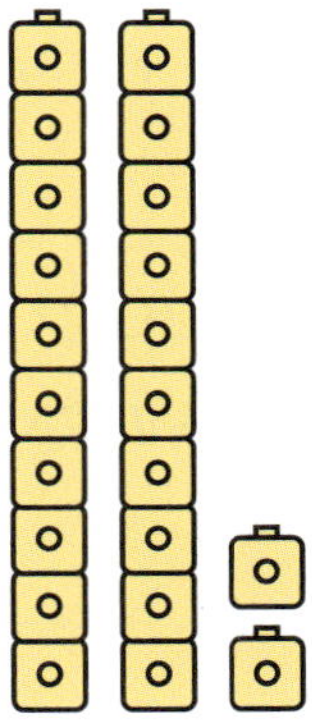

22 ______

PRACTICE

Use mental math.
Write the number that is 10 more.

4. 18 ______	5. 55 ______	6. 20 ______
7. 34 ______	8. 41 ______	9. 90 ______

Problem Solving

10. Leah buys 2 erasers. Then she buys 10 more.
How many erasers does Leah have?
Draw a model to show how you know.

Leah has ______ erasers.

11. Ben says 10 more than 45 is 54.
Jon says 10 more than 45 is 55.
Who is right? Tell how you know.

____

Write About It

12. Write a math story about finding 10 more.
Show how to find the answer.

____

____

Name ______________________________

Mental Math: Find 10 More

Adding 10 more is the same as adding 1 ten.

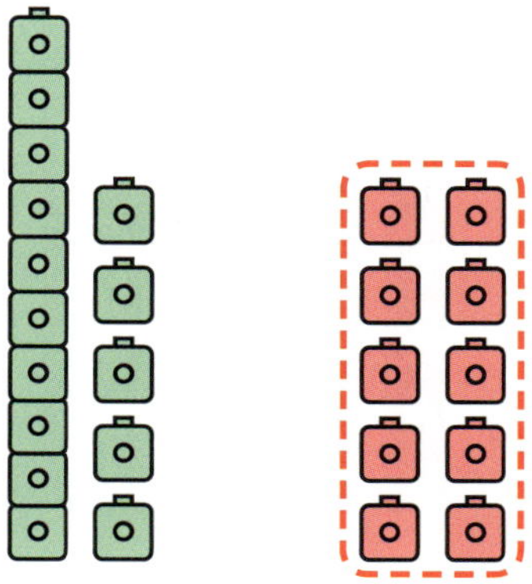

1 ten 5 ones　　10 ones

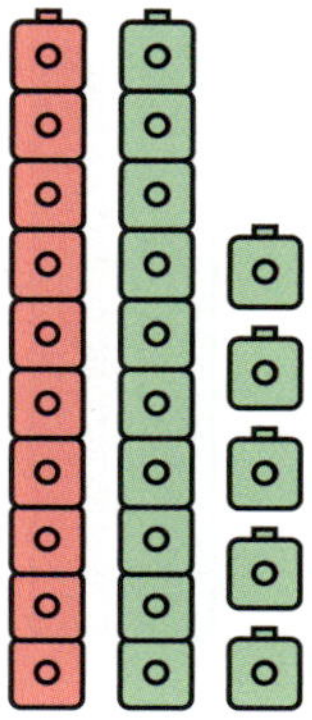

2 tens 5 ones = 25

Adding 10 more is the same as adding 1 ten.

1 ten + 1 ten = 2 tens.
So 15 + 10 = 25.

15 and 10 more make 25.

Count on by tens to check.　　5　15　25　35

MORE PRACTICE

Look at the model.
Write the number that is 10 more.

1.

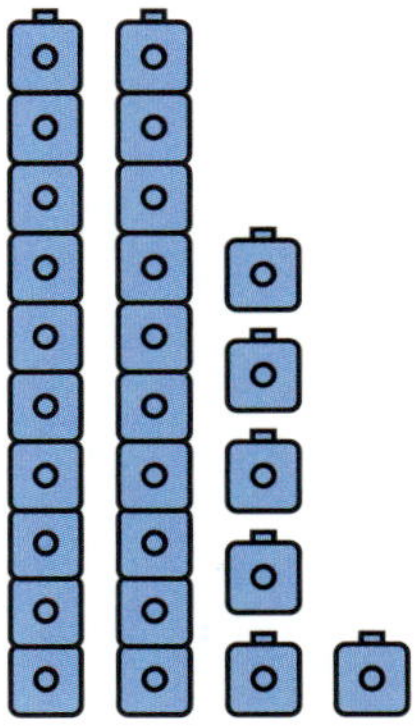

26 ______

2.

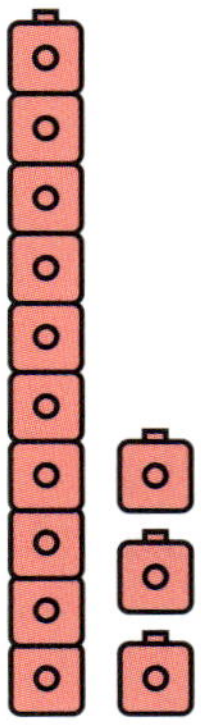

13 ______

3.

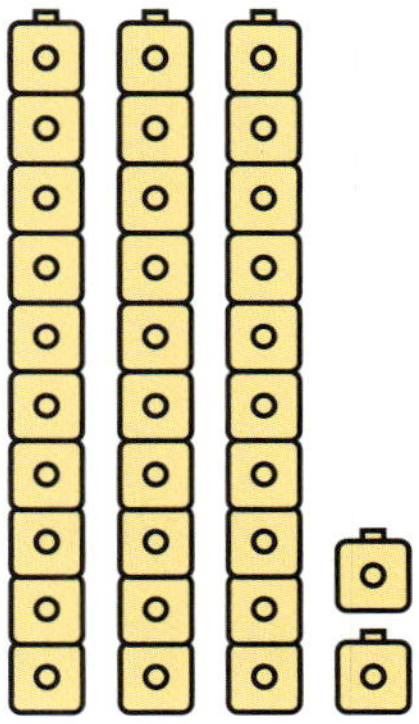

32 ______

HOMEWORK

Look at the model.
Write the number that is 10 more.

1. 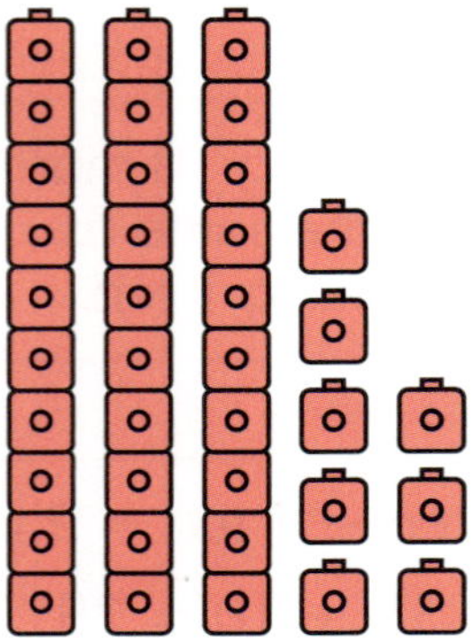

38 ____

2. 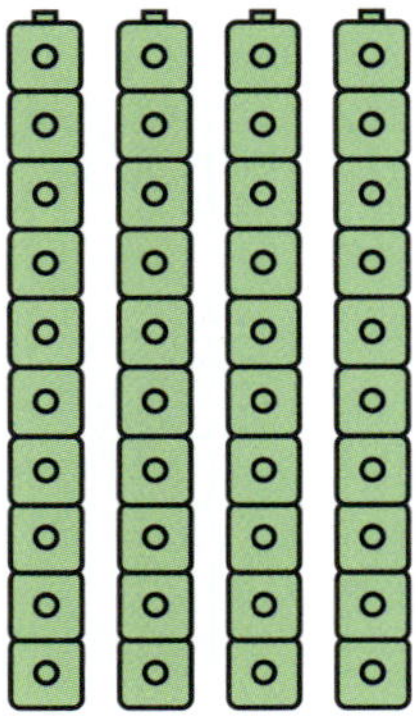

40 ____

3. 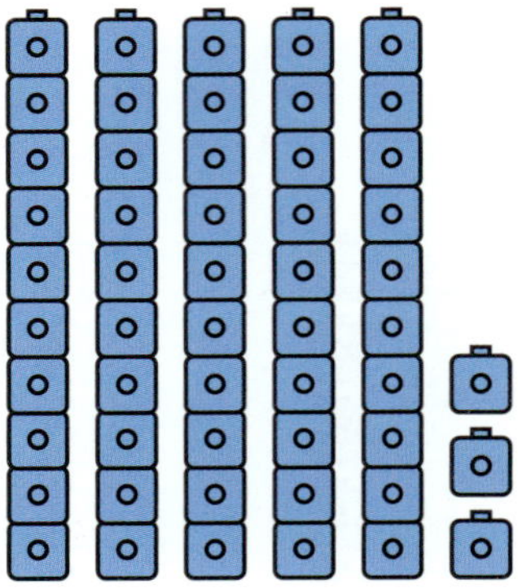

53 ____

Use mental math. Write the number that is 10 more.

4. 39 ____

5. 51 ____

6. 80 ____

Problem Solving

7. Tim has 29 balloons. Sergio has 10 more than Tim. How many balloons does Sergio have?

Sergio has ____ balloons.

Write About It

8. Tell how you can find the number that is 10 more than 23.

____

____

Name ____________________

LESSON 11-2

Objective
- Use models to add multiples of ten.

Math Word
tens

Add Tens

Alexis eats 10 raisins.
Then she eats 20 more raisins.
How many raisins does Alexis eat in all?

To add 10 + 20, think 1 ten + 2 tens.

$$\begin{array}{r} 1 \text{ ten} \\ +\ 2 \text{ tens} \\ \hline 3 \text{ tens} \end{array}$$

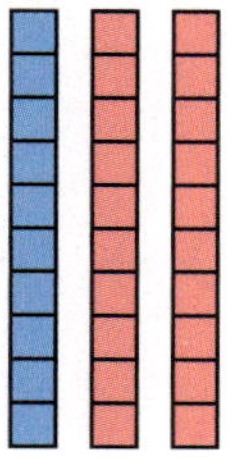

$$\begin{array}{r} 10 \\ +\ 20 \\ \hline 30 \end{array}$$

3 tens = 30 and 10 + 20 = 30.

Alexis eats 30 raisins in all.

PRACTICE

Add. Use  **to help.**

1.

$$\begin{array}{r} 5 \text{ tens} \\ +\ 3 \text{ tens} \\ \hline 8 \text{ tens} \end{array} \qquad \begin{array}{r} \boxed{50} \\ +\ \boxed{30} \\ \hline 80 \end{array}$$

2.

$$\begin{array}{r} 6 \text{ tens} \\ +\ 3 \text{ tens} \\ \hline \_\_\_ \text{ tens} \end{array} \qquad \begin{array}{r} \boxed{} \\ +\ \boxed{} \\ \hline \end{array}$$

3. 1 ten + 5 tens

= _____ tens

_____ + _____ = _____

4. 3 tens + 5 tens

= _____ tens

_____ + _____ = _____

PRACTICE

Add. Use  **to check.**

5. $\begin{array}{r} 40 \\ +50 \\ \hline 90 \end{array}$

6. $\begin{array}{r} 30 \\ +50 \\ \hline \end{array}$

7. $\begin{array}{r} 30 \\ +30 \\ \hline \end{array}$

8. $\begin{array}{r} 60 \\ +10 \\ \hline \end{array}$

9. $\begin{array}{r} 20 \\ +70 \\ \hline \end{array}$

10. 20 + 40 = ____

11. 50 + 20 = ____

12. 30 + 20 = ____

13. 40 + 40 = ____

Problem Solving

14. Lucy has two notebooks. One notebook has 30 sheets of paper. The other notebook also has 30 sheets of paper. How many sheets of paper does Lucy have in all?

Lucy has 30 + 30 = ____ sheets of paper in all.

Write About It

15. Matt hit some baseballs. Look for a pattern in the chart. Complete the chart. Then explain the pattern.

	Baseballs Hit
Morning	10
Afternoon	
Total	20

____

____

Name ____________________

Add Tens

To add 10 + 20, think 1 ten + 2 tens.

$$\begin{array}{r} 1 \text{ ten} \\ +\,2 \text{ tens} \\ \hline 3 \text{ tens} \end{array}$$

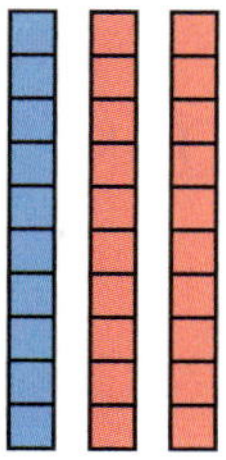

$$\begin{array}{r} 10 \\ +\,20 \\ \hline 30 \end{array}$$

3 tens = 30 and 10 + 20 = 30

MORE PRACTICE

Add. Use  to help.

1.

$$\begin{array}{r} 4 \text{ tens} \\ +\,3 \text{ tens} \\ \hline \underline{\quad} \text{ tens} \end{array} \qquad \begin{array}{r} \square \\ +\,\square \\ \hline \end{array}$$

2.

$$\begin{array}{r} 5 \text{ tens} \\ +\,3 \text{ tens} \\ \hline \underline{\quad} \text{ tens} \end{array} \qquad \begin{array}{r} \square \\ +\,\square \\ \hline \end{array}$$

3.

$$\begin{array}{r} 5 \text{ tens} \\ +\,2 \text{ tens} \\ \hline \underline{\quad} \text{ tens} \end{array} \qquad \begin{array}{r} \square \\ +\,\square \\ \hline \end{array}$$

4.

$$\begin{array}{r} 2 \text{ tens} \\ +\,4 \text{ tens} \\ \hline \underline{\quad} \text{ tens} \end{array} \qquad \begin{array}{r} \square \\ +\,\square \\ \hline \end{array}$$

5. 1 ten + 8 tens = ____ tens

____ + ____ = ____

6. 4 tens + 4 tens = ____ tens

____ + ____ = ____

HOMEWORK

Add. Draw a model to check. Use lines for tens.

1. 10 + 40 = ____

2. 20 + 30 = ____

3. 80 + 10 = ____

4. 10 + 10 = ____

5. $\begin{array}{r} 40 \\ +40 \\ \hline \end{array}$

6. $\begin{array}{r} 10 \\ +50 \\ \hline \end{array}$

7. $\begin{array}{r} 20 \\ +20 \\ \hline \end{array}$

8. $\begin{array}{r} 70 \\ +10 \\ \hline \end{array}$

9. $\begin{array}{r} 30 \\ +40 \\ \hline \end{array}$

Problem Solving

10. Gina reads 20 pages of her book on Monday. She reads 20 more pages on Tuesday. How many pages does Gina read in all?

Gina reads ____ + ____ = ____ pages.

Write About It

11. Explain how to add 30 + 50 by adding tens. Use words and draw a model.

____

____

____

Name ____________________

LESSON 11-3

Objective

- Count on to add tens to a two-digit number.

Math Word

addend

Add Two-Digit Numbers and Multiples of Ten

Trenton picks 42 cherries from one tree.
He picks 20 more cherries from another tree.
How many cherries does Trenton pick in all?

You can count on by tens to add.

Start with the addend 42. Count on 2 tens.

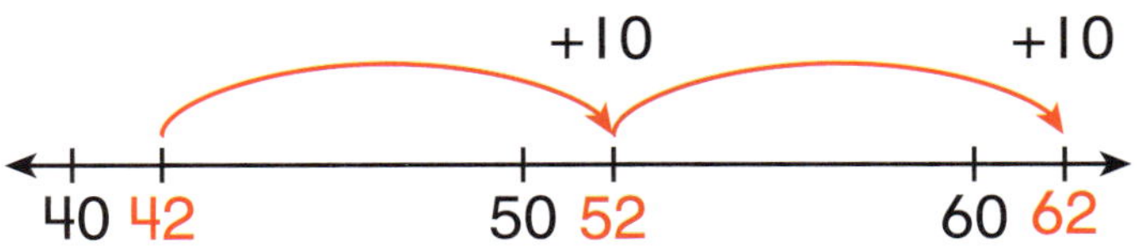

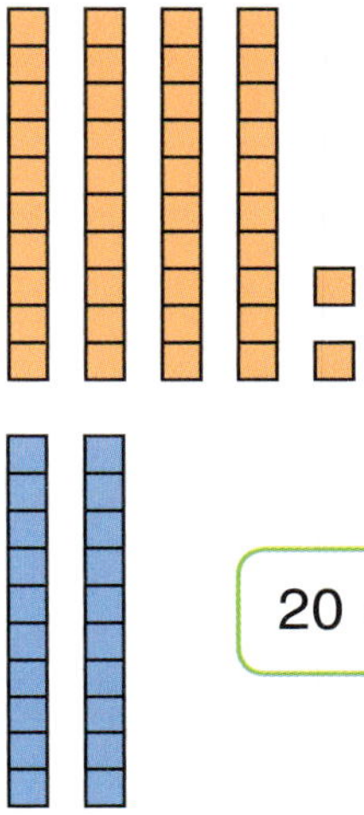

20 = 2 tens

42 + 20 = 62

Trenton picks 62 cherries.

PRACTICE

Model the first addend.
Then count on by tens to add.

1. $\begin{array}{r} 35 \\ +\,20 \\ \hline 55 \end{array}$

2. $\begin{array}{r} 31 \\ +\,10 \\ \hline \end{array}$

3. $\begin{array}{r} 74 \\ +\,20 \\ \hline \end{array}$

4. $\begin{array}{r} 62 \\ +\,20 \\ \hline \end{array}$

5. $\begin{array}{r} 18 \\ +\,50 \\ \hline \end{array}$

6. $\begin{array}{r} 50 \\ +\,30 \\ \hline \end{array}$

7. $\begin{array}{r} 44 \\ +\,40 \\ \hline \end{array}$

8. $\begin{array}{r} 26 \\ +\,30 \\ \hline \end{array}$

9. 56 + 20 = ______

10. 12 + 30 = ______

PRACTICE

Count on by tens to add.

11. $\begin{array}{r} 73 \\ +20 \\ \hline 93 \end{array}$

12. $\begin{array}{r} 36 \\ +20 \\ \hline \end{array}$

13. $\begin{array}{r} 53 \\ +30 \\ \hline \end{array}$

14. $\begin{array}{r} 18 \\ +70 \\ \hline \end{array}$

15. $\begin{array}{r} 26 \\ +40 \\ \hline \end{array}$

16. $\begin{array}{r} 55 \\ +20 \\ \hline \end{array}$

17. $\begin{array}{r} 81 \\ +10 \\ \hline \end{array}$

18. $\begin{array}{r} 13 \\ +30 \\ \hline \end{array}$

19. 50 + 40 = ______

20. 34 + 40 = ______

Problem Solving

21. Devin has 28 blocks. Marty gives him 4 tens. How many blocks does Devin have now?

Devin has ______ blocks.

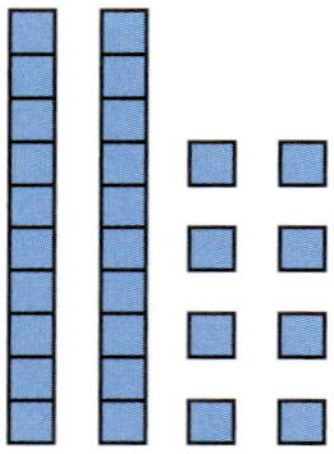

Write About It

22. Look at the addition equations. What do you notice about the addends and sums?

$\begin{array}{r} 55 \\ +20 \\ \hline 75 \end{array}$ $\quad$ $\begin{array}{r} 25 \\ +50 \\ \hline 75 \end{array}$

____

____

____

____

Name ______________________________

Add Two-Digit Numbers and Multiples of Ten

What is 42 + 20?
You can count on by tens to add.

Start with the addend 42.
Count on 2 tens.

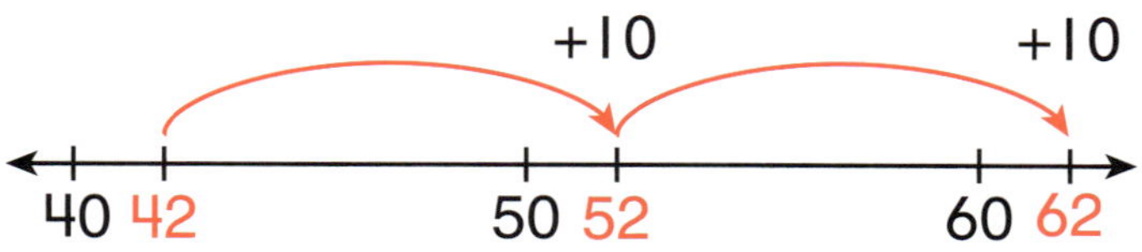

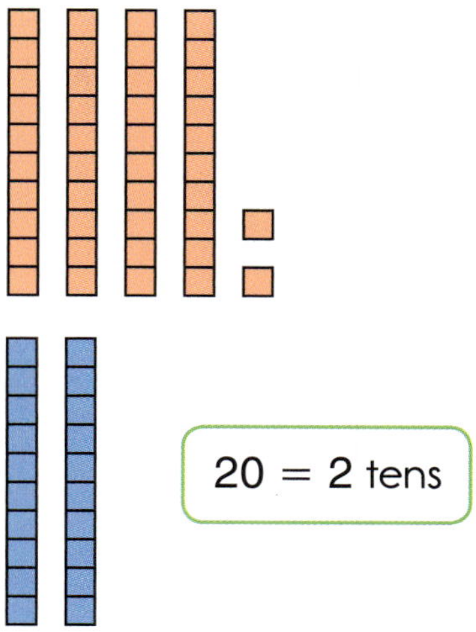

42 + 20 = 62

MORE PRACTICE

Count on by tens to add.
You can draw a model to help.

1. 86 + 10 = _____

2. 18 + 20 = _____

3. 46 + 10 = _____

4. 15 + 30 = _____

HOMEWORK

Count on by tens to add.
You can draw a model to help.

1. $\begin{array}{r} 28 \\ +\ 10 \\ \hline \end{array}$

2. $\begin{array}{r} 22 \\ +\ 20 \\ \hline \end{array}$

3. $\begin{array}{r} 48 \\ +\ 30 \\ \hline \end{array}$

4. 53 + 20 = _____

5. 17 + 30 = _____

Problem Solving

6. Sari finds 21 leaves.
   Then she finds 20 more leaves.
   How many leaves does Sari find in all?

   Sari finds 21 + 20 = _____ leaves in all.

Write About It

7. What is the same about these addition equations? What is different?

   14 + 40 = 54   34 + 20 = 54

   > Look at the tens and ones in the addends and the sums.

   ____

   ____

   ____

Name ________________________________

LESSON 11-4

Objective
- Add a two-digit number and a one-digit number without regrouping.

Math Word
count on

Add Two-Digit and One-Digit Numbers

There are 26 children on a bus.
Then 3 more children get on the bus.
How many children are on the bus now?

Model the two-digit number.

Model the one-digit number.

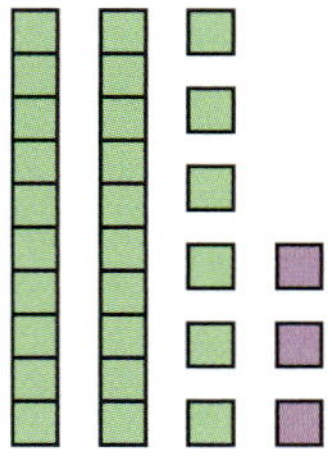

	tens	ones
	2	6
+		3
	2	9

Count on by ones to add.

Start at 26. Count on 3.

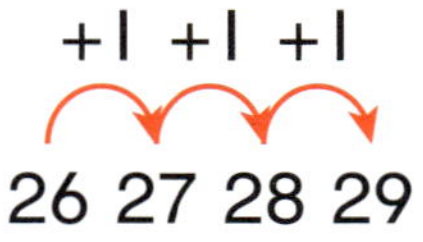

So, 26 + 3 = 29.
There are 29 children on the bus.

PRACTICE

Model the two-digit number.
Count on by ones to add.

1. 2 more than 17
19
17, 18,
19

2. 4 more than 25
______
______, ______,
______, ______,
______

3. 2 more than 31
______
______, ______,
______

PRACTICE

Model the two-digit number. Count on by ones to add.

4. 13 + 5 = ______

______, ______, ______, ______,

______, ______

5. 24 + 4 = ______

______, ______, ______, ______,

______

6. 41 + 3 = ______

______, ______, ______, ______

7. 66 + 2 = ______

______, ______, ______

Problem Solving

8. Ben picks 15 peppers in the garden.
Then he picks 4 more peppers.
How many peppers does Ben pick in all?
Tell how you know.

Ben picks ______ peppers in all.

____

Write About It

9. Bryce says that 3 more than 29 is 31.
Is Bryce right? Tell how you know.

____

____

Name ______________________________

Add Two-Digit and One-Digit Numbers

Add 26 + 3.

Model the two-digit number.

Model the one-digit number.

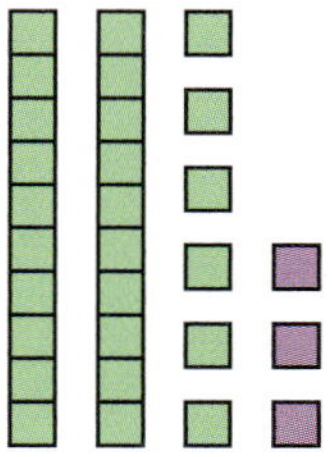

	tens	ones
	2	6
+		3
	2	9

Count on by ones to add.

Start at 26. Count on 3.

+1 +1 +1

26 27 28 29

26 + 3 = 29.

MORE PRACTICE

Count on by ones to add.
You can draw a model to help.

1. 3 more than 35

_____

2. 6 more than 21

_____

3. 2 more than 52

_____

4. 7 more than 43

_____

HOMEWORK

Count on by ones to add.
You can draw a model to help.

1. 24 + 2 = ____

   24, 25, 26

2. 12 + 3 = ____

   12, ____,

   ____, ____

3. 33 + 5 = ____

   33, ____, ____,

   ____, ____, ____

4. 45 + 4 = ____

   45, ____, ____,

   ____, ____

Problem Solving

5. Kevin picks 12 apples.
   Reagan picks 3 more apples than Kevin.
   How many apples does Reagan pick?
   Draw a model to show how you know.

   Reagan picks ____ apples.

Write About It

6. Jordyn says that 4 more than 13 is 16.
   Tim says 4 more than 13 is 17.
   Who is right? Tell how you know.

   ____

   ____

Name ____________________

Make a 10 to Add Two-Digit and One-Digit Numbers

Objective

- Add a two-digit number and a one-digit number with regrouping.

Math Words

two-digit number
ones
tens

Peter has 25 pennies.
Nick has 6 more pennies than Peter.
How many pennies does Nick have?

Add: 25 + 6 = ?

Use a model.

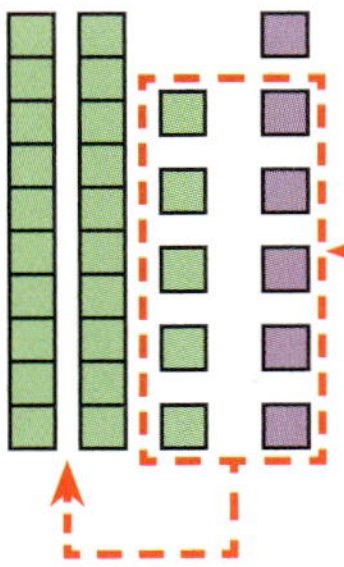

Add the ones.

Make a 10 if there are more than 9 ones.

Add the tens.

Use a place-value chart.

	tens	ones
	1	
	2	5
+		6
	3	1

So, 25 + 6 = 31. Nick has 31 pennies.

PRACTICE

Add. Use the model and place-value chart.

1. 18 + 4 = 22

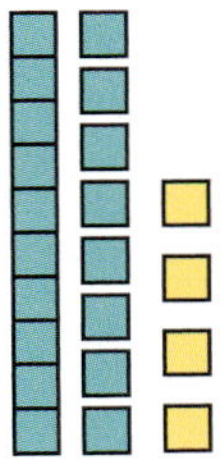

	tens	ones
	1	
	1	8
+		4
	2	2

2. 32 + 7 = ______

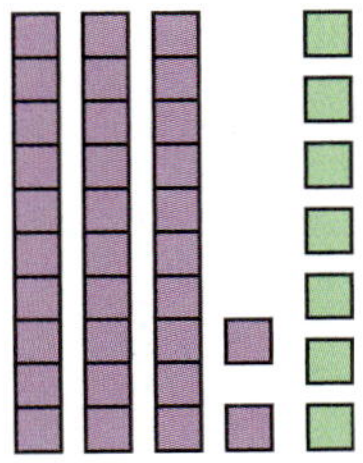

	tens	ones
	3	2
+		7

PRACTICE

Add. Use the model and place-value chart.

3. 47 + 7 = 54

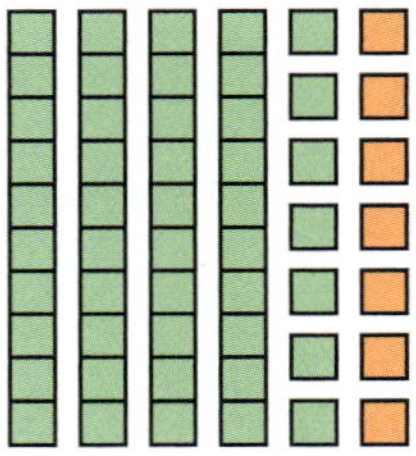

	tens	ones
	4	7
+		7

4. 64 + 6 = ______

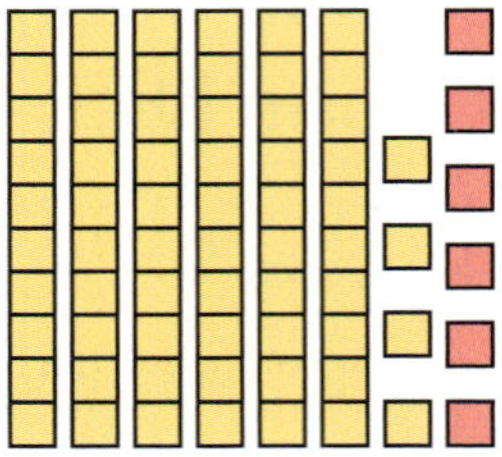

	tens	ones
	6	4
+		6

Problem Solving

5. Kay jumps rope 14 times.
Then she jumps 9 more times.
How many times does Kay jump in all?
Show how you know.

Kay jumps ______ times in all.

Write About It

6. Gina says 27 plus 3 is 29. What error did Gina make? Tell how you know.

____

____

____

Name ______________________________

Make a 10 to Add Two-Digit and One-Digit Numbers

$25 + 6 = ?$

Use a model.

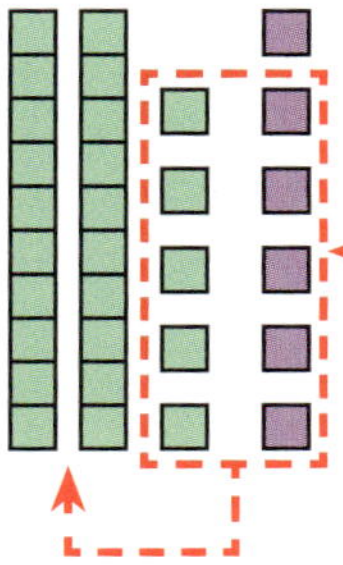

Add the ones.

Make a 10 if there are more than 9 ones.

Add the tens.

Use a place-value chart.

	tens	ones
	1	
	2	5
+		6
	3	1

$25 + 6 = 31$

MORE PRACTICE

Add. Use the model and place-value chart.

1. $36 + 4 =$ ____

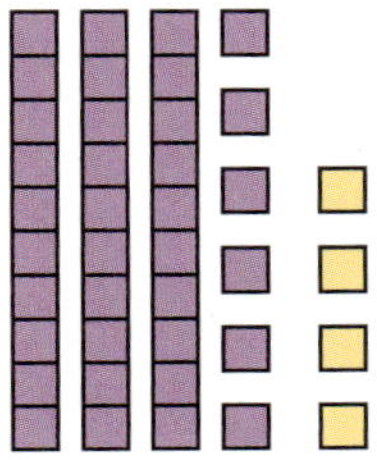

	tens	ones
	3	6
+		4

Did you make a 10?

Yes No

2. $16 + 7 =$ ____

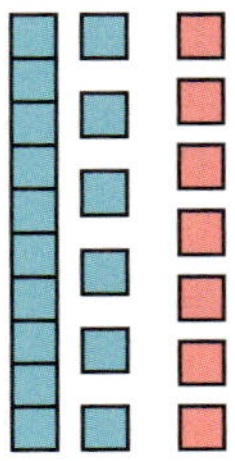

	tens	ones
	1	6
+		7

Did you make a 10?

Yes No

HOMEWORK

Add. Use the model and place-value chart.

1. 54 + 5 = ____

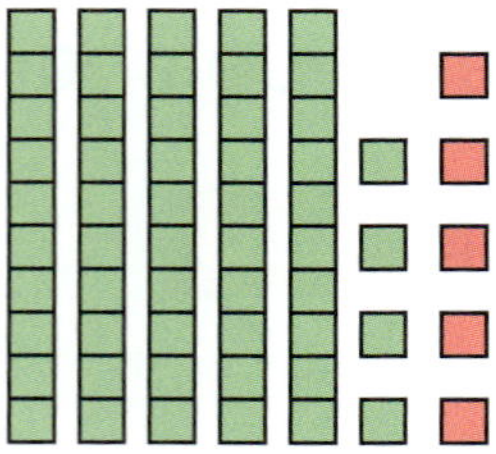

	tens	ones
	5	4
+		5

2. 28 + 2 = ____

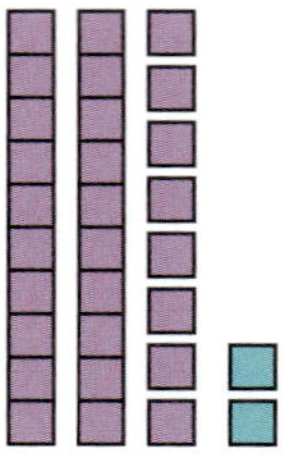

	tens	ones
	2	8
+		2

3. 77 + 4 = ____

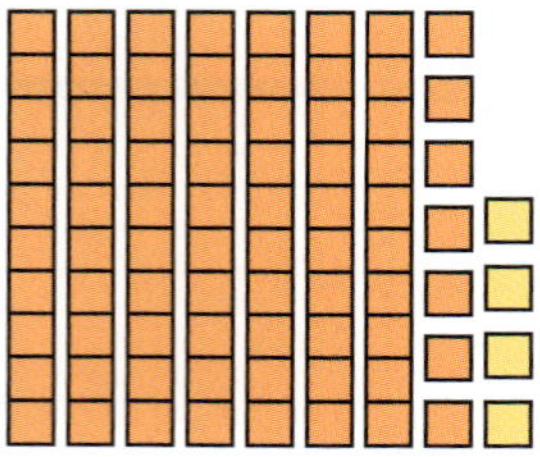

	tens	ones
	7	7
+		4

4. 49 + 6 = ____

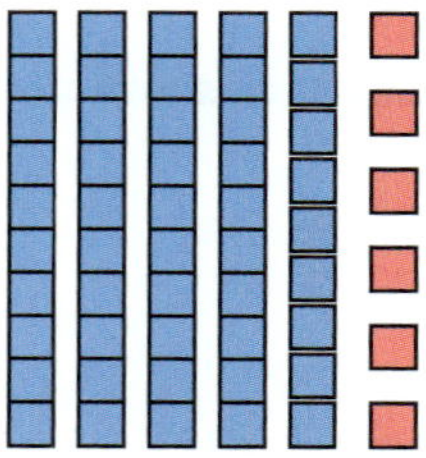

	tens	ones
	4	9
+		6

Problem Solving

5. Alisa found 12 shells, and then 8 more shells. Show how many shells Alisa found in all.

Alisa found ____ shells.

Write About It

6. Harry needs to add 32 + 6. Tell how he can use place value to add.

____

CHAPTER 11
Check Your Progress

Name ____________________

Find the correct answer.

1. Which number is 10 more than 44?

   A. 34
   B. 54
   C. 55

2. 3 tens + 2 tens = ?

   A. 3 tens
   B. 4 tens
   C. 5 tens

3. Which has a sum of 42?

   A. 12 + 30 = ?
   B. 22 + 30 = ?
   C. 32 + 20 = ?

4. Which number is 2 more than 61?

   A. 83
   B. 63
   C. 23

5. $\begin{array}{r} 20 \\ +\,70 \\ \hline \end{array}$

   A. 90
   B. 80
   C. 70

6. Which number is 4 more than 27?

   A. 23
   B. 24
   C. 31

7. 2 tens + 2 ones = ?

   A. 21
   B. 22
   C. 40

8. 2 tens + 2 tens = ?

   A. 21
   B. 22
   C. 40

Find the correct answer.

9.
$$\begin{array}{r} 26 \\ +\ 20 \\ \hline \end{array}$$

A. 46
B. 36
C. 26

10. Mr. Ray has 10 cups. Then he buys 25 more cups. How many cups does Mr. Ray have now?

Mr. Ray has _____ cups.

11. 26 + 2 = ?

_____

12.
$$\begin{array}{r} 35 \\ +\ \ 3 \\ \hline \end{array}$$

_____

13. Drew has 18 blocks. Joey gives him 3 groups of ten blocks. How many blocks does Drew have in all?

Drew has _____ blocks in all.

14. Autumn picks 13 flowers. Kayla picks 3 more flowers than Autumn. How many flowers does Kayla pick?

Kayla picks _____ flowers.

15. 30 + 30 = ?

_____

16. 74 + 3 = ?

_____

17. 5 tens + 4 tens = ?

A. 7 tens
B. 9 tens
C. 10 tens

18. Which TWO have a sum of 40?

A. 30 + 10
B. 2 tens + 2 tens
C. 10 + 20

LESSON 11-6

Name ____________________

Add Two-Digit Numbers

Objective

- Add 2 two-digit numbers without regrouping.

Math Words

tens
ones

Ava has 18 white shells.
She has 21 pink shells.
How many shells does Ava have in all?

18 + 21 = ?

Model the addends.

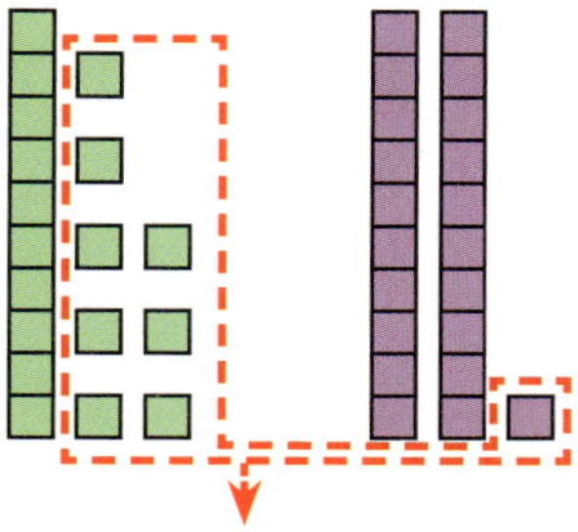

8 ones + 1 one = 9 ones

1 ten + 2 tens = 3 tens

3 tens and 9 ones = 39

Use a place-value chart.

	tens	ones
	1	8
+	2	1
	3	9

Add the ones.

Add the tens.

Ava has 39 shells in all.

PRACTICE

Model the addends.
Add the ones. Add the tens.

1. 27 + 22 = 49

	tens	ones
	2	7
+	2	2
	4	9

2. 26 + 31 = ____

	tens	ones

PRACTICE

Model the addends. Add the ones. Add the tens.

3. 36 + 62 = ____

tens	ones

4. 52 + 13 = ____

tens	ones

5. 66 + 23 = ____

tens	ones

6. 17 + 41 = ____

tens	ones

Problem Solving

7. Isaac has 13 red blocks. He has 24 green blocks. How many blocks does Isaac have in all? Draw a model to show how you know.

Isaac has ____ blocks in all.

Write About It

8. Tell how to add 54 + 14.

____

____

Name ______________________________

Add Two-Digit Numbers

What is 18 + 21?

Model the addends.

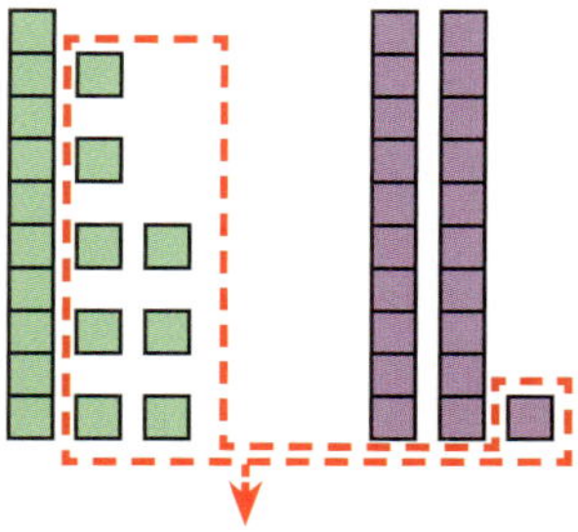

8 ones + 1 one = 9 ones

1 ten + 2 tens = 3 tens

3 tens + 9 ones = 39

18 + 21 = 39

Use place value.

	tens	ones
	1	8
+	2	1
	3	9

Add the ones.

Add the tens.

MORE PRACTICE

Draw a model of the addends.
Add the ones. Add the tens.

1. 15 + 33 = ______

tens	ones

2. 34 + 35 = ______

tens	ones

Draw a model. Add the ones. Add the tens.

1. 63 + 21 = 84

	tens	ones
	6	3
+	2	1
	8	4

2. 25 + 13 = ____

	tens	ones

3. 74 + 22 = ____

	tens	ones

4. 24 + 34 = ____

	tens	ones

Problem Solving

5. Lisa has 11 red feathers. She has 13 blue feathers. How many feathers does Lisa have? Draw a model to show how you know.

Lisa has ____ feathers.

Write About It

6. How do models help you add 65 + 12?

____

____

Name ______________________________

Make a 10 to Add Two-Digit Numbers

Objectives
- Use place value when adding 2 two-digit numbers.
- Add 2 two-digit numbers with regrouping.

Math Words
tens
ones

There are 34 plums and 28 pears in a box. How many pieces of fruit are in the box in all?

Think What is 34 + 28?

Add the ones.

Try to make a ten.

	tens	ones
	1	
	3	4
+	2	8
		2

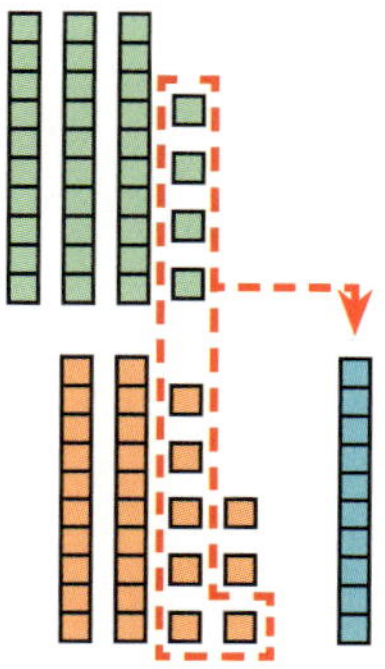

4 + 8 = 12
That is 1 ten and 2 ones.

Then add the tens.

Add any tens you made.

	tens	ones
	1	
	3	4
+	2	8
	6	2

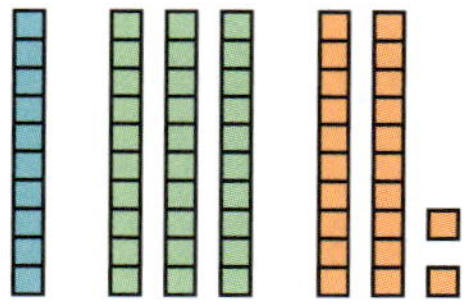

So, 34 + 28 = 62.

There are 62 pieces of fruit in the box.

PRACTICE

Add. Make a ten if you can.

1.

	tens	ones
	1	
	7	1
+	1	9
	9	0

2.

	tens	ones
	5	6
+	2	3

PRACTICE

Add. Make a ten if you can.

3.

	tens	ones
	7	9
+	1	4

4.

	tens	ones
	2	9
+	4	2

5.

	tens	ones
	4	5
+	2	8

Problem Solving

6. Nolan sees 23 yellow fish and 18 blue fish in a tank. How many fish does Nolan see in all? Explain how you know.

Nolan sees ______ fish.

____

____

____

Write About It

7. How do you make a ten to add 26 + 34? Tell how you know.

____

____

____

Name ______________________________

Make a 10 to Add Two-Digit Numbers

34 + 28 = ?

Add the ones.

Try to make a ten.

	tens	ones
	1	
	3	4
+	2	8
		2

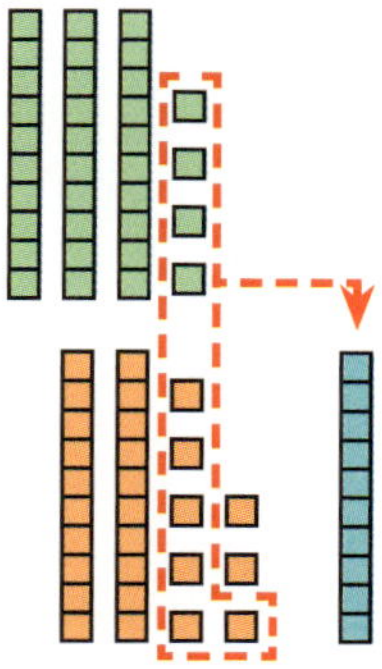

Then add the tens.

Add any tens you made.

	tens	ones
	1	
	3	4
+	2	8
	6	2

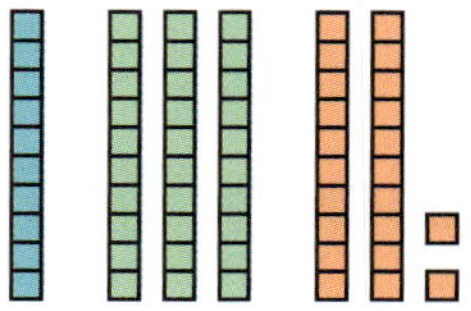

4 + 8 = 12

That is 1 ten and 2 ones.

So, 34 + 28 = 62.

MORE PRACTICE

Add the ones. Make a ten if you can.
Add the tens.

1.

	tens	ones
	7	6
+	1	4

2.

	tens	ones
	2	5
+	3	7

HOMEWORK

**Add the ones. Make a ten if you can.
Add the tens.**

1.

	tens	ones
	2	2
+	3	9

2.

	tens	ones
	7	9
+	1	7

3.

	tens	ones
	5	4
+	2	6

Problem Solving

4. Jim does 24 sit-ups on Monday. He does 17 sit-ups on Tuesday. How many sit-ups does Jim do in all? Show how you know.

Jim does _____ sit-ups in all.

Write About It

5. What is wrong with the addition? Tell how you know.

____

____

____

	tens	ones
	6	8
+	1	4
	7	2

Name ______________________________

Objective
- Break apart addends to add two-digit numbers.

Math Words
addend
sum
expanded form

Break Apart to Add

Kendall counts 26 cars in a parking lot.
Sofia counts 32 cars on the street.
How many cars do they count in all?

Add 26 + 32.

Break apart the addends into tens and ones.

Add the tens.

Add the ones.

Add the sums.

The addends are in expanded form.

$$\begin{array}{r} 26 \\ +32 \\ \hline ? \end{array} \rightarrow \begin{array}{r} 20 + 6 \\ +30 + 2 \\ \hline 50 + 8 = 58 \end{array}$$

Kendall and Sofia count 58 cars.

PRACTICE

Break apart the addends to find the sum.

1. 23 → 20 + 3
   +42 → +40 + 2
   60 + 5 = 65

2. 64 → ☐ + ☐
   +28 → +☐ + ☐
   ___ + ___ = ____

PRACTICE

Break apart the addends to find the sum.

3.

76 → ☐ + ☐

+ 22 → + ☐ + ☐

+ = ____

4.

24 → ☐ + ☐

+ 46 → + ☐ + ☐

+ = ____

Problem Solving

5. Richard's team scores 26 points. Jalen's team scores 25 points. How many points do the two teams score in all? Explain how you know.

The two teams score ____ points in all.

____

____

____

Write About It

6. Trinity is adding two-digit numbers. She breaks apart the addends. Which two-digit numbers could Trinity be adding? Tell how you know.

30 + 50 + 2 + 9

____

____

Name ______________________________

Break Apart to Add

Add 26 + 32.

Break apart the addends into tens and ones.

Add the tens.

Add the ones.

Add the sums.

26 + 32 = 58

The addends are in expanded form.

$$\begin{array}{r} 26 \\ +\,32 \\ \hline ? \end{array} \quad \begin{array}{r} \rightarrow \quad 20 + 6 \\ \rightarrow +30 + 2 \\ \hline 50 + 8 = 58 \end{array}$$

MORE PRACTICE

Break apart the addends to find the sum.

1. 33 → ☐ + ☐
   + 42 → + ☐ + ☐
   ___ + ___ = ___

2. 72 → ☐ + ☐
   + 27 → + ☐ + ☐
   ___ + ___ = ___

3. 35 → ☐ + ☐
   + 23 → + ☐ + ☐
   ___ + ___ = ___

4. 78 → ☐ + ☐
   + 11 → + ☐ + ☐
   ___ + ___ = ___

HOMEWORK

1.
```
  35        [  ] + [  ]
+ 46  →  +  [  ] + [  ]
----     ---------------
                 +      = ____
```

2.
```
  43  →     [  ] + [  ]
+ 24  →  +  [  ] + [  ]
----     ---------------
                 +      = ____
```

3. 65 + 22 = ____

____ + ____ + ____ +

____ = ____

4. 25 + 26 = ____

____ + ____ + ____ +

____ = ____

Problem Solving

5. Kedar has 25 green grapes and 52 red grapes. How many grapes does Kedar have in all?

Kedar has ____ grapes in all.

Write About It

6. Maria broke apart addends to find the sum of 62 + 28 = 80.

Do you agree with her answer? Explain.

____

____

____

Name ______________________________

LESSON 11-9

Objective
- Use bar models to solve two-digit addition problems.

Math Word
bar model

Problem Solving
Read › Plan › Solve › Check

Use a Model

Jane is making bracelets. She has 18 purple beads. She has 6 pink beads. How many beads does she have in all?

Think What is 18 + 6?

Use a bar model to help.

One part is 18.

The other part is 6.

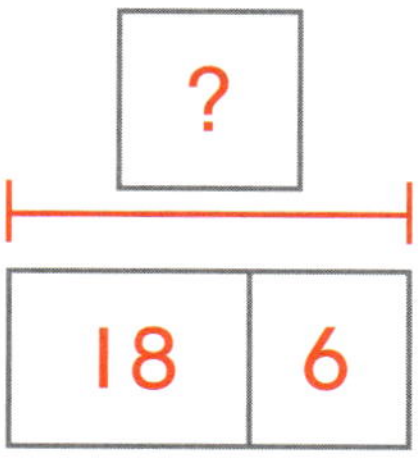

Add to solve.

```
  1
  18
+  6
  24
```

Jane has 24 beads in all.

PRACTICE

Complete the bar model. Find the sum.

1. Jake scores 24 points in a game. Bill scores 16 points. What are the total points scored?

   The total scored is 40 points.

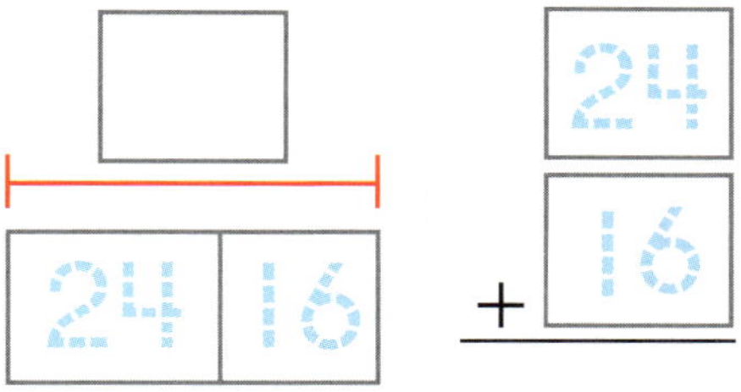

2. A store has the same number of soccer balls and tennis balls. There are 19 soccer balls. How many balls are there in all?

   There are _____ balls in all.

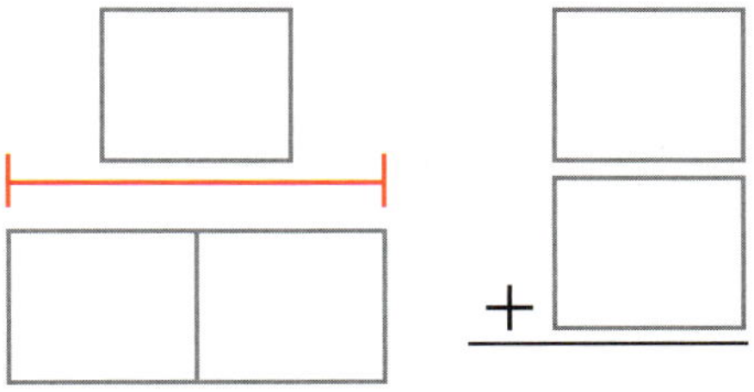

PRACTICE

Complete the bar model. Solve the problem.

3. Joy finds 25 rocks. Cara finds 7 rocks. How many rocks do they find in all?

   They find _____ rocks in all.

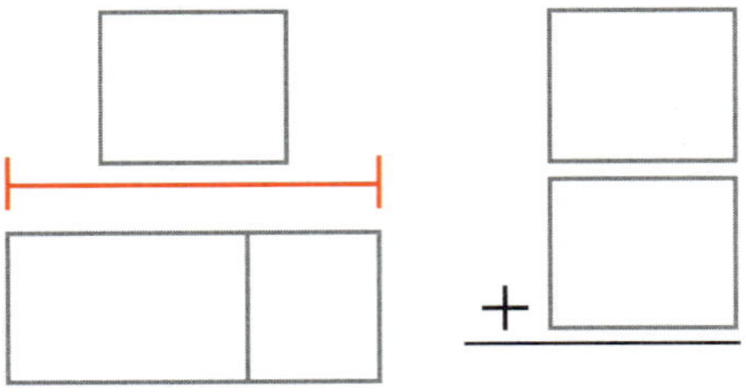

4. Layla gives 17 flowers to Ellen. She has 24 flowers left. How many flowers did Layla have to start?

   Layla started with _____ flowers.

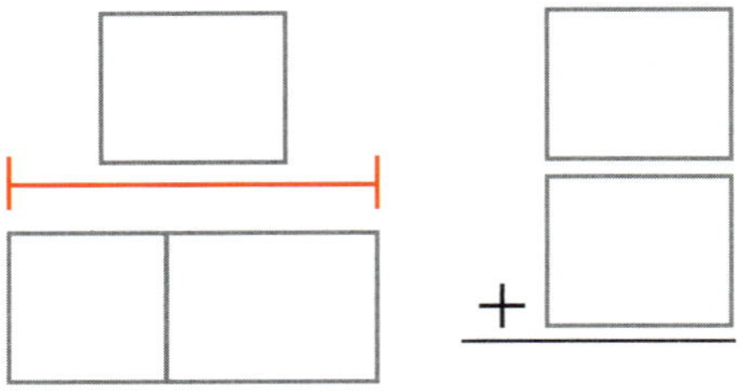

5. Mason plays the violin for 35 minutes. Later he plays for 25 minutes. How many minutes does Mason play in all?

   Mason plays for _____ minutes in all.

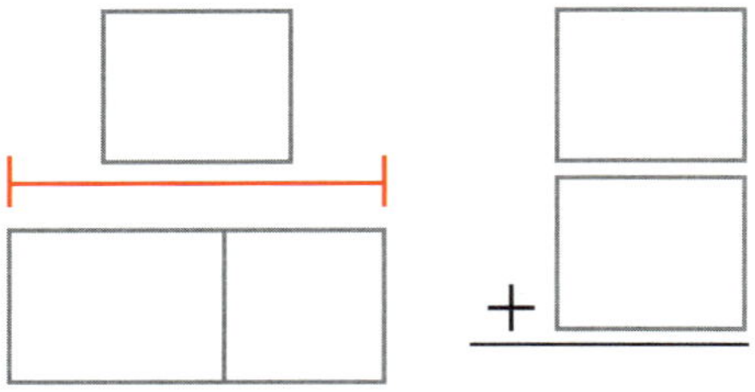

Write About It

6. How can a bar model help you solve an addition problem?

____

____

____

Name ____________________

Problem Solving
Use a Model

Jane is making bracelets. She has 18 purple beads. She has 6 pink beads. How many beads does she have in all?

Use a bar model to help.

One part is 18.

The other part is 6.

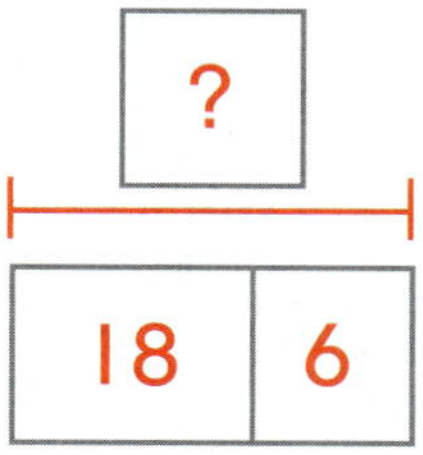

Add to solve.

$$\begin{array}{r} ^{1}\\ 18 \\ +\ \ 6 \\ \hline 24 \end{array}$$

Jane has 24 beads in all.

MORE PRACTICE

Complete the bar model. Find the sum.

1. Ella scores 12 points in a basketball game. Jill scores 7 more points than Ella. How many points does Jill score?

   Jill scores _____ points.

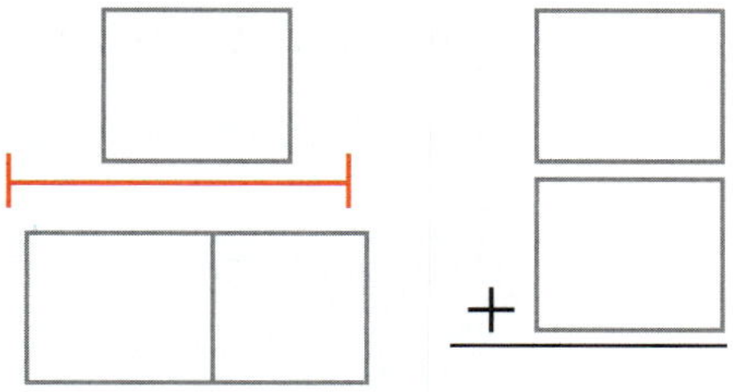

2. Each side of a bus has the same number of seats. There are 17 seats on one side. How many seats are on the bus in all?

   There are _____ seats on the bus in all.

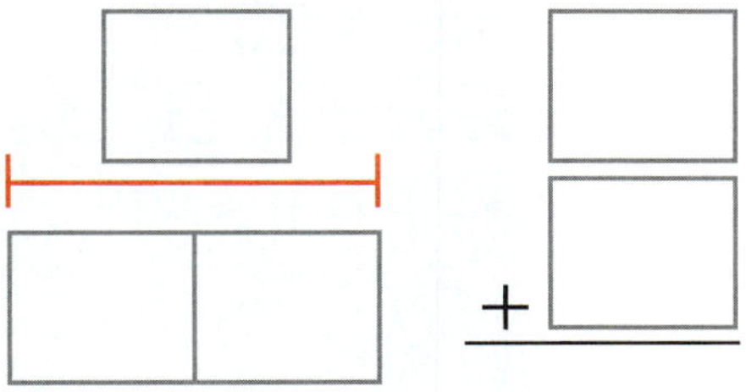

MORE PRACTICE

3. A cat sleeps for 45 minutes.
She then sleeps for 25 more minutes.
How many minutes does the cat sleep in all?

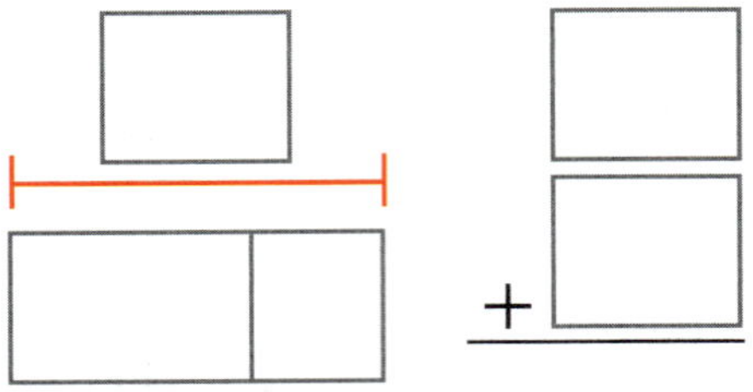

The cat sleeps for _____ minutes in all.

4. Jeremy's team swims 23 laps.
Andy's team swims 20 more laps than Jeremy's team.
How many laps does Andy's team swim?

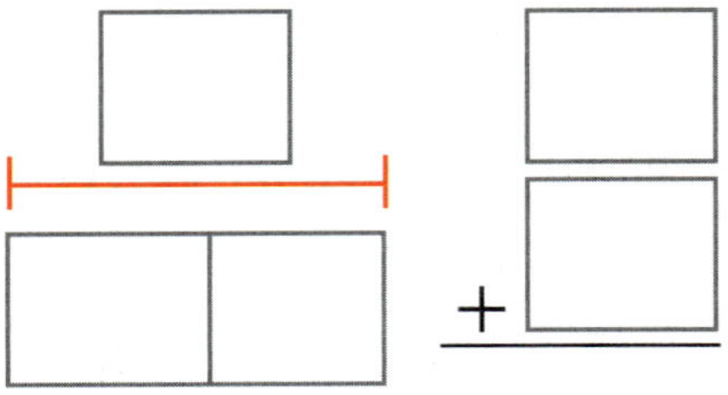

Andy's team swims _____ laps.

5. Gaby takes 18 books off the shelf.
There are 29 books left.
How many books were on the shelf to start?

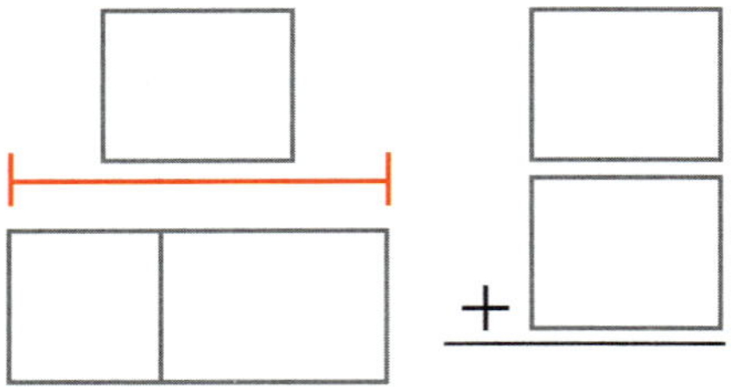

There were _____ books on the shelf.

6. Paul sells 14 pears.
He sells 26 bananas.
How many pieces of fruit does Paul sell?

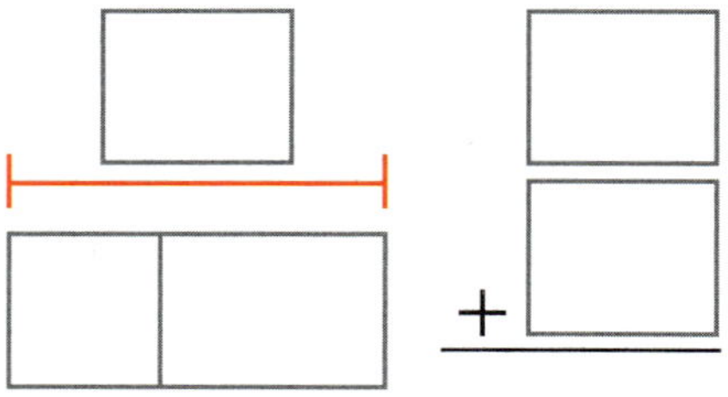

Paul sells _____ pieces of fruit.

Name ______________________________

HOMEWORK

Complete the bar model. Solve the problem.

1. Bella collects 36 white eggs and 45 brown eggs. How many eggs does Bella collect in all?

   Bella collects _____ eggs in all.

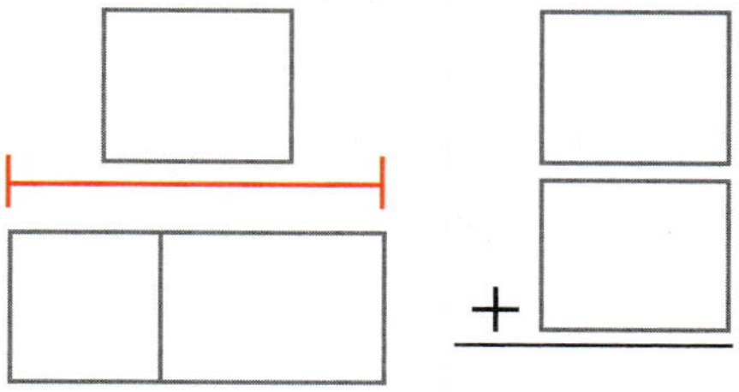

2. Tom plays 21 games. Adrien plays 9 games. How many games do they play in all?

   They play _____ games in all.

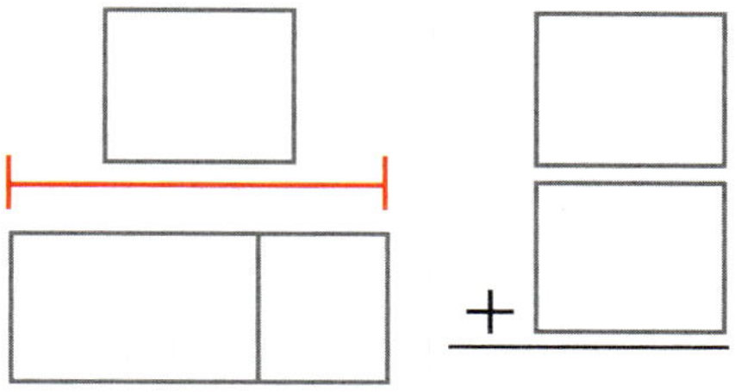

3. Ms. Diaz has 43 math books and 29 reading books. How many books does she have in all?

   Ms. Diaz has _____ books in all.

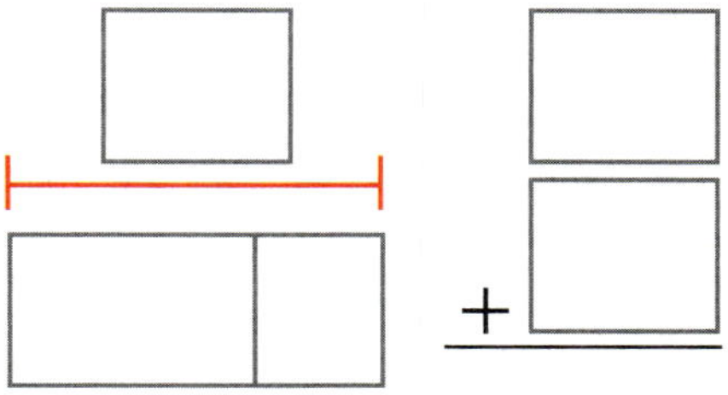

4. Malachi draws 17 squares. He draws 3 more circles than squares. How many circles does Malachi draw?

   Malachi draws _____ circles.

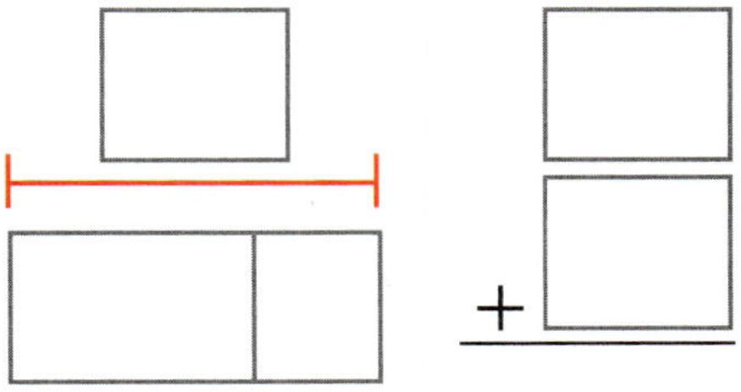

HOMEWORK

5. Jazmin has 67 blocks.
Lilly has 9 more blocks than Jazmin.
How many blocks does Lilly have?

Lilly has _____ blocks.

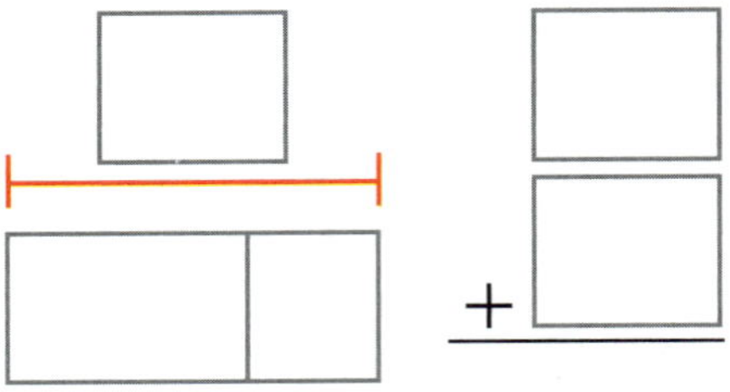

6. There are 15 first graders in the library. There are 16 second graders in the library. How many first and second graders are in the library?

There are _____ first and second graders in the library.

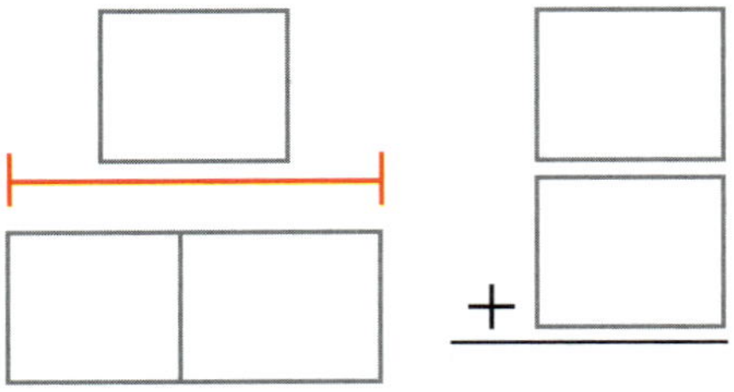

Write About It

7. Read the question.
Is the bar model below correct?
Tell how you know.

Abby scores 19 points in a computer game. Bre scores 20 more points than Abby. How many points do they score in all?

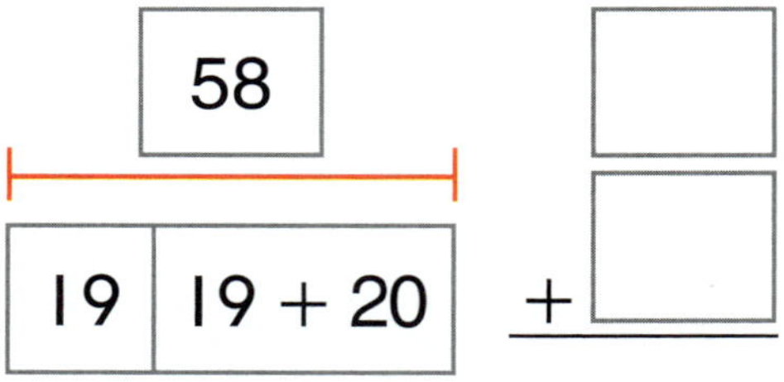

____

____

____

____

Name ______________________________

Find the correct answer.

1. Add.

$$\begin{array}{r} 37 \\ +30 \\ \hline \end{array}$$

A. 13
B. 67
C. 76
D. 77

2. Which number is 10 more than 32?

A. 22
B. 31
C. 42
D. 43

3. Add.

$40 + 50 = ?$

A. 450
B. 405
C. 100
D. 90

4. Which TWO sets of numbers have a sum of 36?

A. 23 and 13
B. 17 and 26
C. 16 and 20
D. 15 and 16

5. Fay finds 38 green leaves. She finds 16 red leaves. How many leaves does Fay find in all?

Fay finds ______ leaves.

6. Sam jumps rope 25 times. Paul jumps 15 more times than Sam. How many times does Paul jump?

Paul jumps ______ times.

7. Which number is 5 more than 22?

A. 17
B. 27
C. 72
D. 77

8. Which TWO sets of numbers have a sum of 41?

A. 21 and 21
B. 20 and 21
C. 33 and 8
D. 40 and 11

9. Which number is 5 more than 66?

A. 51
B. 56
C. 61
D. 71

10. Add.

77 + 13 = ?

A. 90
B. 87
C. 86
D. 77

11. There are 34 red counters and 38 blue counters in a bag. How many counters are in the bag in all?

There are _____ counters in the bag.

12. Sierra has 22 star stickers. She has 16 rainbow stickers. How many stickers does Sierra have in all?

Sierra has _____ stickers in all.

13. Add.

43 + 40 = ?

A. 80
B. 83
C. 90
D. 91

14. Which number is 20 more than 20?

A. 21
B. 30
C. 40
D. 41

Name ____________________

Fran is going to buy some flats to plant bean seeds. The chart shows sizes of different flats.

Flat	Number of Cups in Flat
A	14
B	32
C	28
D	36
E	40

1. Fran wants to buy 2 flats. The flats must have enough cups for 60 bean seeds. There should not be more than 70 cups. Which 2 flats can Fran use? Show your work.

2. Fran decides to also plant pepper seeds. She buys flats A and E. She uses all of the cups in the flats and has 8 seeds left over. How many pepper seeds does Fran plant? Explain how you can count on to find the answer. What other flats could she have bought to have enough cups?

CHAPTER 11
Fluency Practice

Name ______________________

Find the correct answer.

1. Subtract.

$17 - 8 =$ ____

2. Add.

$$\begin{array}{r} 37 \\ +\,23 \\ \hline \end{array}$$

3. Add.

$18 + 19 = ?$

A. 27
B. 28
C. 37
D. 38

4. Find the missing addend.

$13 = ? + 7$

A. 6
B. 7
C. 8
D. 9

5. Subtract.

$$\begin{array}{r} 15 \\ -\,9 \\ \hline \end{array}$$

A. 6
B. 7
C. 8
D. 9

6. Which TWO sets of numbers have a difference of 5?

A. 12 and 7
B. 13 and 6
C. 11 and 8
D. 14 and 9

7. Subtract.

$11 - 9 = ?$

A. 5
B. 4
C. 3
D. 2

8. Which TWO sets of numbers have a sum of 14?

A. 6 and 8
B. 7 and 7
C. 8 and 5
D. 6 and 6

Subtraction: Two-Digit Numbers

CHAPTER 12

A nursery is a place that grows plants to sell. The plants are grown in plastic flats. Each flat has rows of cups with seeds planted in soil.

Some plants only last one year. They are called annual plants. Some plants regrow year after year. They are called perennial plants.

By the Numbers

- Some flats hold 16, 20, or 25 plants.
- Some plants, like impatiens, can grow from a seed in 5 to 7 days.

What You Can Do

- Visit a nursery or garden center. Or, look for pictures of plant flats.
- Count how many plants are in each flat.
- Draw pictures of flats and compare.

Dear Family,

In this chapter, we will be learning about subtracting two-digit numbers.

Here are the Key **Math Words** for this chapter:

10 less	**count back**
tens	**guess and test**
difference	

You can use the glossary to check out the definition of each word and help your child make flash cards to study each day we work on the lessons for this chapter.

During the Chapter Opener and the Performance Assessment, we will be making STEAM connections with the number of plants nursery flats hold. Read the opening to the chapter together and discuss the **By the Numbers** and **What You Can Do** statements. If it is not possible to visit a nursery, look for pictures of plant flats in magazines or on the Internet.

Keep Your Skills Sharp

Here is a **Keep Your Skills Sharp** activity to do at home to prepare for this chapter.

Practice single-digit subtraction by giving your child two numbers between 0 and 9. Ask your child to find the difference between the two numbers. Use small objects such as dried pasta or beans to model the problems if needed.

Name ____________________

Mental Math: Find 10 Less

Objective
- Use mental math to find 10 less.

Math Word
10 less

Kylee scored 84 points bowling.
Lucy scored 10 less than Kylee.
How many points did Lucy score bowling?

You can use mental math to find 10 less. Start at 84.

74 ← 84

Think Count back 10.

tens	ones
7	4

tens	ones
8	4

74 is 10 less than 84.

74 is 1 ten less than 84.

Lucy scored 74 total points bowling.

PRACTICE

Use mental math.
Circle the number that is 10 less.

1. 45 — 35 44
2. 51 — 11 41
3. 76 — 66 75
4. 23 — 13 33
5. 67 — 57 66
6. 19 — 9 29
7. 64 — 44 54
8. 82 — 72 81
9. 38 — 27 28
10. 91 — 90 81
11. 49 — 39 29
12. 62 — 72 52

PRACTICE

Use mental math.
Write the number that is 10 less.

13. 73 83

14. ____ 65

15. ____ 41

Use mental math. Match each number to the number that is 10 less.

16. 98 a. 77

17. 78 b. 68

18. 87 c. 88

Problem Solving

19. Noah scores 37 points. Luke scores 10 less points than Noah. Justin scores 10 less points than Luke. How many points does Justin score?

____ ____

Justin scores ____ points.

Write About It

20. Tell how to use mental math to find the number that is 10 less than 22. Use words or numbers.

____

____

Name ______________________________

Mental Math: Find 10 Less

You can use mental math to find 10 less than 84.
Start at 84. Count back 10.

74 ← 84

10 less is 1 ten less.

tens	ones
7	4

tens	ones
8	4

74 is 10 less than 84.

74 is 1 ten less than 84.

MORE PRACTICE

Use mental math.
Circle the number that is 10 less.

1. 65
   55 64

2. 71
   51 61

3. 96
   86 95

4. 43
   33 53

5. 87
   77 86

6. 39
   29 49

7. 84
   64 74

8. 12
   2 21

Use mental math. Match each number to the number that is 10 less.

9. 88	a. 57
10. 67	b. 68
11. 78	c. 78

HOMEWORK

Use mental math.
Write the number that is 10 less.

1. ______ 53	2. ______ 35	3. ______ 11
4. ______ 24	5. ______ 47	6. ______ 62

Problem Solving

7. Jessica has 22 coins. Jill has 10 less coins than Jessica. Leah has 10 less coins than Jill. How many coins does Leah have?

______ ______

Leah has ______ coins.

8. Maxwell writes the number 24 and a number that is 10 less on a piece of paper. What number did he write with 24?

Maxwell wrote ______.

Write About It

9. Zoe's mother makes 25 muffins.
After the bake sale, she has 10 less muffins.
How many muffins are left? Tell how you know.

____

____

Name ____________________

Objective
- Subtract tens from tens.

Math Word
tens

Subtract Tens

There are 90 beads in a box. Carly uses 40 beads. How many beads are left?

To find how many are left, subtract tens.

9 tens	90
− 4 tens	− 40
5 tens	50

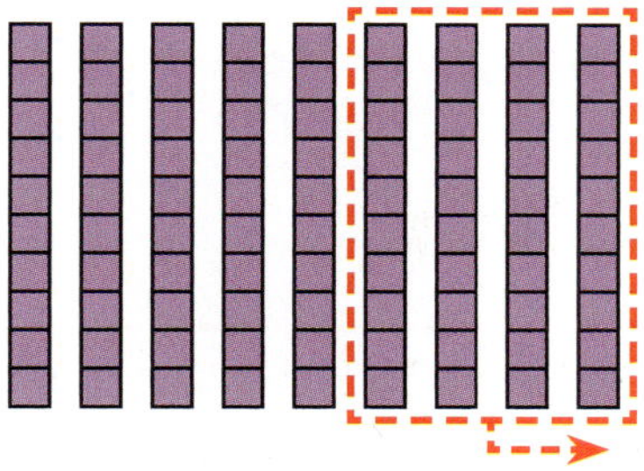

There are 50 beads left.

PRACTICE

Subtract. Use ten rods to help.

1. 5 tens − 2 tens = 3 tens; 50 − 20 = 30

2. 8 tens − 6 tens = ____ tens; ____ − ____ = ____

3. 6 tens − 5 tens = ____ tens; ____ − ____ = ____

4. 8 tens − 4 tens = ____ tens; ____ − ____ = ____

5. 6 tens − 3 tens = ____ tens

____ − ____ = ____

6. 3 tens − 1 ten = ____ tens

____ − ____ = ____

PRACTICE

Subtract. Use ten rods to help.

7. $\begin{array}{r} 80 \\ -\ 40 \\ \hline 40 \end{array}$	8. $\begin{array}{r} 70 \\ -\ 50 \\ \hline \end{array}$	9. $\begin{array}{r} 90 \\ -\ 30 \\ \hline \end{array}$	10. $\begin{array}{r} 50 \\ -\ 10 \\ \hline \end{array}$
11. $\begin{array}{r} 30 \\ -\ 20 \\ \hline \end{array}$	12. $\begin{array}{r} 90 \\ -\ 70 \\ \hline \end{array}$	13. $\begin{array}{r} 60 \\ -\ 40 \\ \hline \end{array}$	14. $\begin{array}{r} 20 \\ -\ 10 \\ \hline \end{array}$

15. 80 − 30 = _____

16. 90 − 20 = _____

17. 30 − 10 = _____

18. 50 − 40 = _____

Problem Solving

19. John has 40 grapes. He gives 20 grapes to his brother. How many grapes does John have left?

John has _____ grapes left.

Write About It

20. Tell how you can use a model to help you subtract 60 − 20.

____

____

____

Name ______________________________

Subtract Tens

Subtract 90 − 40.

90 − 40 is the same as
9 tens − 4 tens.

9 tens	90
− 4 tens	− 40
5 tens	50

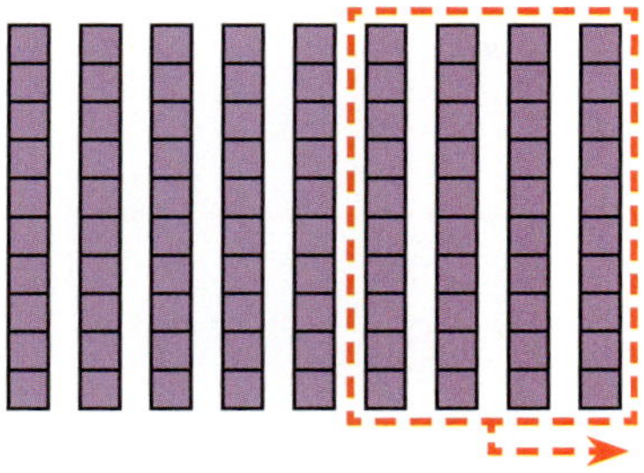

MORE PRACTICE

Subtract. Draw ten rods to help.

1. 4 tens − 2 tens = ____ tens

   ____ − ____ = ____

2. 8 tens − 6 tens = ____ tens

   ____ − ____ = ____

3. 6 tens − 3 tens = ____ tens

   ☐ − ☐ = ____

4. 7 tens − 6 tens = ____ tens

   ☐ − ☐ = ____

HOMEWORK

Subtract. Draw ten rods to help.

1. $\begin{array}{r} 90 \\ -\ 80 \\ \hline \end{array}$

2. $\begin{array}{r} 50 \\ -\ 20 \\ \hline \end{array}$

3. $\begin{array}{r} 80 \\ -\ 20 \\ \hline \end{array}$

4. $\begin{array}{r} 90 \\ -\ 10 \\ \hline \end{array}$

5. $\begin{array}{r} 70 \\ -\ 20 \\ \hline \end{array}$

6. $\begin{array}{r} 40 \\ -\ 30 \\ \hline \end{array}$

7. $70 - 10 =$ _____

8. $90 - 50 =$ _____

Problem Solving

9. Mariah finds 30 red leaves in the park.
She finds 10 yellow leaves.
How many more red leaves does Mariah find?

Mariah finds _____ more red leaves.

Write About It

10. What would you tell a friend about how to subtract tens? Use words or pictures.

____

____

____

____

Name ____________________

LESSON **12-3**

Objective
- Relate addition and subtraction to subtract multiples of ten.

Math Word
difference

Think Addition to Subtract Tens

Nate wants to read 60 pages of a book. He has read 40 pages. How many more pages does Nate need to read?

$60 - 40 = ?$

You can use addition to find the difference.

Think:
$? + 40 = 60$
$20 + 40 = 60$

$$\begin{array}{r} 60 \\ -\ 40 \\ \hline ? \end{array} \qquad \begin{array}{r} ? \\ +\ 40 \\ \hline 60 \end{array} \qquad \begin{array}{r} 20 \\ +\ 40 \\ \hline 60 \end{array} \qquad \begin{array}{r} 60 \\ -\ 40 \\ \hline 20 \end{array}$$

So $60 - 40 = 20$.
Nate needs to read 20 more pages.

PRACTICE

Use addition to find the difference.

1. $90 - 20 = ?$

70 $+ 20 = 90$

$90 - 20 =$ 70

2. $80 - 50 = ?$

_____ $+ 50 = 80$

$80 - 50 =$ _____

3.

$$\begin{array}{r} 40 \\ -\ 10 \\ \hline ? \end{array} \qquad \begin{array}{r} \square \\ +\ 10 \\ \hline 40 \end{array} \qquad \begin{array}{r} 40 \\ -\ 10 \\ \hline \end{array}$$

4.

$$\begin{array}{r} 50 \\ -\ 40 \\ \hline ? \end{array} \qquad \begin{array}{r} \square \\ +\ 40 \\ \hline 50 \end{array} \qquad \begin{array}{r} 50 \\ -\ 40 \\ \hline \end{array}$$

PRACTICE

Use addition to find the difference.

5. $60 - 50 =$ _____

_____ $+ 50 = 60$

6. $90 - 30 =$ _____

_____ $+ 30 = 90$

7.
$$\begin{array}{r} 70 \\ -\ 10 \\ \hline \end{array} \qquad \begin{array}{r} \square \\ +\ 10 \\ \hline 70 \end{array}$$

8.
$$\begin{array}{r} 80 \\ -\ 30 \\ \hline \end{array} \qquad \begin{array}{r} \square \\ +\ 30 \\ \hline 80 \end{array}$$

9.
$$\begin{array}{r} 30 \\ -\ 20 \\ \hline \end{array} \qquad \begin{array}{r} \square \\ +\ 20 \\ \hline 30 \end{array}$$

Problem Solving

10. Mrs. Jones had 70 paper clips in a cup.
She spilled some on the floor and had 20 left.
How many did she spill? Tell how you know.

____

____

____

Write About It

11. Explain how to use addition to find a difference.
Use words or numbers.

____

____

Name ______________________

Think Addition to Subtract Tens

You can use addition to find the difference.

$$\begin{array}{r} 60 \\ -\ 40 \\ \hline ? \end{array} \qquad \begin{array}{r} ? \\ +\ 40 \\ \hline 60 \end{array} \qquad \begin{array}{r} 20 \\ +\ 40 \\ \hline 60 \end{array} \qquad \begin{array}{r} 60 \\ -\ 40 \\ \hline 20 \end{array}$$

Think
? + 40 = 60 or
60 − 40 = ?

60 − 40 = 20

MORE PRACTICE

Use addition to find the difference.

1. 80 − 10 = ?

_____ + 10 = 80

80 − 10 = _____

2. 60 − 40 = ?

_____ + 40 = 60

60 − 40 = _____

3.

$$\begin{array}{r} 20 \\ -\ 10 \\ \hline ? \end{array} \qquad \begin{array}{r} \square \\ +\ 10 \\ \hline 20 \end{array} \qquad \begin{array}{r} 20 \\ -\ 10 \\ \hline \end{array}$$

4.

$$\begin{array}{r} 80 \\ -\ 40 \\ \hline ? \end{array} \qquad \begin{array}{r} \square \\ +\ 40 \\ \hline 80 \end{array} \qquad \begin{array}{r} 80 \\ -\ 40 \\ \hline \end{array}$$

5. 70 − 40 = ?

_____ + 40 = 70

70 − 40 = _____

6. 80 − 20 = ?

_____ + 20 = 80

80 − 20 = _____

HOMEWORK

Use addition to find the difference.

1. $\begin{array}{r} 90 \\ -\ 70 \\ \hline \end{array}$ $\begin{array}{r} \square \\ +\ 70 \\ \hline 90 \end{array}$

2. $\begin{array}{r} 70 \\ -\ 60 \\ \hline \end{array}$ $\begin{array}{r} \square \\ +\ 60 \\ \hline 70 \end{array}$

3. $\begin{array}{r} 50 \\ -\ 20 \\ \hline \end{array}$ $\begin{array}{r} \square \\ +\ 20 \\ \hline 50 \end{array}$

4. 60 − 50 = _____

   _____ + 50 = 60

5. 30 − 30 = _____

   _____ + 30 = 30

Problem Solving

6. Isabelle plays two games. She scores 30 points in the first game. She scores 80 points in all. How many points does she score in the second game? Show how you know.

   Isabelle scores _____ points in the second game.

Write About It

7. If you subtract any tens number from itself, will you always get the same answer? Tell how you know.

   ____

   ____

Name ______________________________

Find the correct answer.

1. Which number is 10 less than 67?

A. 37
B. 57
C. 77

2. Which addition equation can you use to subtract 90 − 40?

A. 50 + 40 = 90
B. 60 + 30 = 90
C. 80 + 10 = 90

3. Subtract.

$$\begin{array}{r} \text{5 tens} \\ -\ \text{1 ten} \\ \hline \end{array}$$

A. 2 tens
B. 3 tens
C. 4 tens

4. Subtract.

$$\begin{array}{r} 70 \\ -50 \\ \hline \end{array}$$

A. 20
B. 30
C. 40

5. Which number is 10 less than 99?

A. 88
B. 89
C. 98

6. Subtract.

80 − 30 = ?

A. 30
B. 40
C. 50

Find the correct answer.

7. Subtract.

   30 − 20 = ____

8. What number is 10 less than 43?

   ____

9. Bailey and Diana are jumping rope. Bailey jumps 40 times in a row. Diana jumps 20 times in a row. How many more times does Bailey jump in a row than Diana?

   A. 0
   B. 10
   C. 20

10. Gracie and Delaney are playing a game. Gracie scores 67 points. Delaney scores 10 less points. How many points does Delaney score?

   A. 37
   B. 57
   C. 77

11. Justin is reading a book. It has 50 pages. He reads 30 pages. How many more pages does Justin have left to read?

   A. 20 pages
   B. 40 pages
   C. 60 pages

12. Grant has 20 balloons. He has 10 red balloons. The rest are blue. How many blue balloons does Grant have?

   A. 10 balloons
   B. 20 balloons
   C. 30 balloons

Name ____________________

Subtract Multiples of Ten from Two-Digit Numbers

Objective
- Subtract tens from two-digit numbers.

Math Word
count back

Eva picks 45 cherries.
Chloe picks 20 fewer cherries than Eva.
How many cherries does Chloe pick?

Subtract: 45 − 20 = ?

You can count back by 10s to solve.
Start at 45. Count back by 10s.

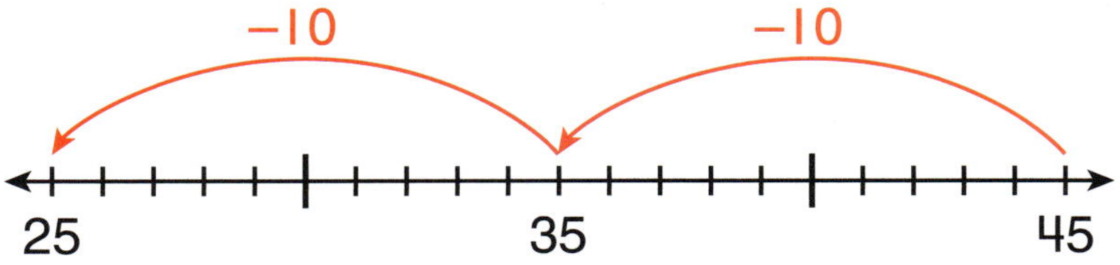

So, 45 − 20 = 25.

Chloe picks 25 cherries.

PRACTICE

Count back by 10s to subtract. Use the number line to help. Write the difference.

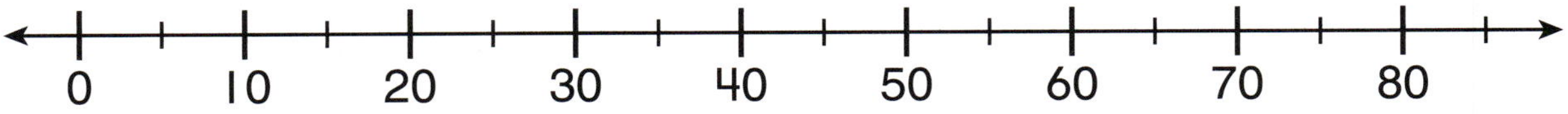

1. 57 − 30 = 27

2. 68 − 20

3. 55 − 50

4. 46 − 30

5. 83 − 20

6. 74 − 40

PRACTICE

Count back by 10s to subtract. Write the difference.

7. $\begin{array}{r} 67 \\ -\ 30 \\ \hline \end{array}$

8. $\begin{array}{r} 78 \\ -\ 20 \\ \hline \end{array}$

9. $\begin{array}{r} 66 \\ -\ 60 \\ \hline \end{array}$

10. $\begin{array}{r} 77 \\ -\ 60 \\ \hline \end{array}$

11. $\begin{array}{r} 13 \\ -\ 10 \\ \hline \end{array}$

12. $\begin{array}{r} 84 \\ -\ 40 \\ \hline \end{array}$

13. 37 − 10 = _____

14. 24 − 10 = _____

Problem Solving

15. Dean needs 38 points to win a game. He has 20 points. How many more points does Dean need to win?

Count back by 2 tens.

38 − _____ = _____

Dean needs _____ more points.

Write About It

16. Which is greater, the difference of 59 − 30 or the difference of 45 − 20? Tell how you know.

____

____

____

Name ______________________________

Subtract Multiples of Ten from Two-Digit Numbers

Subtract: 45 − 20 = ?

You can count back by 10s to solve.
Start at 45. Count back by 10s.

Change the tens digit when counting back by 10.

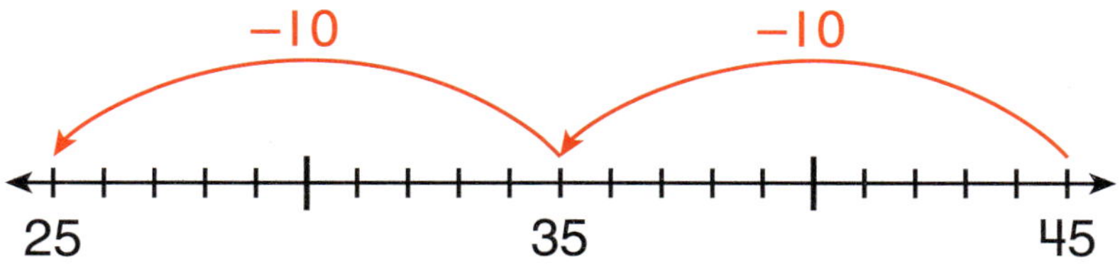

So, 45 − 20 = 25.

MORE PRACTICE

Count back by 10s to subtract. Use the number line to help. Write the difference.

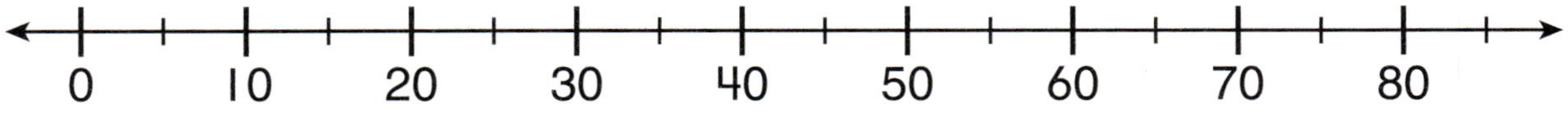

1. 25 − 10 = ____

2. 64 − 30 = ____

3. 57 − 40 = ____

4. 32 − 30 = ____

5. 73 − 20 = ____

6. 81 − 50 = ____

7. 36 − 10 = ____

8. 62 − 50 = ____

9. 57 − 40 = ____

10. 77 − 70 = ____

HOMEWORK

Count back by 10s to subtract. Write the difference.

1. $\begin{array}{r} 15 \\ -\ 10 \\ \hline \end{array}$

2. $\begin{array}{r} 34 \\ -\ 20 \\ \hline \end{array}$

3. $\begin{array}{r} 57 \\ -\ 40 \\ \hline \end{array}$

4. $\begin{array}{r} 42 \\ -\ 30 \\ \hline \end{array}$

5. $\begin{array}{r} 23 \\ -\ 20 \\ \hline \end{array}$

6. $\begin{array}{r} 71 \\ -\ 50 \\ \hline \end{array}$

7. 26 − 10 = ______

8. 82 − 50 = ______

9. 65 − 30 = ______

10. 33 − 30 = ______

Problem Solving

11. Sara wants to collect 17 cans to recycle. She has collected 10 so far. How many more cans does Sara need to collect?

Count back by 1 ten.

17 − ______ = ______

Sara needs to collect ______ more cans.

Write About It

12. Which difference is greater, 60 − 40 or 70 − 50? Tell how you know.

____

____

Name ______________________________

Problem Solving
Read › Plan › Solve › Check

Guess and Test

Objective
- Use the guess and test method to solve problems.

Math Word
guess and test

Kate's book is about a group of 90 stars. She draws a picture of stars for her book report. How many more stars are in the book than in Kate's drawing?

To solve the problem, you can guess and test.

Make a guess.	80 more	
Subtract to test.	90	90 stars in book
	− 10	10 stars in drawing
The guess is correct.	80	

There are 80 more stars in the book than Kate's drawing.

If the guess is not correct, make another guess.

PRACTICE

Make a guess. Then subtract to test.

1. Levi has 70 stamps. He has 20 small stamps. The rest are large stamps. How many large stamps does Levi have?

   Guess: ______________________________

   Test: ______________________________

   Levi has ______ large stamps.

PRACTICE

Make a guess. Then subtract to test.

2. Faith makes 50 bookmarks.
   She sells 30 bookmarks.
   How many bookmarks does Faith have left?

   Guess: ____________________

   Test: ____________________

   Faith has _____ bookmarks left.

The table shows how many rocks each friend collects. Use the table to guess and test the answer to the question.

	Number of Rocks
Sara	80
Rose	30
Maya	50

3. How many more rocks does Sara have than Rose?

   Guess: ____________________

   Test: ____________________

   Sara has _____ more rocks than Rose.

Write About It

4. Write a math story that could be solved using guess and test. Explain the final answer.

   ____

   ____

   ____

Name ______________________________

Problem Solving
Guess and Test

Kate's book is about a group of 90 stars. She draws a picture of stars for her book report. How many more stars are in the book than in Kate's drawing?

Make a guess.	80 more	
Subtract to test.	90	90 stars in book
	− 10	10 stars in drawing
The guess is correct.	80	

There are 80 more stars in the book.

MORE PRACTICE

Make a guess. Then subtract to test.

1. A store has 80 T-shirts. The store has 60 white T-shirts. The rest are blue. How many blue T-shirts does the store have?

   Guess: ______________________________

   Test: ______________________________

   The store has ______ blue T-shirts.

MORE PRACTICE

2. Leslie has 20 dolls. She has 10 paper dolls. The rest are rag dolls. How many rag dolls does Leslie have?

   Guess: ______________________

   Test: ______________________

   Leslie has ____ rag dolls.

---

3. Randy makes 40 bracelets. He gives 20 bracelets to his friends. How many bracelets does Randy have left?

   Guess: ______________________

   Test: ______________________

   Randy has ____ bracelets left.

The table shows how many stamps each friend has. Use the table to guess and test to answer the question.

	Number of Stamps
Paul	90
Lucas	20
Julian	60

4. How many more stamps does Paul have than Lucas?

   Guess: ______________________

   Test: ______________________

   Paul has ____ more stamps than Lucas.

Name ____

HOMEWORK

Make a guess. Then subtract to test.

1. Jonas has 50 trading cards. He gives 20 cards to his brother. How many trading cards does Jonas have left?

   Guess: ____

   Test: ____

   Jonas has _____ trading cards left.

2. A bakery sells 80 pans of bread. They sell 50 pans of wheat bread. The rest of the pans they sell are raisin bread. How many pans of raisin bread does the bakery sell?

   Guess: ____

   Test: ____

   The bakery sells _____ pans of raisin bread.

3. Nevaeh buys 20 tulips. She gives away 10 tulips. How many tulips does Nevaeh have left?

   Guess: ____

   Test: ____

   Nevaeh has _____ tulips left.

HOMEWORK

4. Seth collects 60 cans to recycle. He also collects 80 bottles to recycle. How many more bottles than cans does Seth collect?

Guess: ______________________

Test: ______________________

Seth collects _____ more bottles than cans.

Three friends collect stickers. The table shows how many stickers each friend has. Use the table to answer the question.

	Number of Stickers
Mariah	10
Jazmin	30
Isabelle	50

5. Jazmin gives 20 stickers to some friends. How many stickers does she have now?

Guess: ______________________

Test: ______________________

Jazmin has _____ stickers now.

Write About It

6. Jimmy used the guess and test method to solve a problem. His first guess was wrong. What should Jimmy do next?

____

____

Name ____________________

Find the correct answer.

1. Which number is 10 less than 17?

   A. 6
   B. 7
   C. 16
   D. 27

2. Which addition equation can you use to subtract 90 − 70?

   A. 20 + 70 = 90
   B. 30 + 60 = 90
   C. 40 + 50 = 90
   D. 50 + 40 = 90

3. Subtract.

$$\begin{array}{r} 6 \text{ tens} \\ -\,3 \text{ tens} \\ \hline \end{array}$$

   A. 1 ten
   B. 2 tens
   C. 3 tens
   D. 9 tens

4. Subtract.

$$\begin{array}{r} 80 \\ -\,40 \\ \hline \end{array}$$

   A. 20
   B. 40
   C. 60
   D. 80

5. Subtract.

   71 − 40 =

   A. 21
   B. 31
   C. 41
   D. 51

6. What number is 10 less than 62?

   A. 22
   B. 32
   C. 42
   D. 52

7. Kelly writes a story that has 80 words. There are 50 words on the first page. The rest of the words are on the second page. Which addition equation can Kelly use to find how many words are on the second page?

A. $20 + 60 = 80$
B. $30 + 50 = 80$
C. $40 + 40 = 80$
D. $70 + 10 = 80$

8. The table shows how long each friend studies.

	Time (minutes)
Elias	40
Dylan	30
Adam	50

How many more minutes does Elias study than Dylan?

A. 10
B. 20
C. 70
D. 80

9. Ellie gets 90 points on her test. Ava gets 10 less points than Ellie. How many points does Ava get on her test?

A. 60
B. 70
C. 80
D. 90

10. The Bulldogs scored 77 points in the basketball game. They beat the Tigers by 20 points. How many points did the Tigers score?

A. 37
B. 57
C. 77
D. 97

Name ______________________________

CHAPTER 12
Performance Assessment

Mr. Kym uses 4 flats for plants in his nursery. There are 66 cups in all.

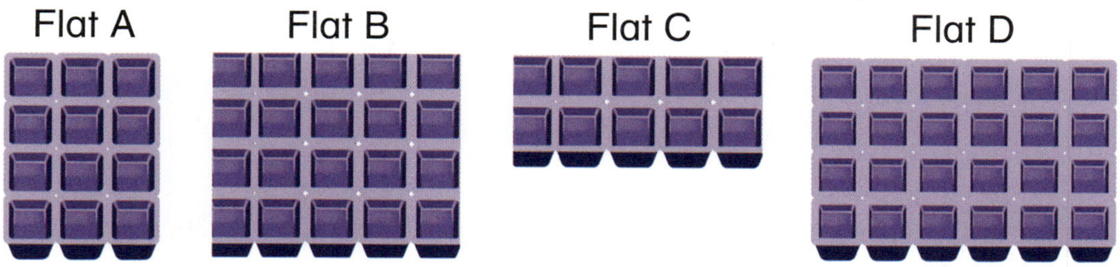

1. Mr. Kym fills the flats with plants. He moves the flats to his garden. He forgets to bring one of the flats. The total number of plants he moves to the garden is fewer than 50 plants. Which flat could he have forgotten to bring to the garden? Explain how you know.

____

____

2. Draw two of your own flats. Follow the rules:

- One flat must have 10 less cups than the other flat.
- The total number of cups in both flats must be a two-digit number.
- The total number of cups in both flats cannot be greater than 45.

Name ______________________

Find the correct answer.

1. What number is 10 less than 65?

   A. 45
   B. 55
   C. 50
   D. 40

2. Subtract.

   90 − 50 = ?

   A. 20
   B. 30
   C. 40
   D. 45

3. Subtract.

   70 − 20 = ?

   A. 20
   B. 50
   C. 70
   D. 90

4. Which number is 10 less than 43?

   A. 3
   B. 23
   C. 33
   D. 53

5. Add.

   3 + 7 + 9 = ?

   A. 10
   B. 12
   C. 16
   D. 19

6. Subtract.

   8 − 6 = ?

   A. 2
   B. 6
   C. 8
   D. 14

Geometry

CHAPTER
13

Since ancient Roman times, people have been using shapes of different-colored glass. They put the shapes together to make stained glass windows and sun catchers.

By the Numbers

- Some of the tallest stained glass windows in the world are over 80 feet tall.
- One of the largest stained glass windows weighs 1 ton.

What You Can Do

- Look at a picture of a stained glass window. How many different shapes do you see?
- Use colored tissue paper and clear contact paper to make shapes for a sun catcher.

Dear Family,

In this chapter, we will be learning about two-dimensional and three-dimensional shapes.

Here are the Key **Math Words** for this chapter:

closed shapes
corner
open shapes
vertex
two-dimensional shape
three-dimensional shape
face
side
edge

You can use the glossary to check out the definition of each word and help your child make flash cards to study each day we work on the lessons for this chapter.

During this chapter about geometric shapes, we will also be making some STEAM connections about geometric shapes in stained glass designs. Read the opening to the chapter together and discuss the **By the Numbers** and **What You Can Do** statements.

Keep Your Skills Sharp

Here are **Keep Your Skills Sharp** activities to do at home to prepare for this chapter.

Ask your child to draw a triangle, square, and rectangle, and cut out the shapes. Give your child a description of a shape based on its defining attributes (number of sides or corners), and have your child hand you that shape.

Name ____

Two-Dimensional Shapes

Objective

- Understand the defining and non-defining attributes of two-dimensional shapes.

Math Words

- two-dimensional shape
- closed shape
- open shape
- square
- rectangle
- triangle
- side
- vertex (vertices)
- corner

Some shapes are two-dimensional.
They are flat and have no thickness.
This shape has sides that can be measured.

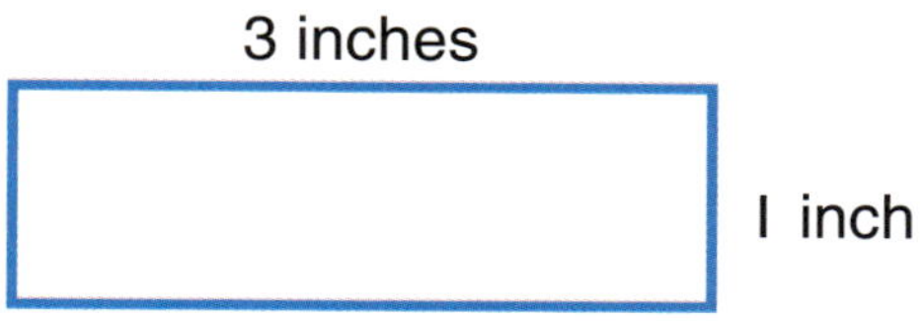

Closed shapes have connected lines.

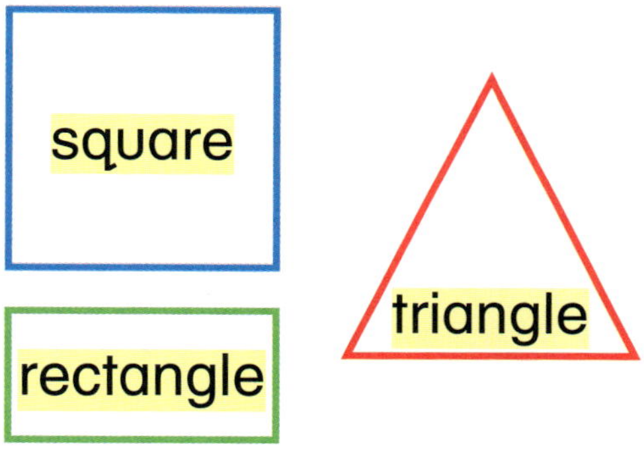

Open shapes have a line missing.

Size and color do not matter when naming a shape.

The closed shapes shown have sides that are straight lines.

The point where two sides meet is called a vertex, or corner.

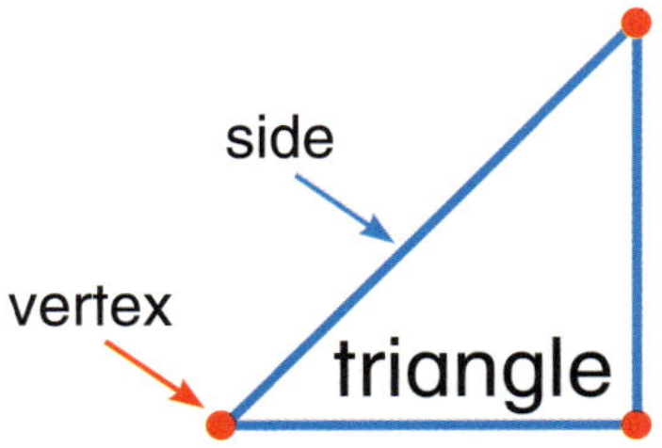

3 sides
3 vertices or corners

PRACTICE

Trace each shape. Draw a • at each corner.
Write how many sides and corners.

1\. 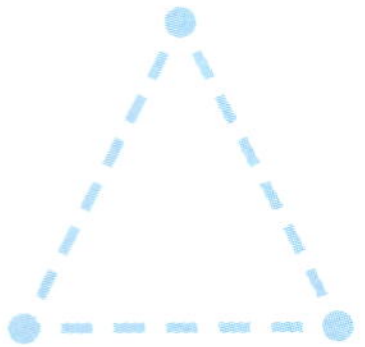

3 sides

3 corners

2\. 

_____ sides

_____ corners

3\. 

_____ sides

_____ corners

Problem Solving

4\. Jan draws a shape. Her shape has 3 sides and 3 corners. Does Jan draw a closed or open shape? Draw a picture to help.

____

Write About It

5\. Mason says you can tell if a shape is closed by looking at its size and color. Do you agree? Tell how you know.

____

____

____

Name ______________________________

Two-Dimensional Shapes

These are closed shapes. The sides of these shapes are straight lines.

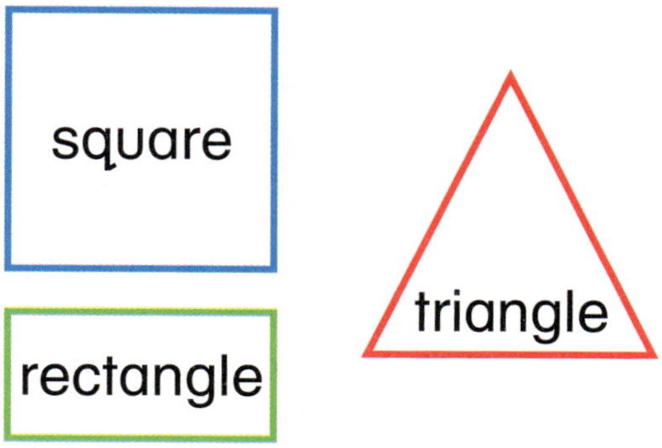

These are open shapes. There is a side missing in these shapes.

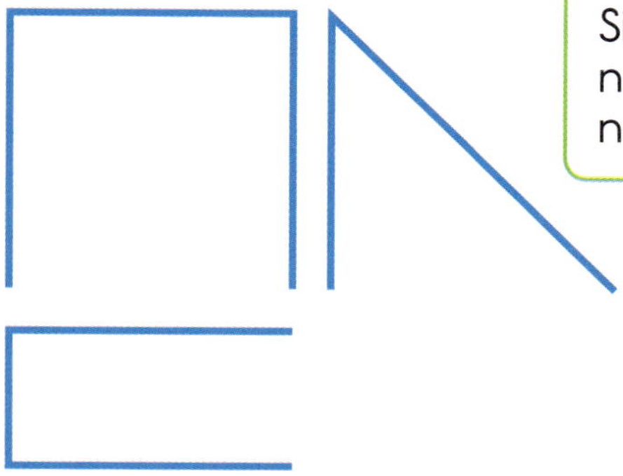

Size and color do not matter when naming a shape.

The point where two sides meet is called a corner, or vertex.

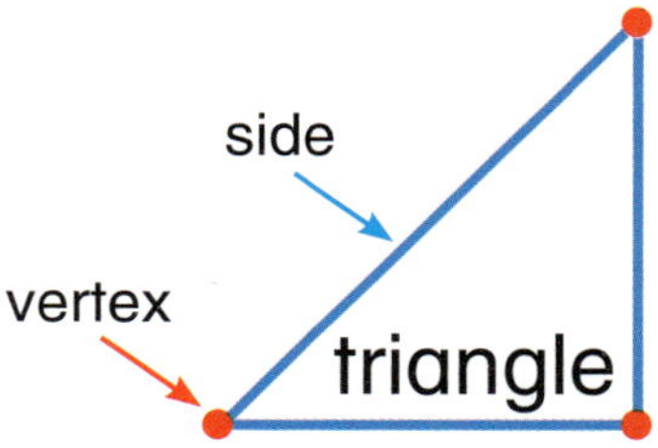

3 sides
3 corners

A closed flat shape is a two-dimensional shape.

MORE PRACTICE

Color the closed shapes.

1. 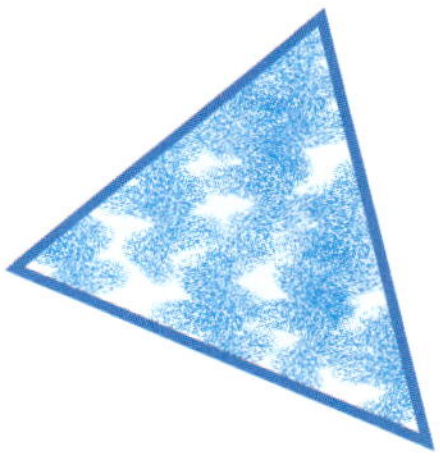

2. 

3. 

4. 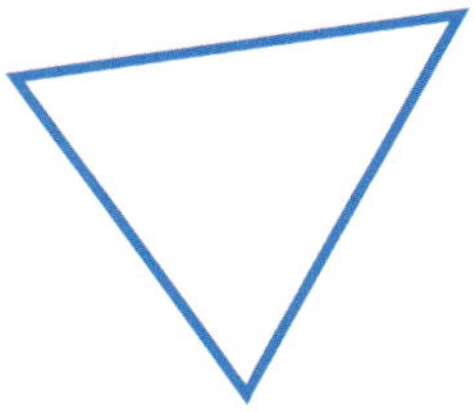

HOMEWORK

Trace each shape. Draw a • at each corner.
Write how many sides and corners.

1.

4 sides

4 corners

2.

_____ sides

_____ corners

3.

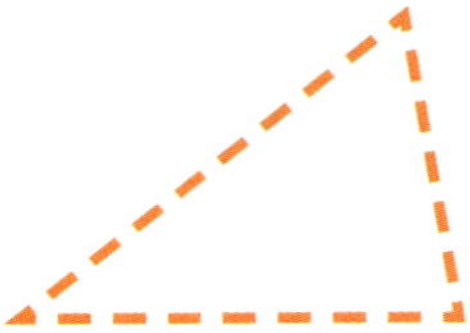

_____ sides

_____ corners

Problem Solving

4. Tim and Al draw closed shapes. Jack draws an open shape. Tim's shape has the most sides. Which shape does each child draw?

____

____

____

Write About It

5. How are these shapes the same?

How are they different?

____

____

Name ______________________________

Attributes of Two-Dimensional Shapes

Objective

- Understand the defining and non-defining attributes of two-dimensional shapes.

Math Words

closed shape
open shape
circle
hexagon
rhombus
trapezoid
side
corner

Tammy draws a small closed shape.
It has 6 sides and 6 corners.
What shape does Tammy draw?

These are closed shapes.

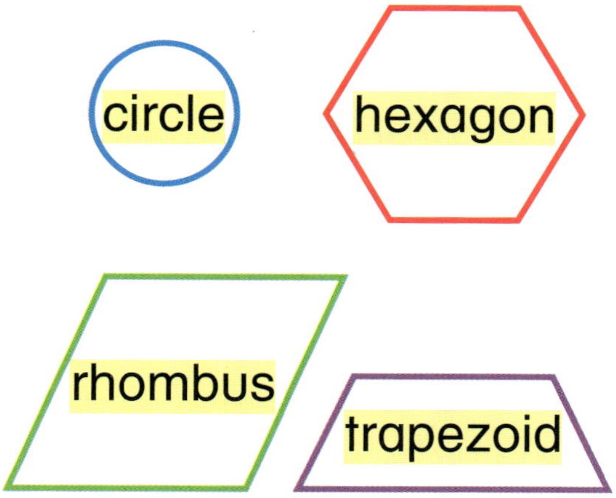

These are open shapes.

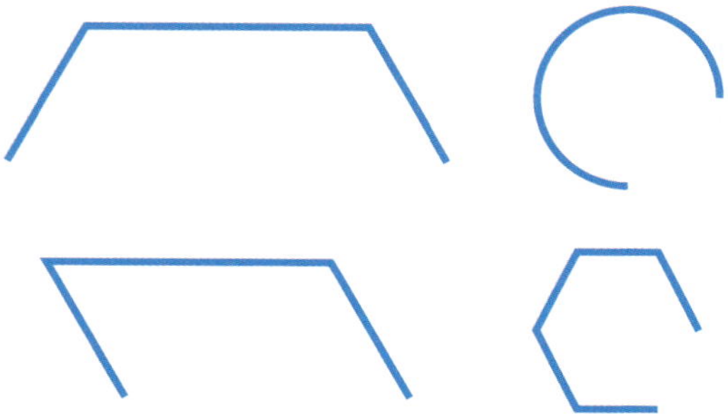

Some closed shapes have sides and corners.

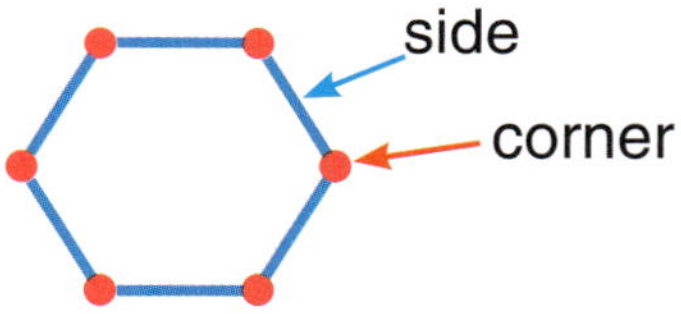

6 sides 6 corners

A circle does not have sides or corners.

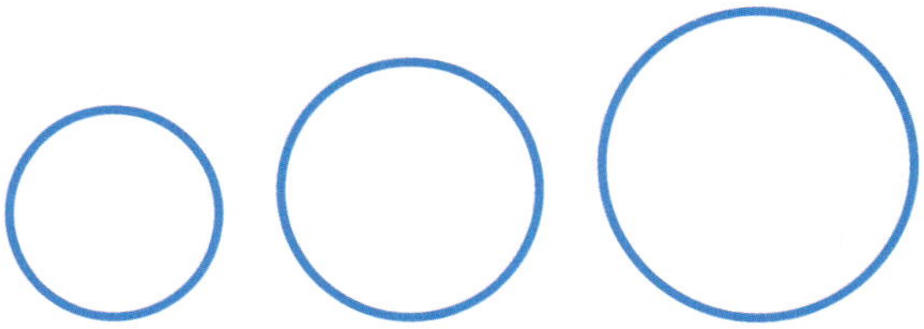

Size, color, and position do not matter when you name a shape.

A hexagon has 6 sides and 6 corners.
Tammy draws a hexagon.

PRACTICE

Color each closed shape.

1. 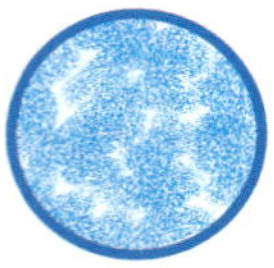

2. 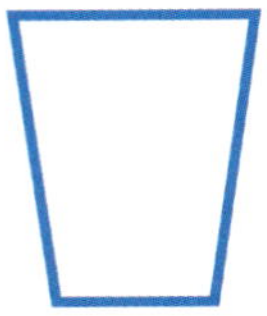

3. 

4. 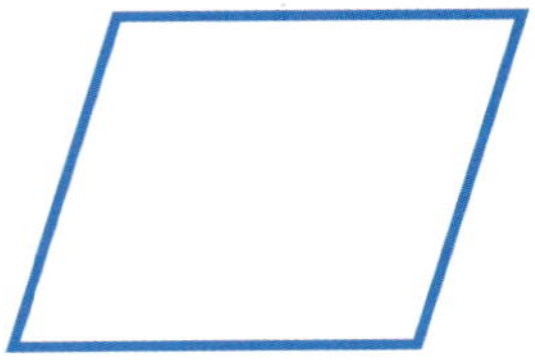

Problem Solving

5. Sally draws a shape that does not have corners. Beth draws a shape with 3 sides. Which closed shape could each child draw?

______ 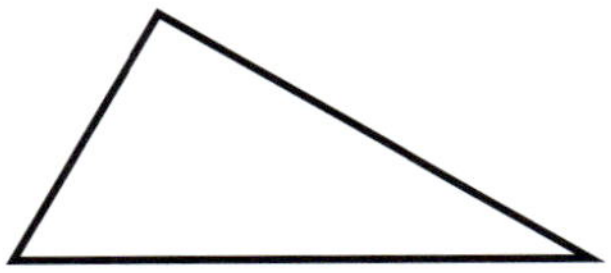 ______ 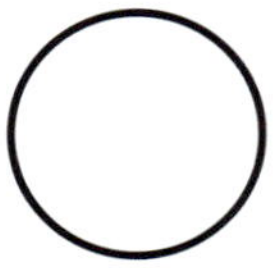

Write About It

6. Cory draws two shapes and says they are the same. Is he correct? Tell how you know.

____

____

____

Name ______________________________

Attributes of Two-Dimensional Shapes

These are closed shapes.

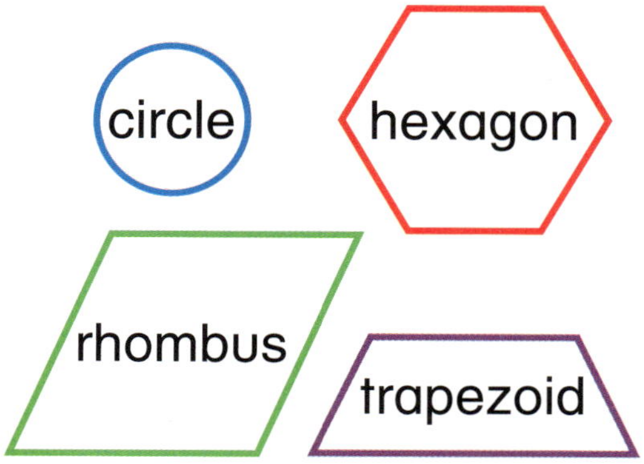

These are open shapes.

Some closed shapes have sides and corners.

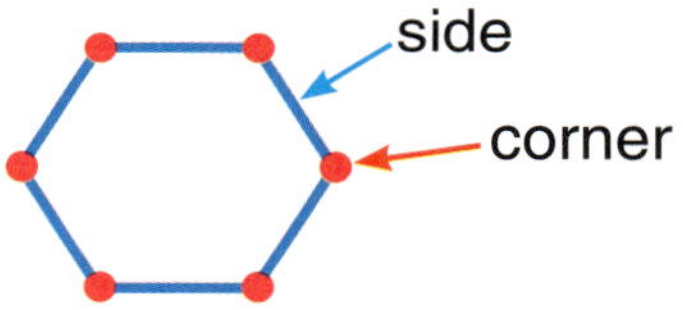

6 sides 6 corners

A circle does not have sides or corners.

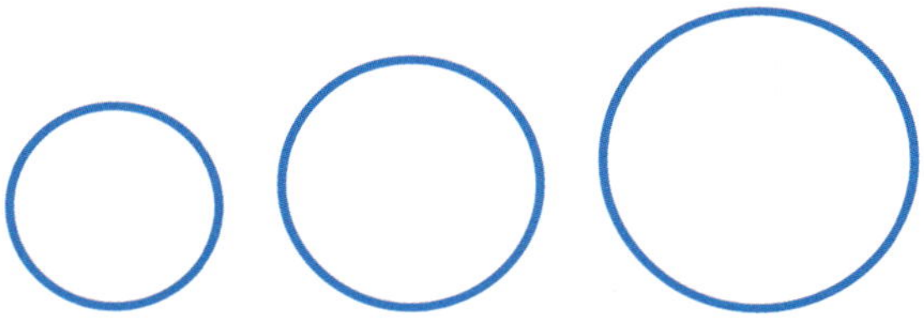

Size, color, and position do not change a shape.

MORE PRACTICE

Color each closed shape.

1. 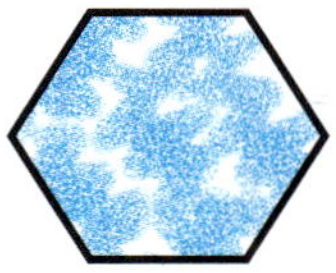
2. 
3. 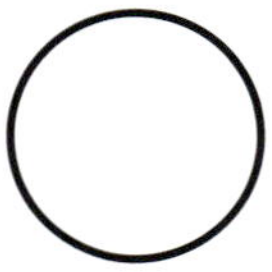
4. 
5. 
6. 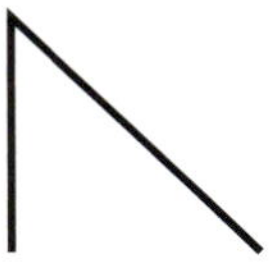
7. 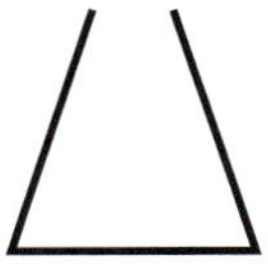
8. 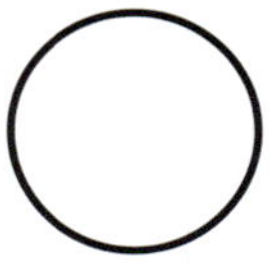

HOMEWORK

Trace each shape. Draw a • at each corner. Write how many sides and corners.

1. 

4 sides

4 corners

2. 

_____ sides

_____ corners

3. 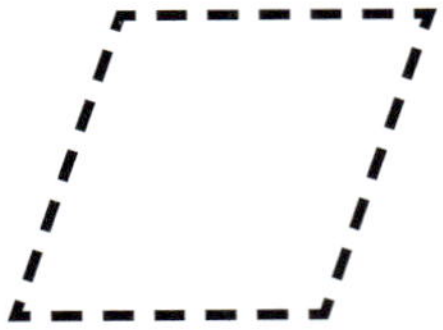

_____ sides

_____ corners

Problem Solving

4. Andy draws an open shape. Matt and Fred draw closed shapes. Matt's shape has more sides than a square. Which shape does each child draw?

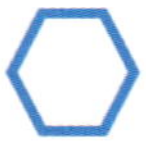 ____________________

 ____________________

 ____________________

Write About It

5. What makes these two shapes the same?

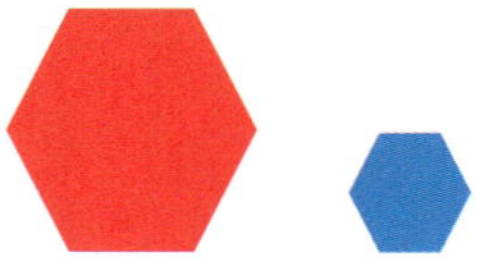

____

____

Name ______________________

LESSON 13-3

Objective

- Compose two-dimensional shapes using triangles, trapezoids, rhombuses, and hexagons.

Math Words

triangle
rhombus
trapezoid
hexagon

Compose Two-Dimensional Shapes

Jackson uses and to make new shapes.
How many make 1 ?
How many make 1 ?

One way to make a is to use 3 .

3 triangles   1 trapezoid

Jackson uses 3 to make 1 .

One way to make a is to use 3 .

3 rhombuses   1 hexagon

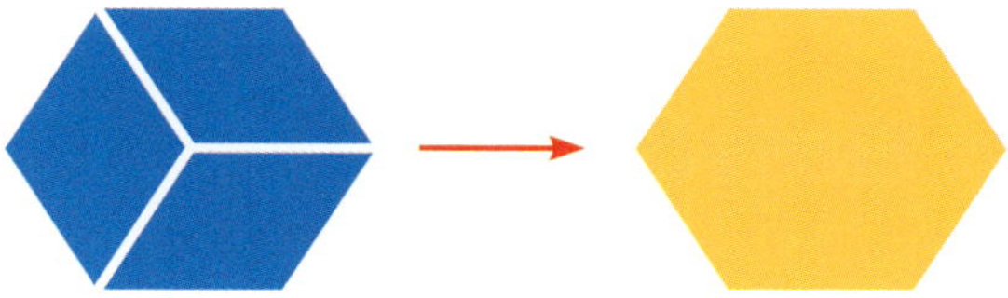

Jackson uses 3 to make 1 .

PRACTICE

Use pattern blocks to make a new shape.
How many of each pattern block did you use?

1. Use to make a .

2 make 1 .

2. Use to make a .

____ make ____ .

3. Use to make a .

____ make 1 .

4. Use and to make a .

____ and ____ make 1 .

PRACTICE

**Use the pattern blocks to make a new shape.
Draw a line to match the shape you made.**

5. 2 trapezoids

6. 1 triangle and 1 trapezoid

7. 1 rhombus and 1 trapezoid

a. 

b. 

c. 

Problem Solving

8. Jane makes this larger shape with
3 smaller pattern blocks.
The 3 pattern blocks are the same shape.
Circle the pattern block Jane uses.

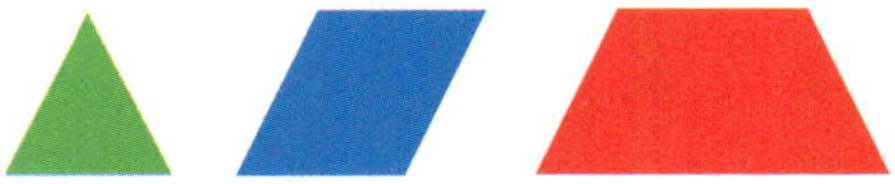

Write About It

9. Make a shape with 1 triangle and 1 hexagon.
Trace the shape. Tell how to count
the number of sides in the new shape.

Name ______________________________

Compose Two-Dimensional Shapes

One way to make a is to use 3 .

3 triangles 1 trapezoid

One way to make a is to use 3 .

3 rhombuses 1 hexagon

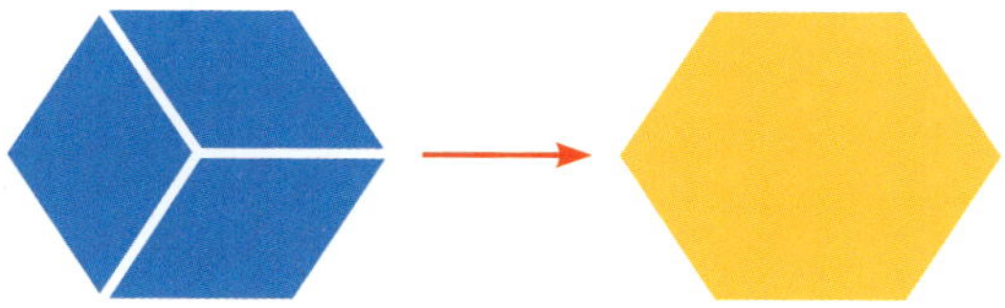

MORE PRACTICE

Draw the smaller shapes to make a new shape. How many of each smaller shape did you draw?

1. Use to make a .
   6 make 1 .

2. Use to make a .
   ____ make ____ .

3. Use to make a .
   ____ make ____ .

4. Use and to make a .
   ____ and ____ make 1 . Or, ____ and ____ .

5. Use to make a .
   ____ make 1 .

6. Use and to make a .
   ____ and ____ make 1 .

HOMEWORK

The triangles can go together to make a new shape. Draw a line to match the new shape.

1. 2 ▲ — a. 

2. 6 ▲ — b. 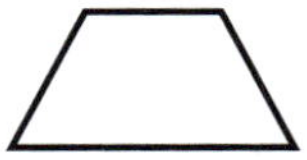

3. 4 ▲ — c. 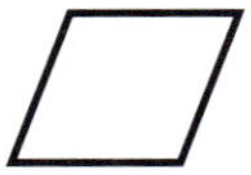

4. 3 ▲ — d. 

Problem Solving

5. Jen makes a shape with 1 ▲ and 1 ▱.
Mia makes a shape with 2 ⏢.
Which shape does each child draw?

 ____________ 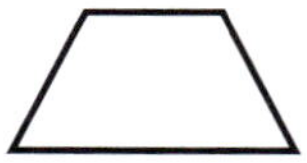 ____________

Write About It

6. Use 1 ▲ and 1 ⏢. How can you use both shapes together to make a new shape with 3 sides? Draw your shape.

____

____

Name ______________________________

Compose More Two-Dimensional Shapes

Objective

- Compose two-dimensional shapes using rectangles, squares, circles, and parts of circles.

Math Words

curved
square
rectangle
circle

Sara has  and .
She makes these new shapes.

Start with 2 curved shapes.	Make a new shape.	Start with 2 squares.	Make a rectangle.

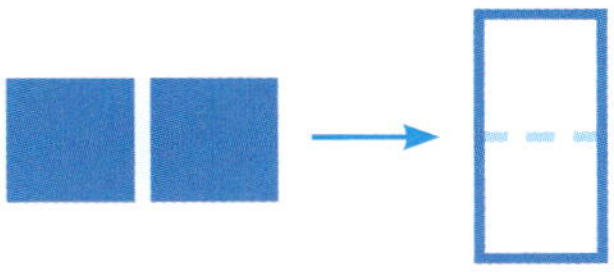

Use the 2 new shapes.	Make a circle.	Use 2 rectangles.	Make a new shape.

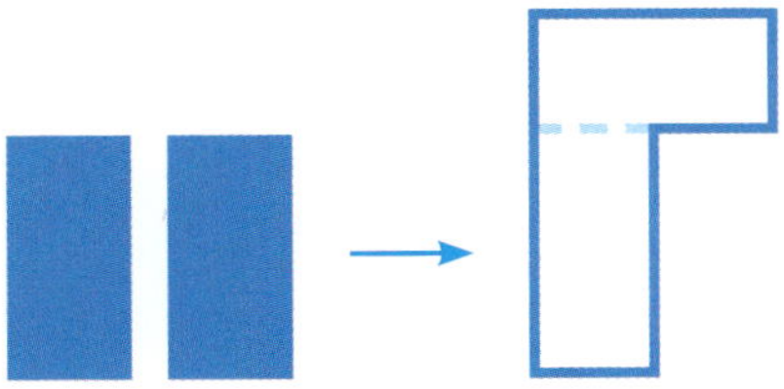

PRACTICE

Draw lines to show how to use the two-dimensional shapes to make a new shape.

1. 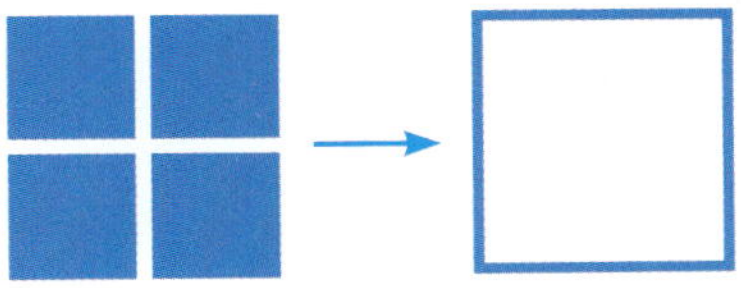

2. 

PRACTICE

Draw lines to show how to use the two-dimensional shapes to make a new shape.

3. 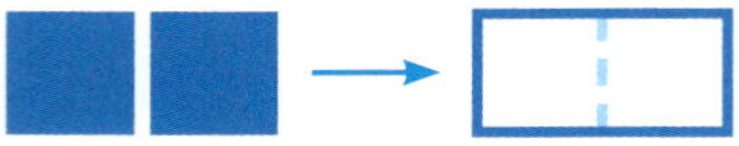

4. 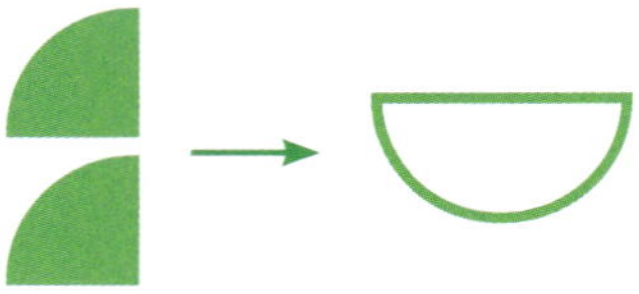

5. 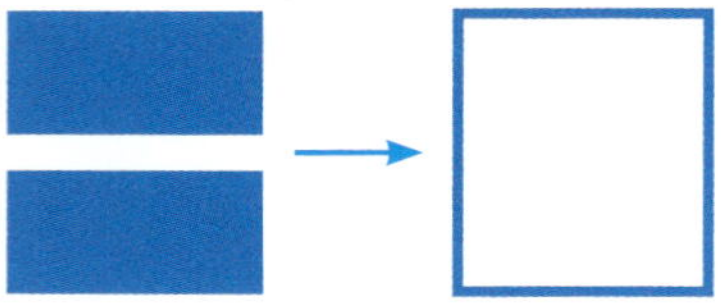

6. 

Problem Solving

7. Draw lines to show how you can make shape A with squares. Draw lines to show other shapes you could use to make shape B.

A. 

B. 

Write About It

8. How can you use 2  and 1 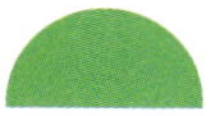 to make a circle? Draw lines to show. Then tell what you did.

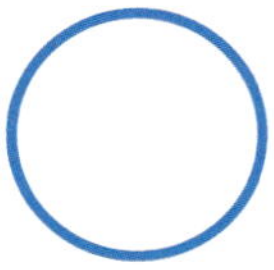

Name ______________________________

Compose More Two-Dimensional Shapes

Start with 2 curved shapes. | Make a new shape.

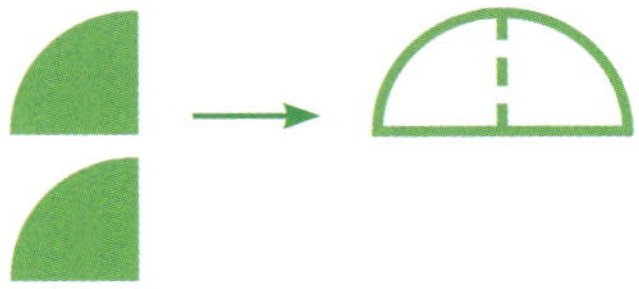

Start with 2 squares. | Make a rectangle.

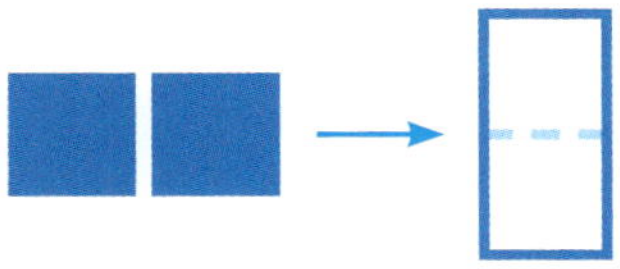

Use the 2 new shapes. | Make a circle.

Use 2 rectangles. | Make a new shape.

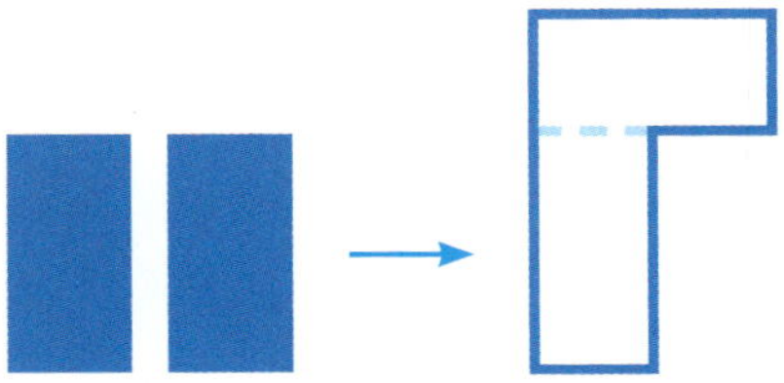

MORE PRACTICE

Draw lines to show how to use the two-dimensional shapes to make a new shape.

1. 2 

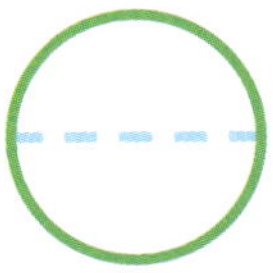

2. 4 

3. 4 

4. 2 

5. 4 

6. 3 

HOMEWORK

The smaller shapes can make a new shape. Draw a line to match the new shape.

1. 2 
2. 3 
3. 4 
4. 3 

a. 

b. 

c. 

d. 

Problem Solving

5. Use 2  to draw a shape with 4 sides or 6 sides.

Write About It

6. Tell how to use 4  to make a larger square.

____

____

____

Name ____________________

Find the correct answer.

1. Which shape is closed?

A. 

B. 

C. 

2. Which shape has 3 sides and 3 corners?

A. 

B. 

C. 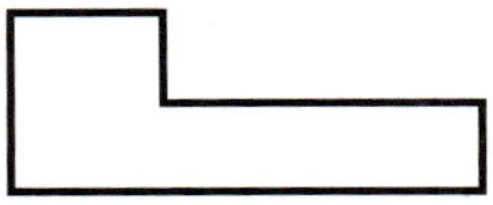

3. How many corners does this shape have?

A. 4
B. 5
C. 6

4. Which shape can you make with 3 ?

A. 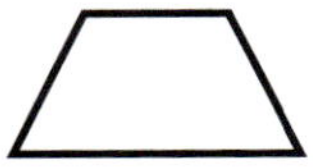

B. 

C. 

5. Which shape can you make with 3 ?

A. 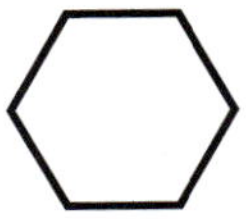

B. 

C. 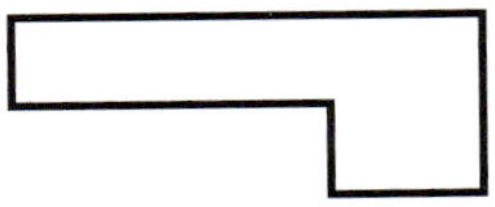

6. Which shape is open?

A. 

B. 

C. 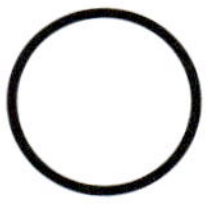

Find the correct answer.

7. Nick makes this shape with 6 of the same pattern blocks. Which pattern block does Nick use?

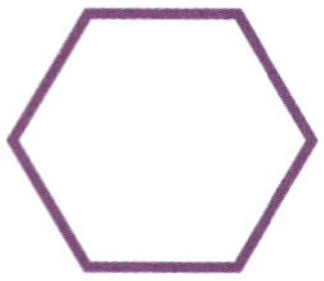

A. 

B. 

C. 

8. How many sides and corners does this shape have?

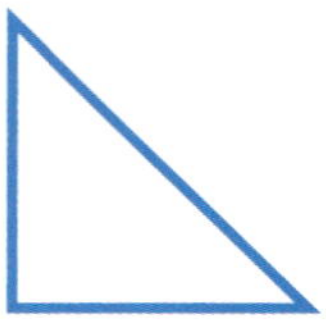

_____ sides _____ corners

9. How many sides and corners does this shape have?

_____ sides _____ corners

10. Draw lines to show how to make this shape with 3 .

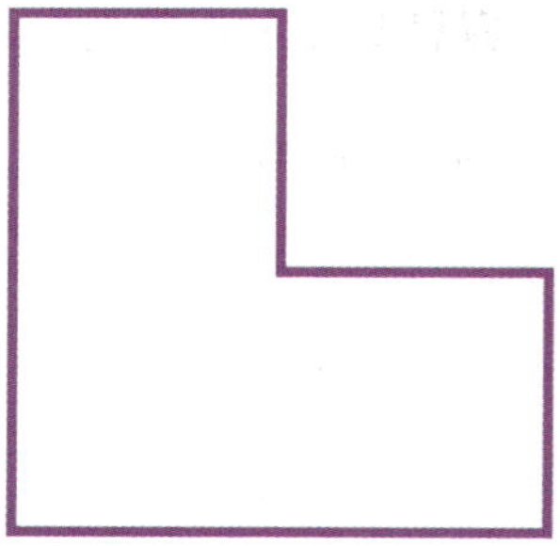

11. Draw lines to show how to make this shape with 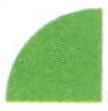.

12. Select the shape that has 4 sides and 4 corners.

A. 

B. 

C. 

Name ______________________________

Three-Dimensional Shapes

Objective

- Understand the defining and non-defining attributes of three-dimensional shapes.

Math Words

solid shape
three-dimensional shape
cube
rectangular prism
cone
cylinder
sphere

Sally has different kinds of blocks.
They are solid shapes and are not flat.
The blocks are three-dimensional.
This solid shape shows 3 measured lengths.

4 inches

3 inches 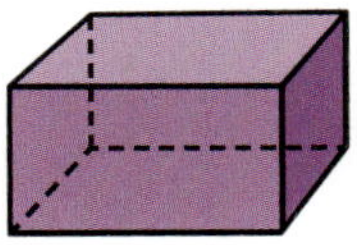 2 inches

How can Sally sort her blocks?

These shapes can be stacked.

cube 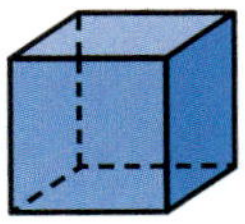

rectangular prism 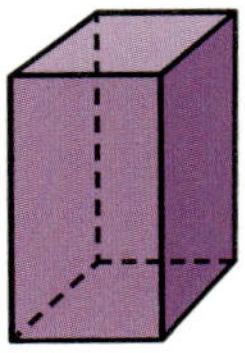

cylinder 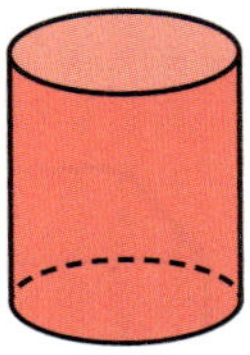

These shapes can roll.

cone 

cylinder 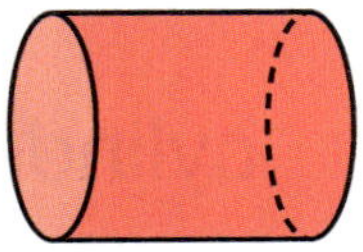

sphere 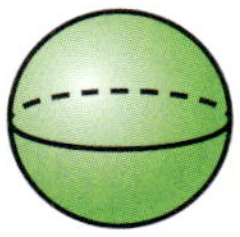

Sally can sort the blocks into solid shapes that can be stacked and can roll.

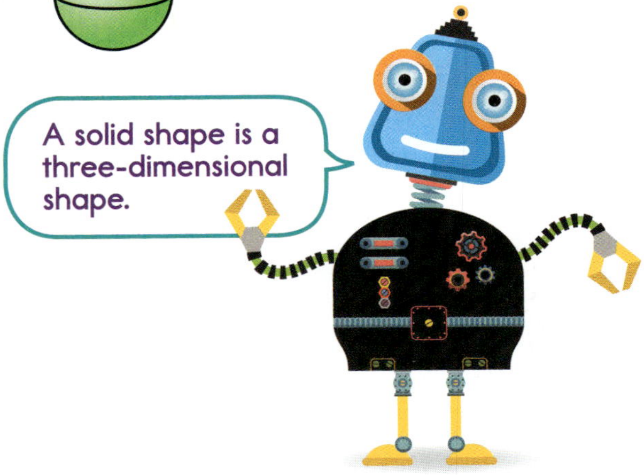

PRACTICE

Color the shapes that match.

Solid shapes are not flat.

1. 

cone

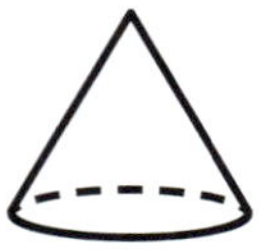 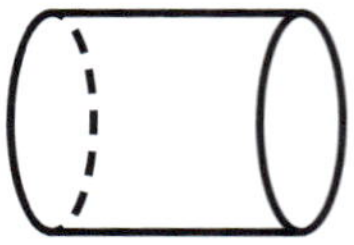  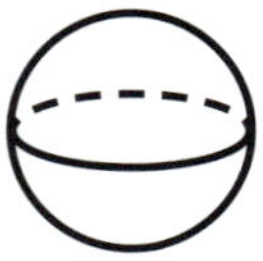

Circle the real objects that are shaped like the solid shape.

2. 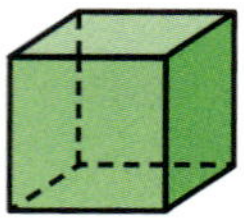

cube

Problem Solving

3. Tim pulls out a block from a bag. He can stack his block and roll his block. Which solid shape does Tim have? Circle the name of the shape.

cone   cube   cylinder

Write About It

4. How are these solid shapes the same or different?

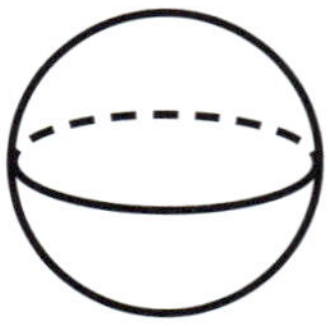 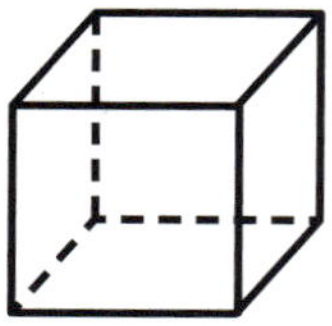

____

____

____

Name ______________________________

Three-Dimensional Shapes

These shapes can be stacked.

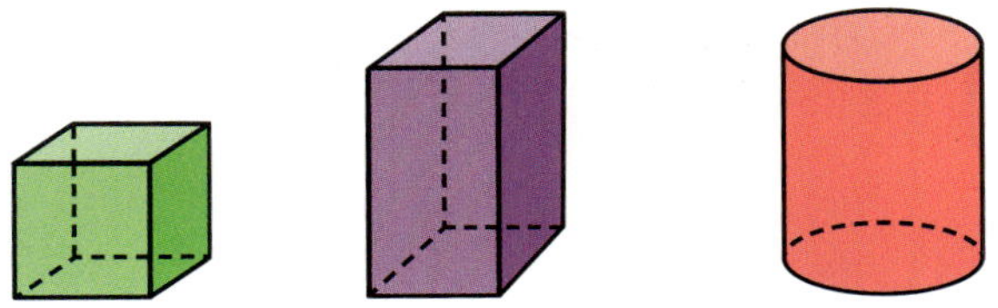

cube | rectangular prism | cylinder

These shapes can roll.

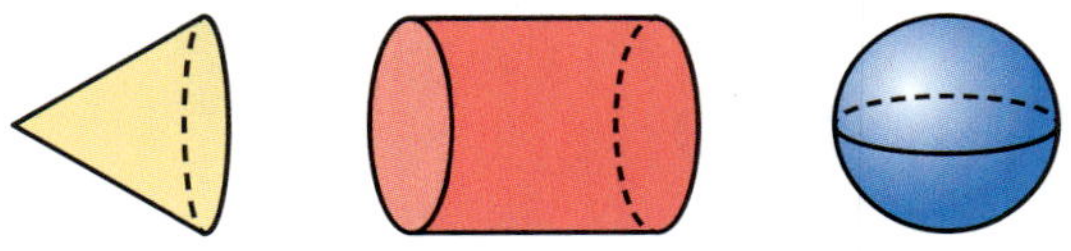

cone | cylinder | sphere

A solid shape is a three-dimensional shape.

MORE PRACTICE

Color the shapes that match.

1. 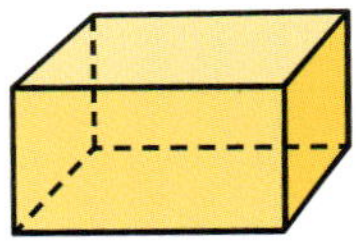

rectangular prism

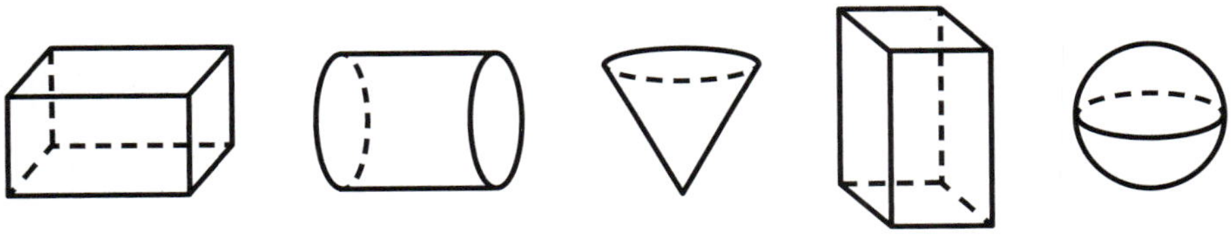

2. 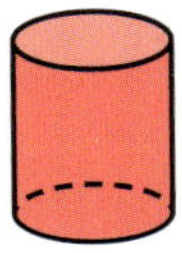

cylinder

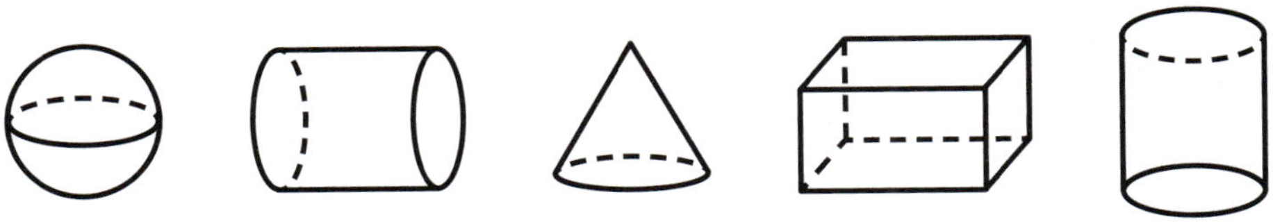

3. 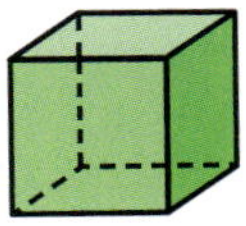

cube

HOMEWORK

Circle the real objects that are shaped like each solid shape.

1. 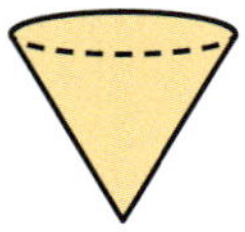

cone

2. 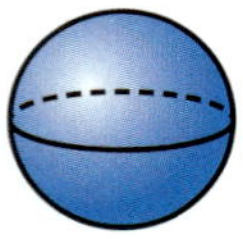

sphere

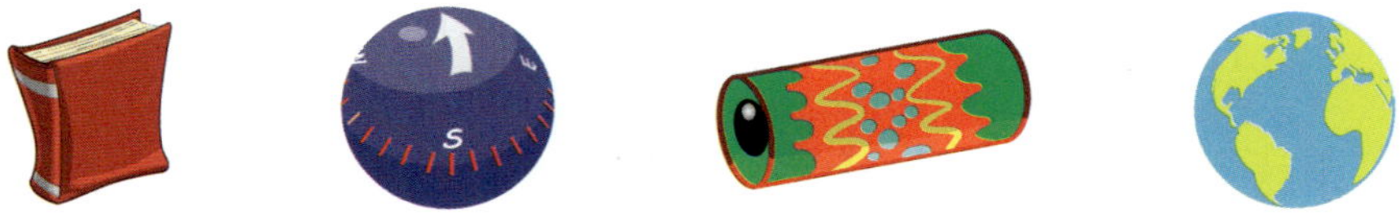

Problem Solving

3. Maya and Pearl each draw a shape that rolls. Kim draws a shape that does not roll. Pearl's shape can be stacked.

Which shape does each child draw?

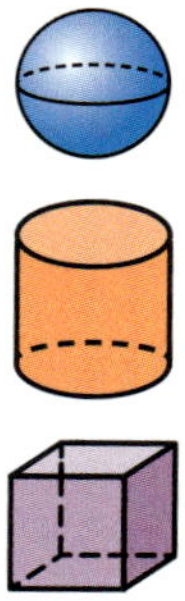

______

______

______

Write About It

4. How are these solid shapes the same or different?

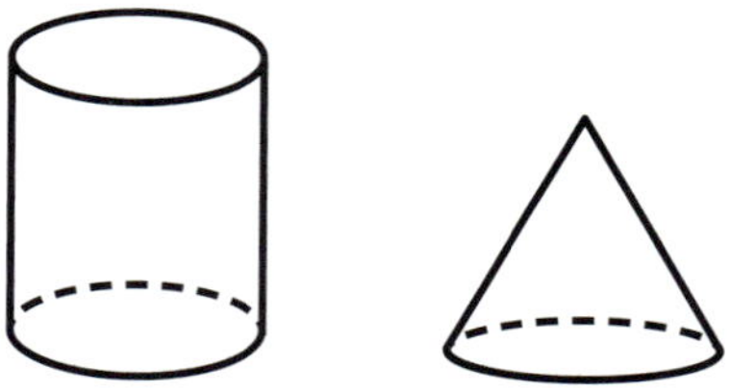

______

______

______

Name ______________________________

Objective

- Understand the defining and non-defining attributes of three-dimensional shapes.

Math Words
face
edge
vertex (vertices)
corner
flat surface
curved surface

Attributes of Three-Dimensional Shapes

Yin has two blocks.
One is a cube.
One is a cylinder.

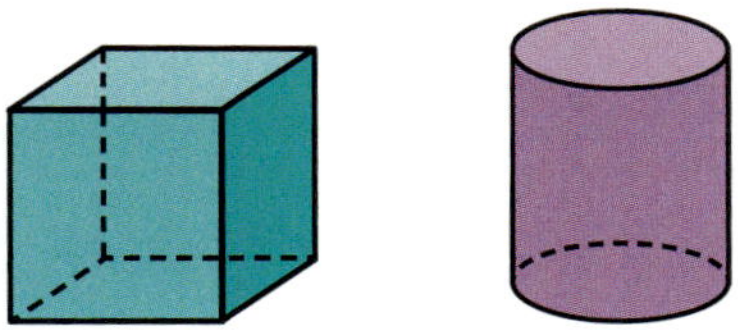

Compare how they are the same or different.

The cube has 6 square faces, vertices or corners, and edges.

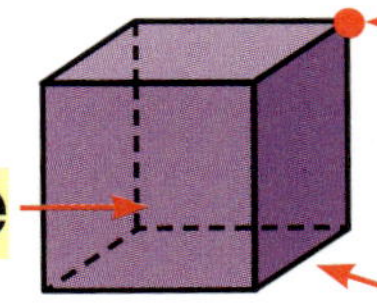

The cylinder has 2 flat surfaces that are circles and a curved surface.

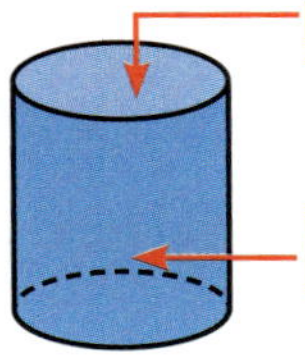

PRACTICE

Circle the part that each arrow points to.

1.

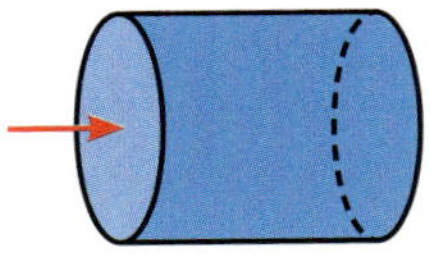

curved surface

flat surface

2.

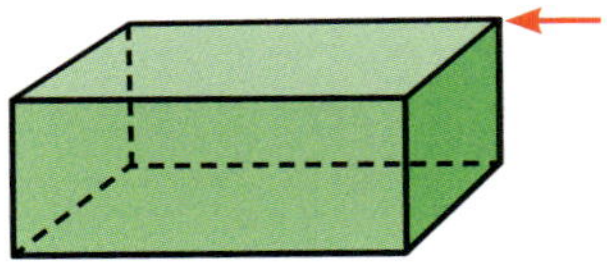

curved surface

vertex

3.

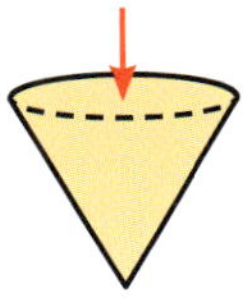

edge

flat surface

PRACTICE

Circle the shapes that have the same name.

4. 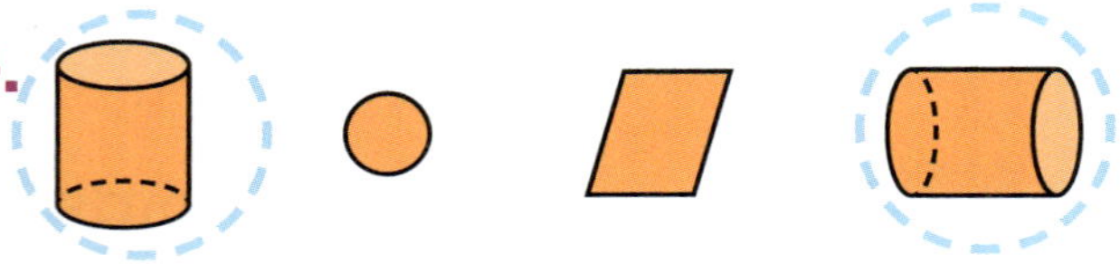

5. 

6. 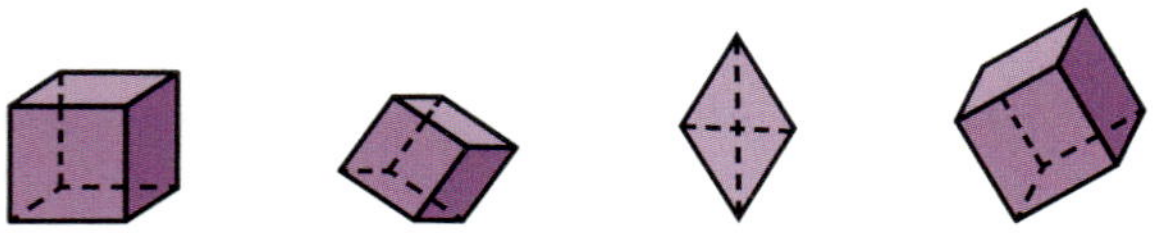

Problem Solving

7. Sid draws either a cone or a cylinder.
The shape has 2 flat surfaces.
Which solid shape does Sid draw?
Draw a picture.

Sid draws a ______________.

Write About It

8. Tell how each flat surface of a cylinder is different than each flat surface of a cube.

____

____

Name ____

Attributes of Three-Dimensional Shapes

Some solid shapes have faces, vertices or corners, and edges.

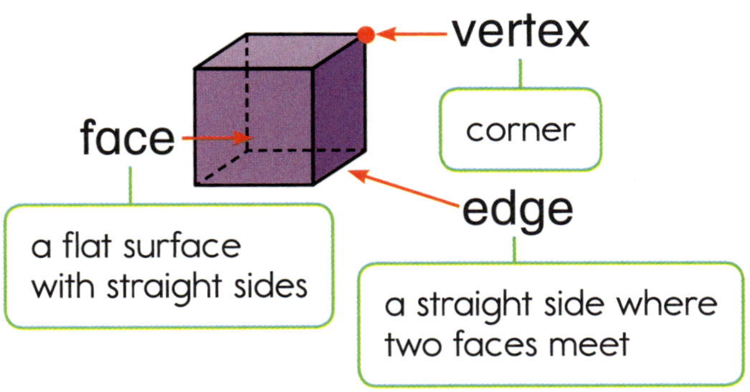

Some solid shapes have curved surfaces and flat surfaces.

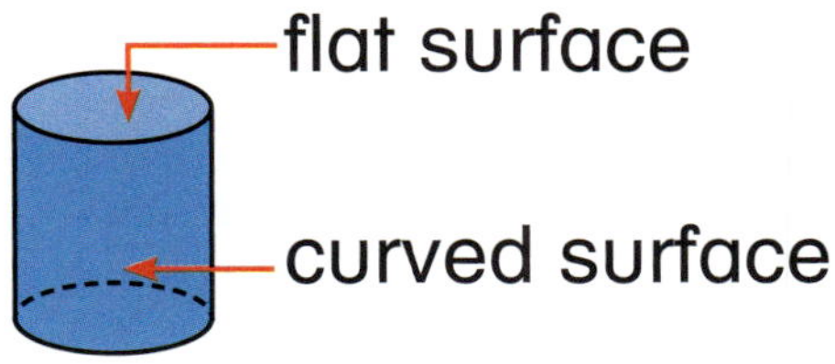

MORE PRACTICE

Circle the correct math words that describe what each arrow points to.

1. 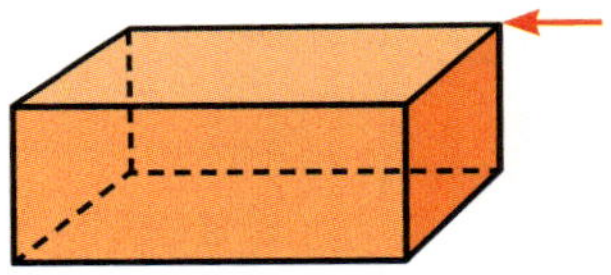

corner

edge

2. 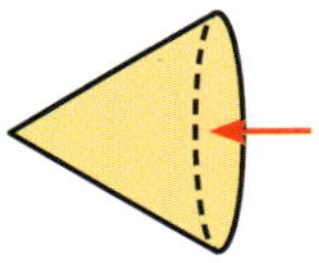

vertex

flat surface

3. 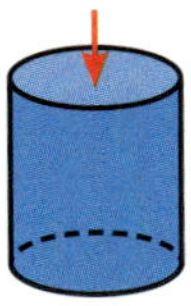

flat surface

curved surface

4. 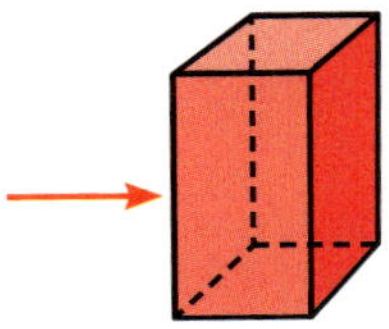

edge

corner

5. 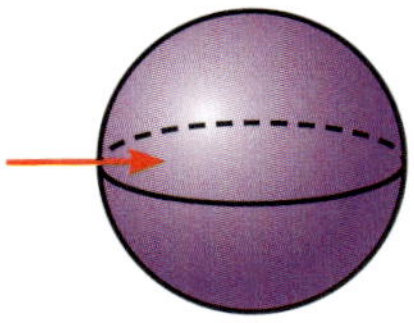

flat surface

curved surface

6. 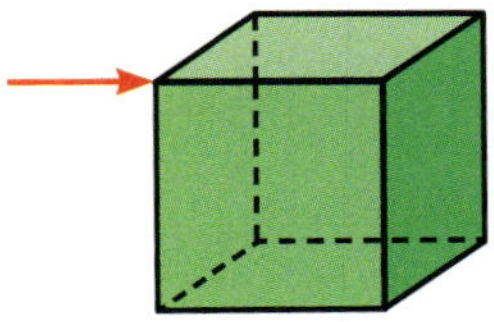

vertex

edge

HOMEWORK

Circle the shapes that have the same name.

1. 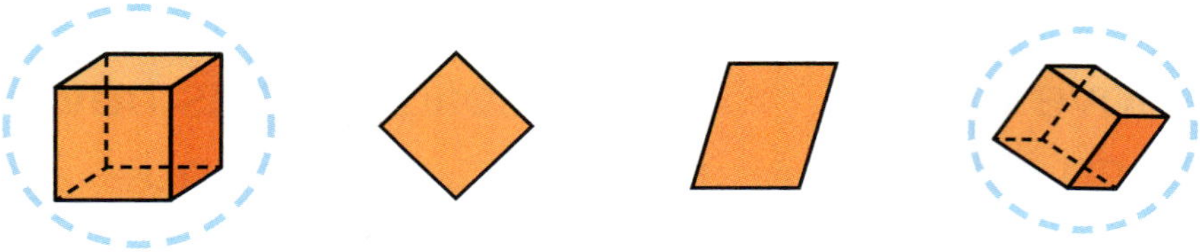

2. 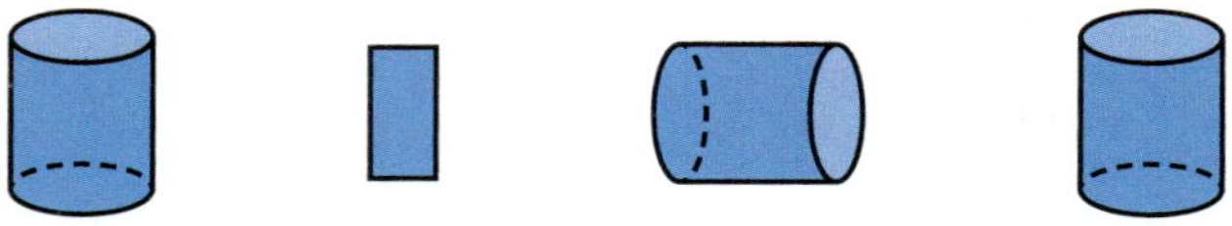

3. 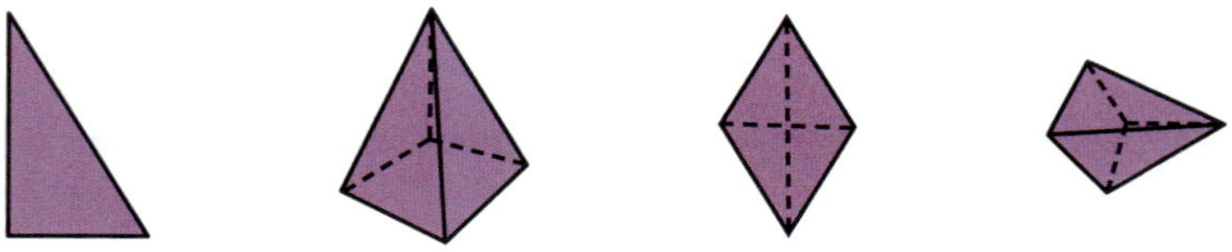

Problem Solving

4. Joe draws a solid shape with faces. Luca and Sam draw shapes with curved surfaces. Luca's shape has a flat surface. Which shape does each child draw?

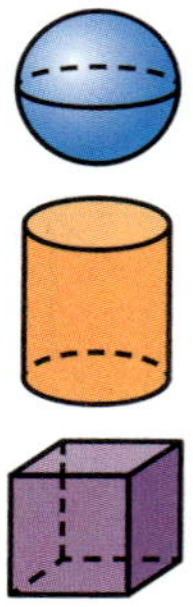

______

______

______

Write About It

5. How would you sort these shapes?

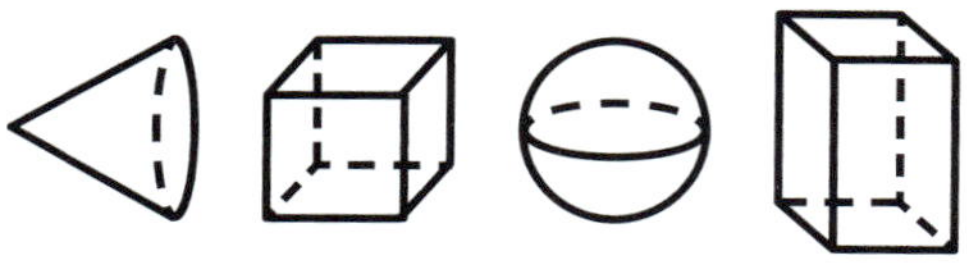

______

______

Name ______________________________

Objective

- Identify two-dimensional shapes as flat surfaces of three-dimensional shapes.

Math Word

plane shape

Compare Two-Dimensional and Three-Dimensional Shapes

Frank traces one flat surface of a cube. What shape does Frank trace?

The flat surfaces of solid shapes are two-dimensional. They are also called plane shapes.

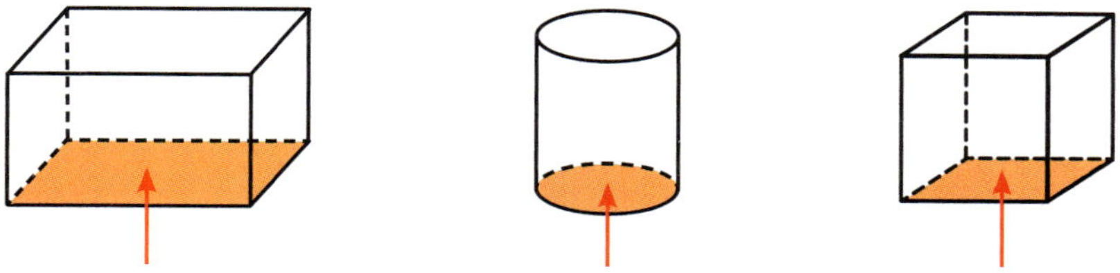

rectangle circle square

The rectangle, circle, and square are all plane shapes.

The flat surfaces of a cube are squares.

Frank traces a square on his cube.

PRACTICE

Draw a line to match the plane shape with the flat surface of the solid shape.

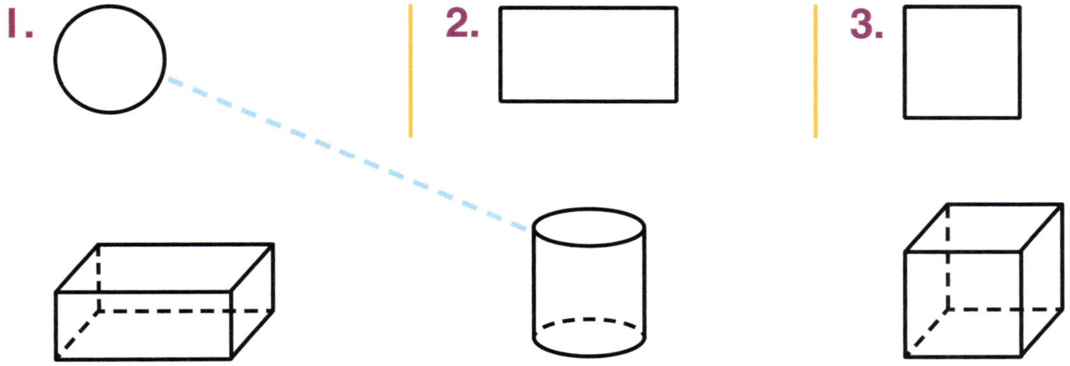

PRACTICE

Look at the pictures of solid shapes.

4. Use  to color any solid shape you could use to trace a circle.

5. Use  to color any solid shape you could use to trace a square.

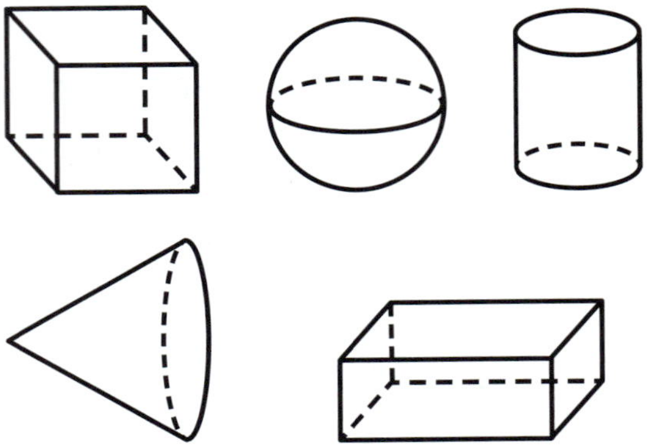

Problem Solving

6. Ed has a solid shape with only 2 flat surfaces. Circle the shape.

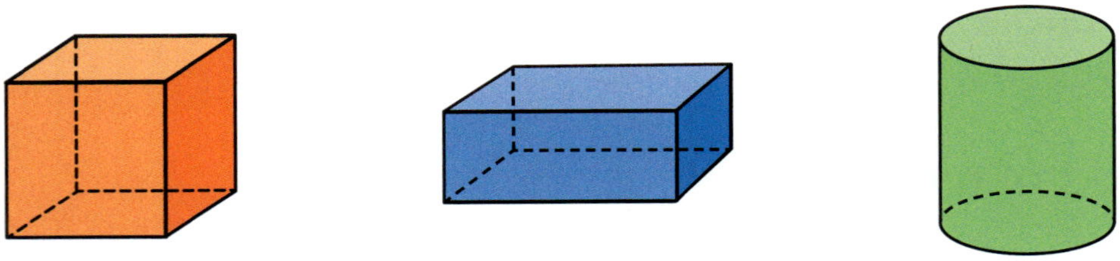

Write About It

7. What solid shape can you make using the faces shown? Explain.

____

____

____

Name ______________________________

Compare Two-Dimensional and Three-Dimensional Shapes

The flat surfaces of solid shapes are two-dimensional and are called plane shapes.

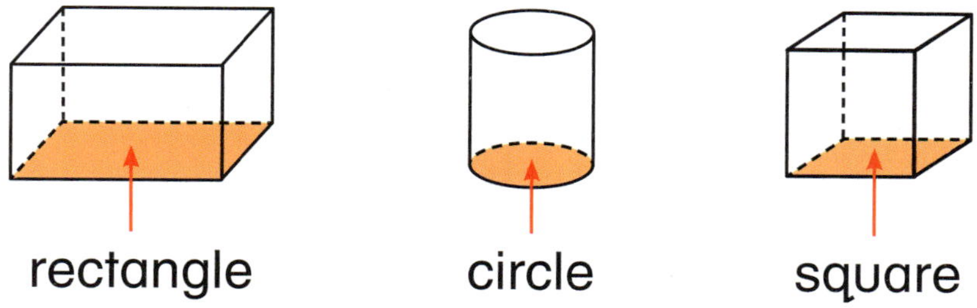

The rectangle, circle, and square are all plane shapes.

MORE PRACTICE

Circle any solid shape with a flat surface that matches the plane shape at the beginning of each row.

1. 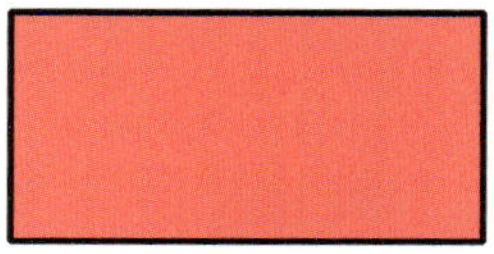

2. 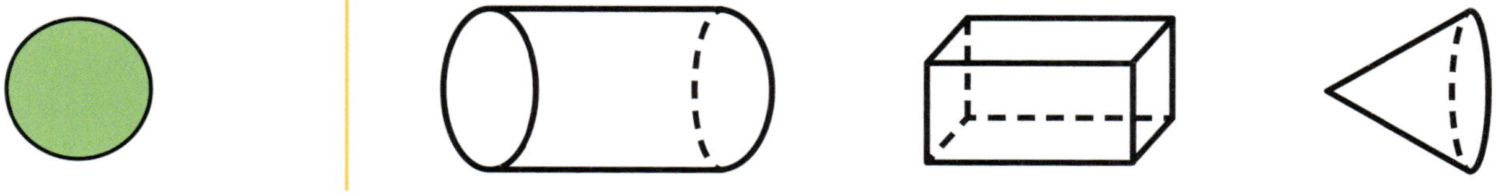

3. 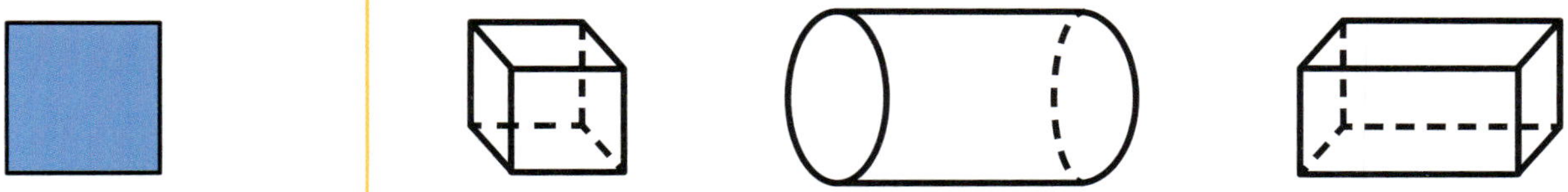

HOMEWORK

Match the plane shape with the shaded flat surface on the solid shape.

1. square

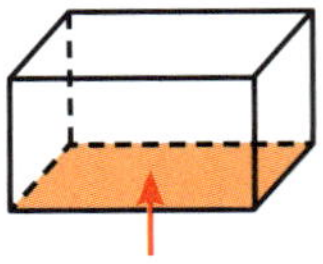

2. circle

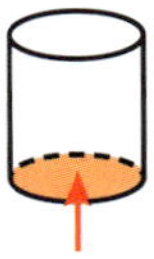

3. rectangle

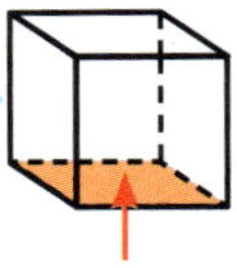

Problem Solving

4. Pam draws a solid shape with flat surfaces. Eva and Lucy draw shapes with curved surfaces. Eva can trace her shape to make a circle. Which person draws each shape?

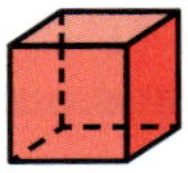 ____________

 ____________

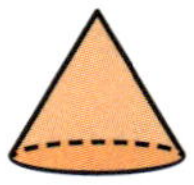 ____________

Write About It

5. Stephen and Josh look at a solid shape.
It has only 1 flat surface that is a circle.
Stephen says it is a cylinder.
Josh says it is a cone.
Who is right? Explain.

____

____

____

Name ______________________________

LESSON 13-8

Sort Two-Dimensional and Three-Dimensional Shapes

Objective
- Identify and sort two-dimensional and three-dimensional shapes.

Math Words
plane shape
solid shape

Lily sorts cards that show plane shapes and solid shapes. Tell where Lily should place this card.

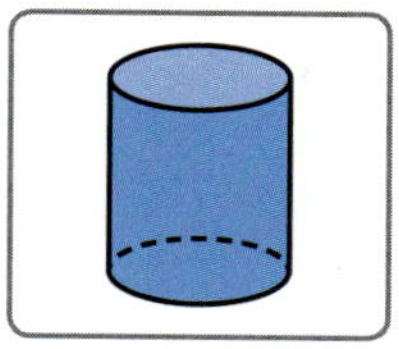

Plane Shapes	Solid Shapes
	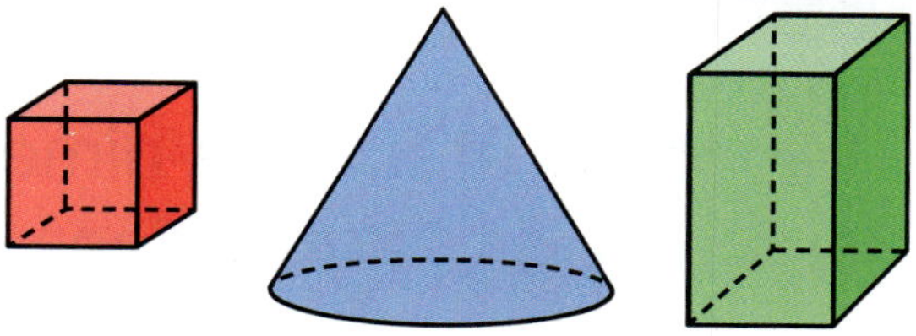

Lily's card shows a solid shape because it is three-dimensional. It is not flat.

Lily should place the card with the solid shapes.

PRACTICE

Circle the shapes that should be in each group.

1.

Group	Shapes
3 sides	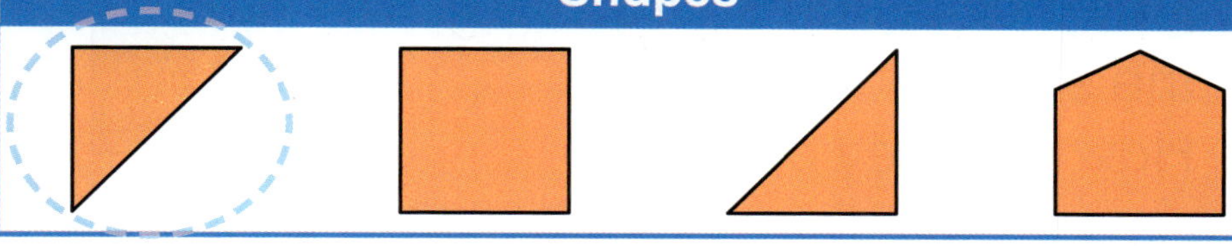

2.

Group	Shapes
0 corners	

PRACTICE

Circle the objects that should be in the group.

3.

Group	Real Objects
4 corners and 4 sides	

Problem Solving

4. Mia looks at a three-dimensional shape that has only one flat surface. Where should Mia put the shape?

Cylinders	Cones

Mia should put the shape with the ________________.

Write About It

5. How are squares and cubes the same?
How are they different?

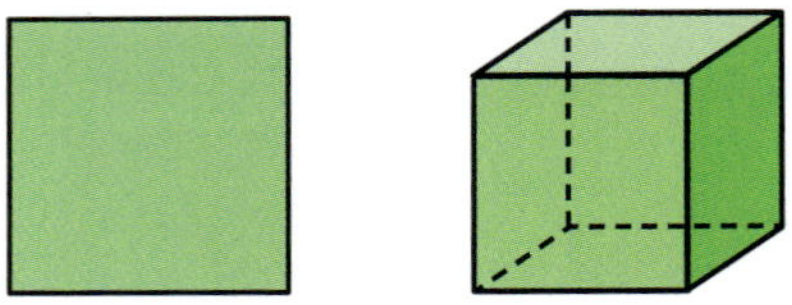

____

____

____

Name ______________________________

Sort Two-Dimensional and Three-Dimensional Shapes

Shapes can be sorted by comparing faces, corners, and sides or edges.

Remember, plane shapes are flat.

Plane Shapes	Solid Shapes
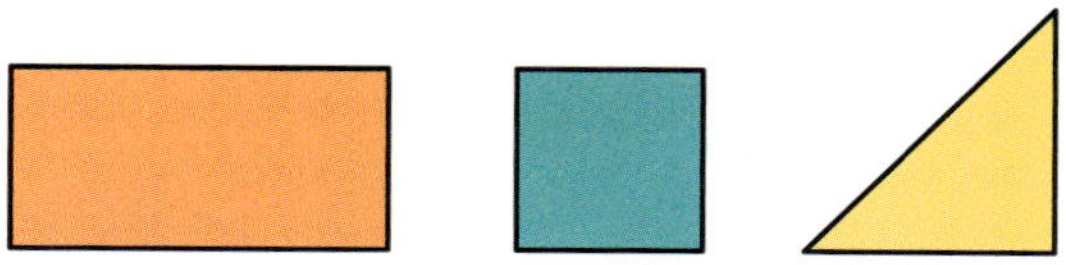	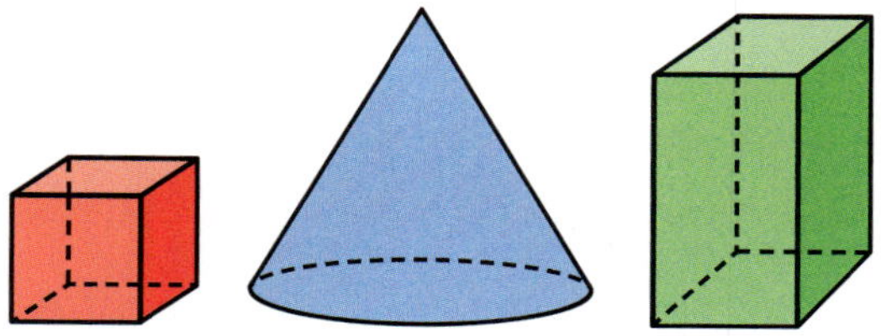

MORE PRACTICE

Circle the shapes that should be in each group.

1.

Group	Shapes
4 corners and 4 sides	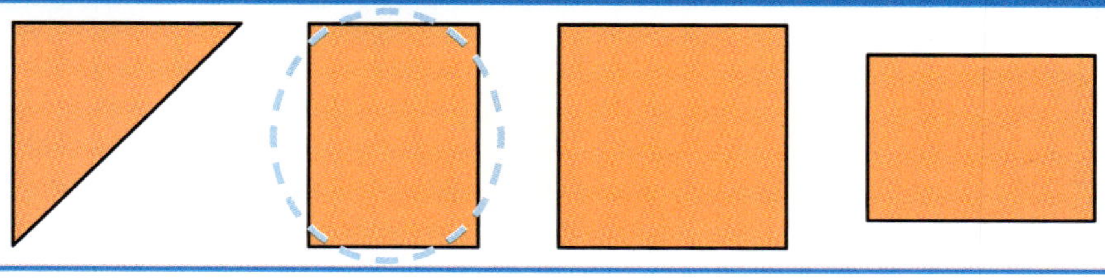

2.

Group	Shapes
solid shapes	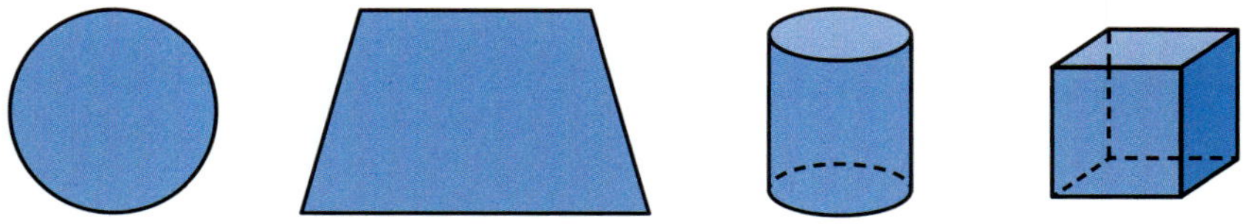

HOMEWORK

Circle the shapes that should be in each group.

1.

Group	Shapes
4 corners and 4 sides	

2.

Group	Shapes
0 corners	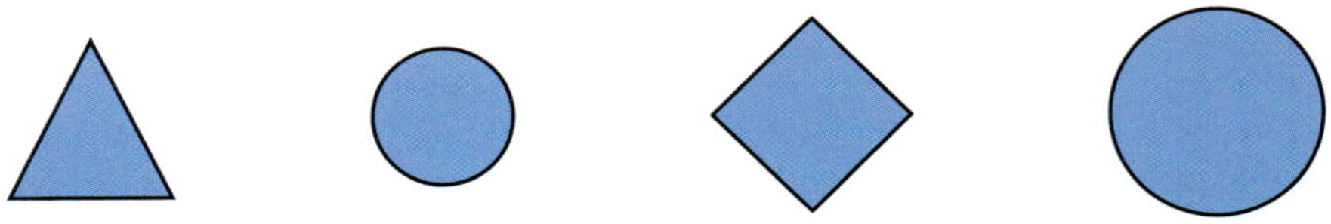

Problem Solving

3. Ted sorts shapes. He only picks objects that are two-dimensional. Circle the objects Ted picks.

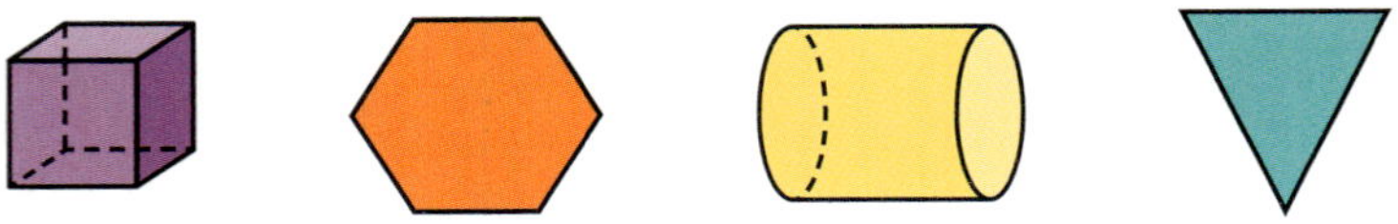

Write About It

4. How are circles and spheres the same? How are they different?

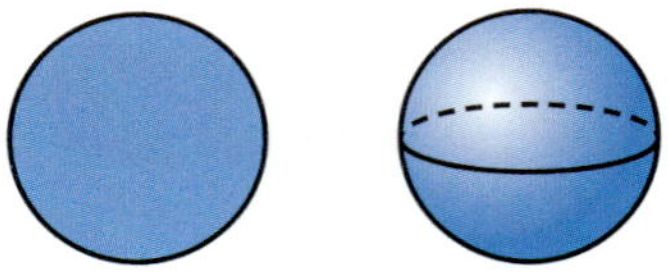

Name ______________________________

LESSON 13-9

Objective
- Compose three-dimensional shapes using cubes, cones, cylinders, and rectangular prisms.

Math Word
three-dimensional shape

Compose Three-Dimensional Shapes

Tina makes a three-dimensional T using other solid shapes.
Which solid shapes does she use?

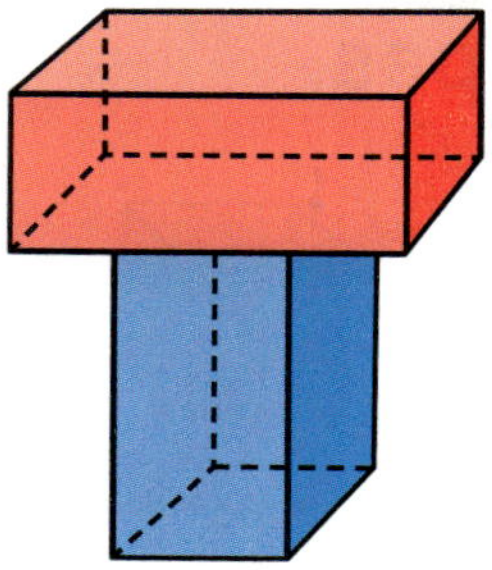

Solid shapes are three-dimensional shapes.

You can put together solid shapes to make new three-dimensional shapes.

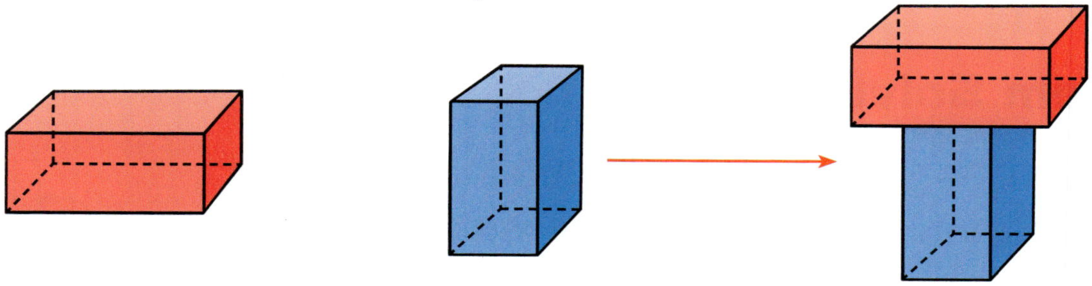

rectangular prism | rectangular prism | new three-dimensional shape

Tina uses two rectangular prisms to make a T.

PRACTICE

Circle the two solid shapes that make the new three-dimensional shape.

1.

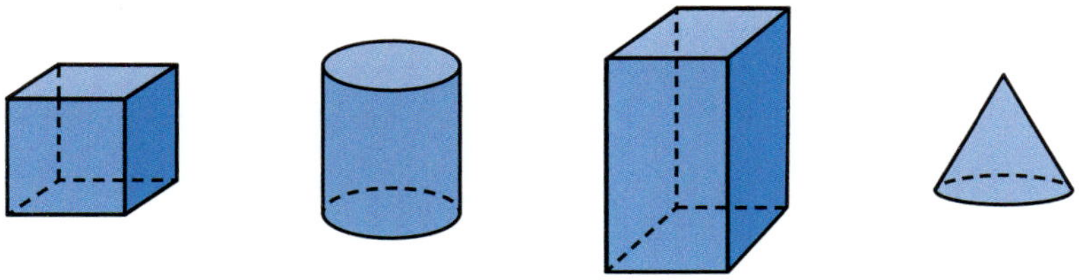

New Shape

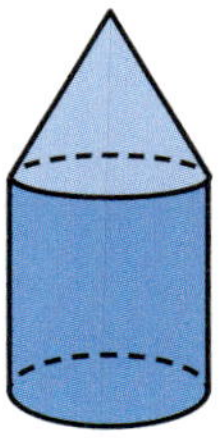

PRACTICE

Circle the new shape you can make with two of the given shapes.

2. 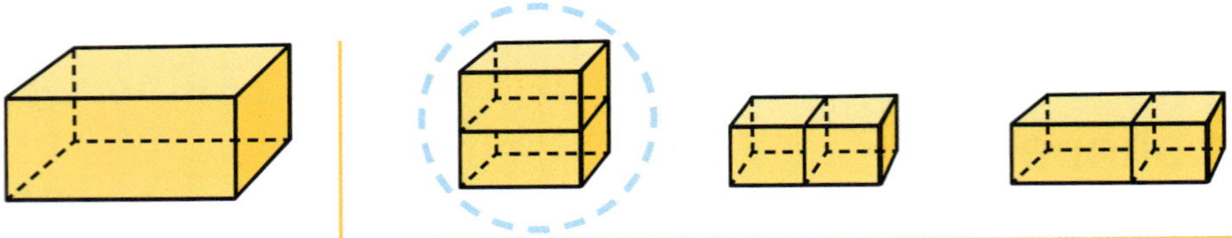

3. 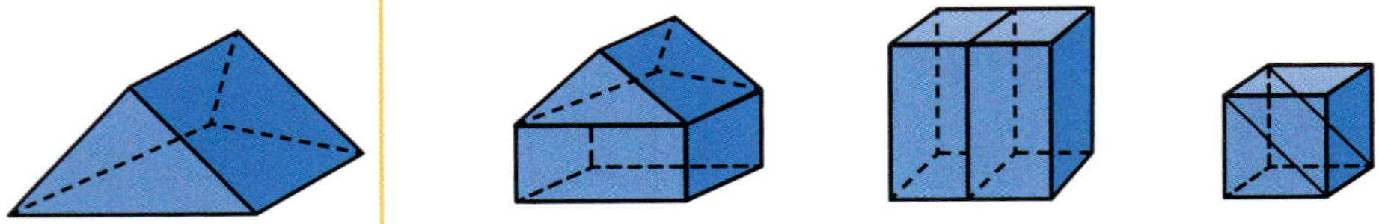

Problem Solving

4. Ryan uses 3 cubes to make the three-dimensional shape shown. He wants to use his new shape to make other three-dimensional shapes. Circle two shapes Ryan could make.

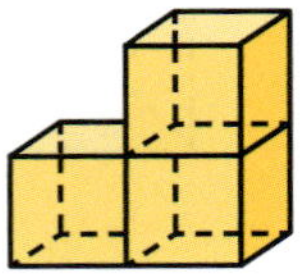

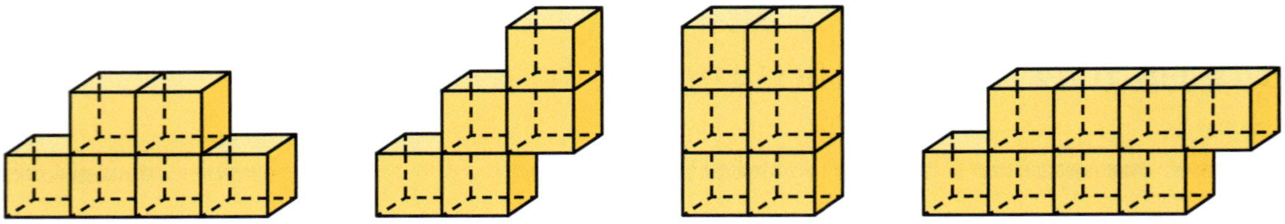

Write About It

5. Two triangles can make a square. Can 2 cones make a cube? Explain.

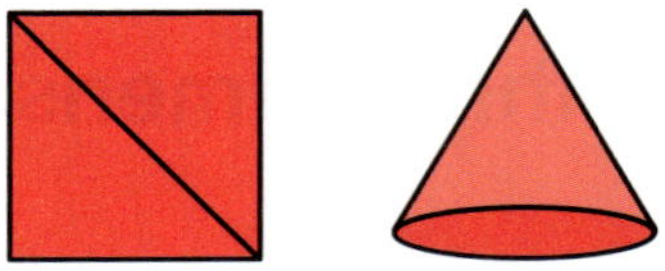

____

____

____

Name ______________________

Compose Three-Dimensional Shapes

You can put together solid shapes to make new three-dimensional shapes.

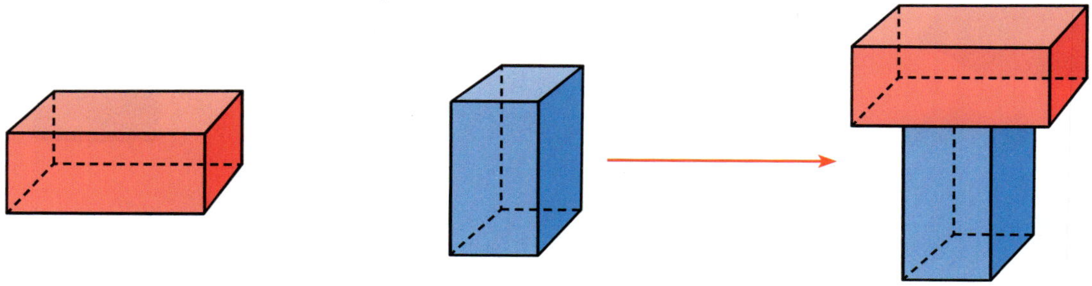

rectangular prism

rectangular prism

new three-dimensional shape

MORE PRACTICE

Circle the new three-dimensional shape you can make from the two solid shapes.

1.

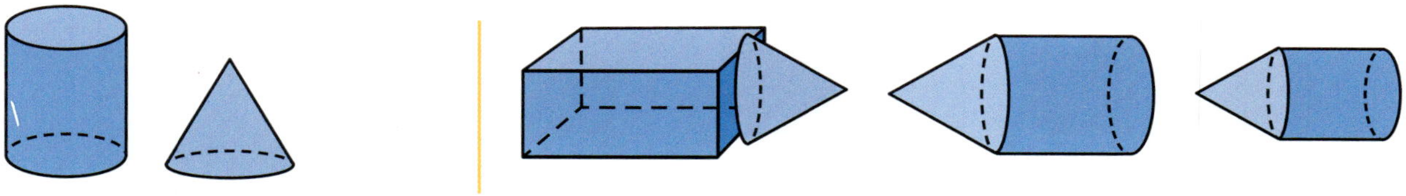

2.

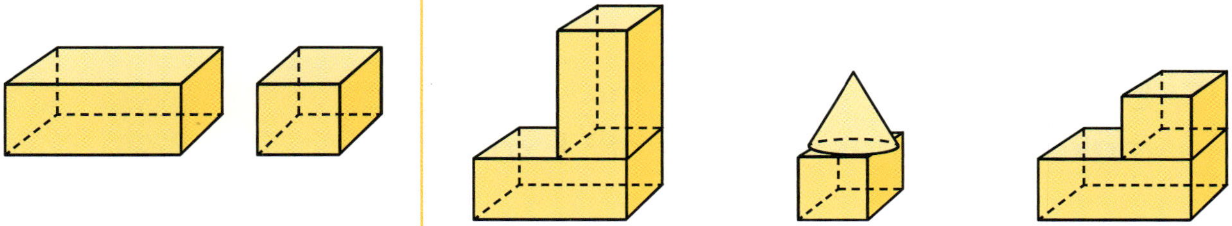

3.

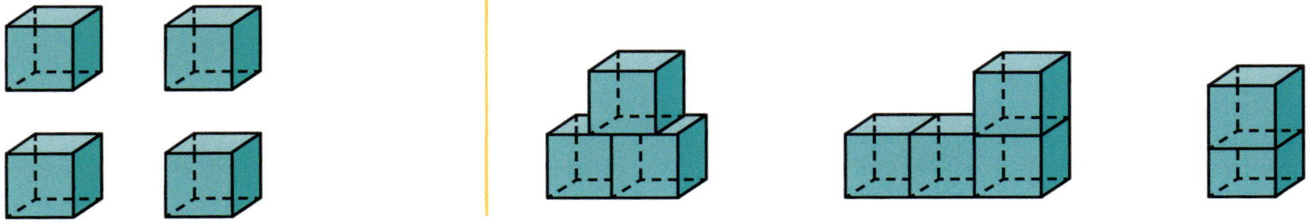

HOMEWORK

Circle the two solid shapes that make the new three-dimensional shape.

1. 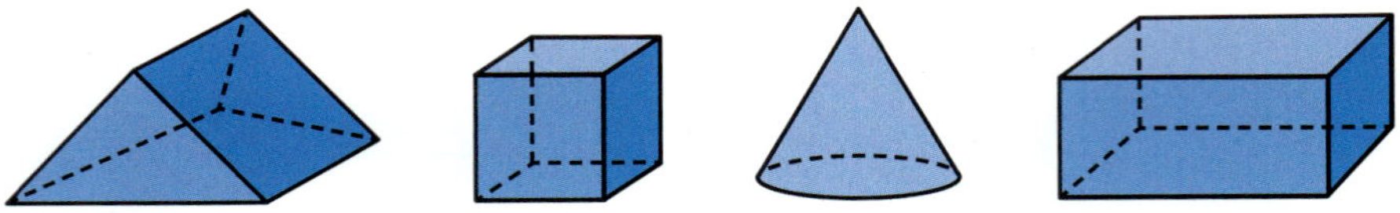

New Shape

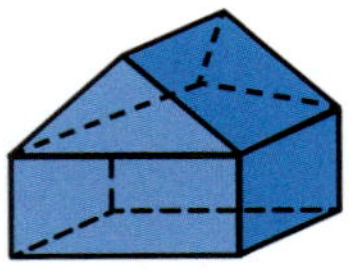

Problem Solving

2. Abby uses 4 connecting cubes to make this three-dimensional shape. She wants to use two of her new shapes to make another three-dimensional shape. Circle the shape Abby could make.

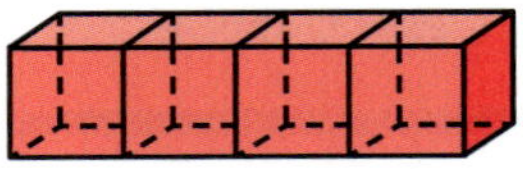

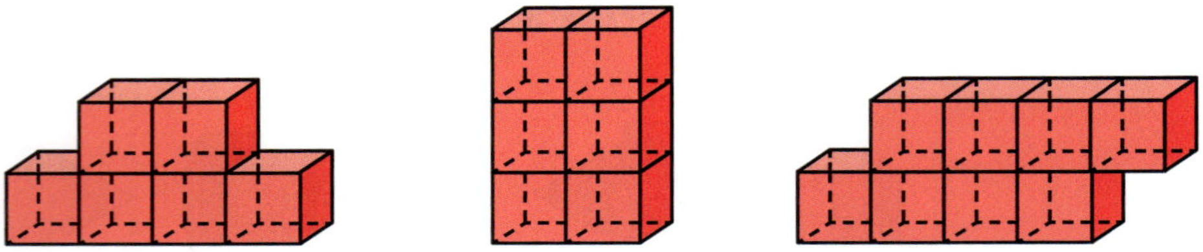

Write About It

3. Simon says he can combine 2 cubes to make a cylinder. Is he right? Explain.

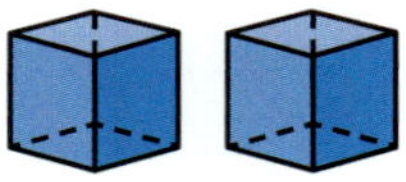

Name ____________________

Problem Solving

Read › Plan › Solve › Check

Use Logical Reasoning

Objective
- Use logical reasoning to solve problems.

Math Word
logical reasoning

Amy, Niki, and Jody each have a shape.
Amy and Niki have shapes with flat surfaces.
Amy has a shape with 8 corners.
Who has each shape shown?

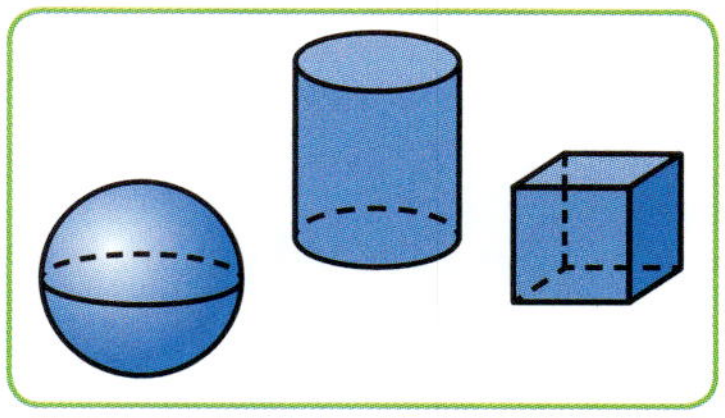

You can use reasoning to solve problems.

Read the first clue.
Amy and Niki have shapes with flat surfaces.
This means Jody has the sphere.

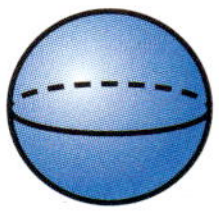
Jody

Read the next clue.
Amy has a shape with 8 corners.
This means Amy has the cube.

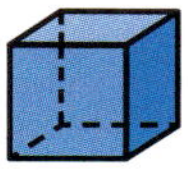
Amy

Find what is left and solve.
Niki has the shape that is left.
This means Niki has the cylinder.

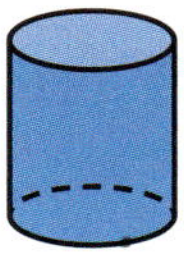
Niki

PRACTICE

Use reasoning. Complete the sentences.

1. Alana has 50 solid shapes. 10 are cubes.
How many of the shapes are not cubes?

Read the first clue. Alana has _____ solid shapes.

Read the next clue. There are _____ cubes.

Subtract to solve. _____ − _____ = _____

There are _____ shapes that are not cubes.

PRACTICE

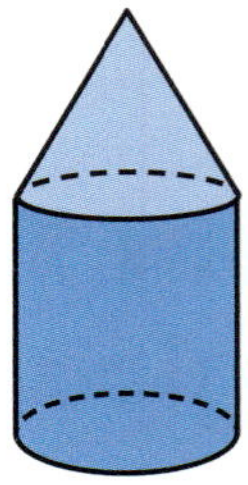

2. Edwin wants to make towers like the one shown. He has 7 cones and 5 cylinders. How many towers can Edwin make?

Read the first clue. Edwin wants to make towers with ____ cone and ____ cylinder.

Read the next clue. Edwin has ____ cones and ____ cylinders.

Solve. Edwin can make ____ towers.

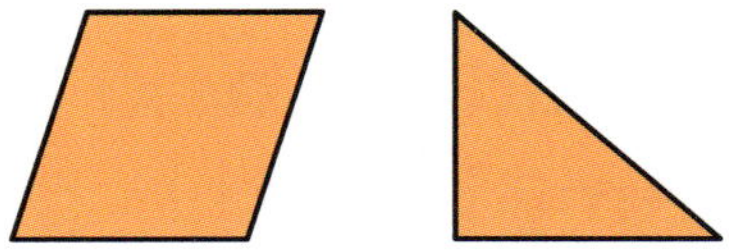

3. Tom and Henry each draw a shape shown. Both are closed shapes. Henry's shape has 4 sides. Who draws a triangle?

Read the first clue. Both shapes are ________.

Read the next clue. Henry's shape has ____ sides.

Solve. ______ draws the triangle.

Write About It

4. How many cubes are in this shape? Tell how you know.

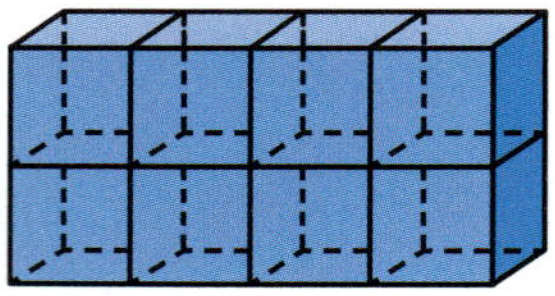

The shape has ____ cubes.

____

____

Name ______________________________

Problem Solving
Use Logical Reasoning

Amy, Niki, and Jody each have a shape.
Amy and Niki have shapes with flat surfaces.
Amy has a shape with 8 corners.
Who has each shape shown?

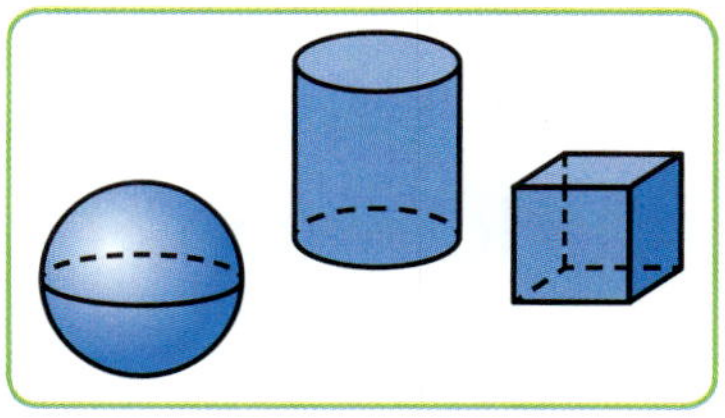

You can use reasoning to solve problems.

Read the first clue.
Amy and Niki have shapes with flat surfaces.
This means Jody has the sphere.

Jody

Read the next clue.
Amy has a shape with 8 corners.
This means Amy has the cube.

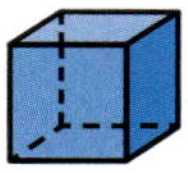

Amy

Find what is left and solve.
Niki has the shape that is left.
This means Niki has the cylinder.

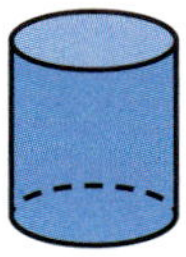

Niki

MORE PRACTICE

Use reasoning. Complete the sentences.

1. Hayden's shape has a curved surface. It cannot be stacked. What shape does he have?

Read the first clue. The shape has a ________ surface.

Read the next clue. The shape cannot be ________.

Solve. Hayden has a ____________.

Use reasoning. Complete the sentences to solve the problems.

2. Gabriella uses 39 blocks to build a castle. There are 20 rectangular prisms in the castle. How many blocks are not rectangular prisms?

Read the first clue. Gabriella uses _____ blocks to build a castle.

Read the next clue. She uses _____ rectangular prisms.

Subtract to solve. _____ − _____ = _____

There are _____ blocks that are not rectangular prisms.

---

3. Stephen, Austin, and Ben each make a shape with triangles. Stephen and Austin use more than 2 triangles. Stephen uses the most triangles. Which shape does each child make?

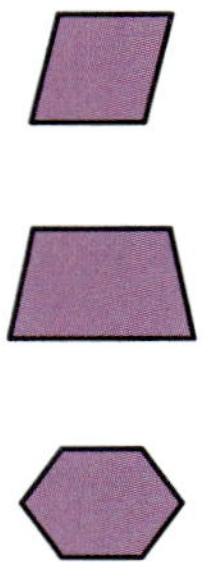

____

____

____

Read the first clue. Stephen and Austin use more than _____ triangles.

Read the next clue. Stephen uses the _______________ triangles.

Label the shapes to solve.

Name ______________________________

Problem Solving
Use Logical Reasoning

HOMEWORK

Use the clues and reasoning to solve.

1. Tim and Brayden can make a circle using their shapes.

   Tim needs 4 of his shape to make a circle.

   Carson's shape has all straight edges. Which shapes do they have?

   ____
   ____
   ____

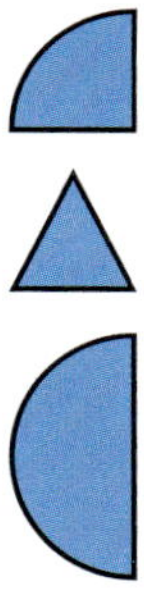

2. Alice makes this shape using blocks. How many total blocks does she need to make 2 of these shapes?

   Alice needs ____ blocks.

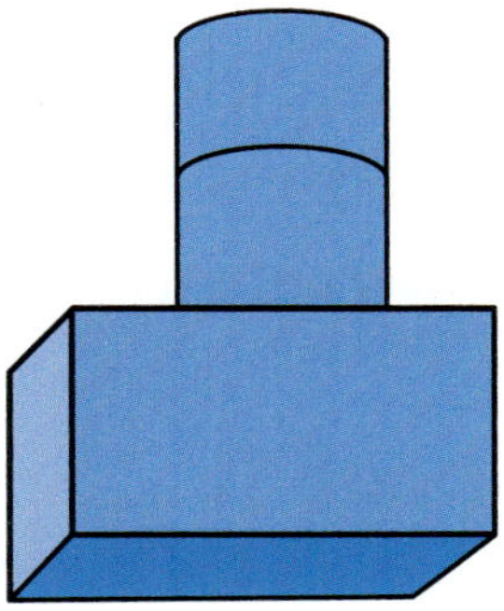

3. Kirk makes a train. He uses 3 solid shapes. Two of the shapes are the same and have 6 square faces. The flat surfaces on the other shape are circles. Name or draw the 3 shapes.

HOMEWORK

Use the clues and reasoning to solve.

4. Remy and Jamal's shapes have curved surfaces. Remy's shape has 2 circles. Andy's shape has no curves. Which shape does each child have?

5. Three friends draw shapes. Denise's shape has 6 sides. Abigail's has 2 long sides and 2 shorter sides. Kathryn's shape has 4 equal sides. Who draws each shape?

Write About It

6. How can you use  to make 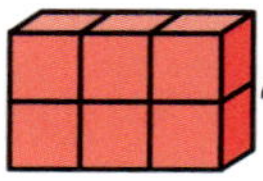?

Trace the smaller shape inside the larger shape to help.

Name ______________________________

Find the correct answer.

1. Which shape is open?

A. 

B. 

C. 

2. Which shape has 4 sides and 4 corners?

A. 

B. 

C. 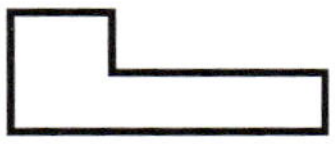

3. Which shape can you make with 6 ?

A. 

B. 

C. 

4. Which is a solid shape that can roll?

A. cube

B. cylinder

C. circle

5. What does the arrow point to?

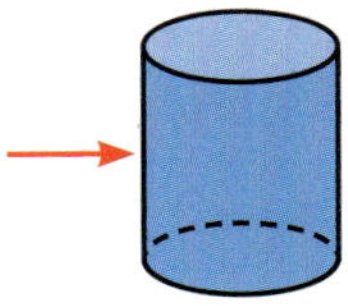

A. curved surface

B. flat surface

C. vertex

6. All the shapes in a group have a curved surface. Which shapes are in this group?

A. cube

B. sphere

C. cone

Find the correct answer.

7. Which plane shape is a flat surface on this solid?

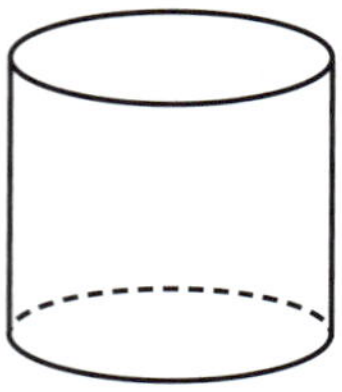

A. square
B. circle
C. triangle

8. Which solid shape has this flat surface?

A. 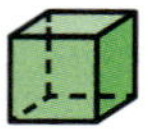
B. 
C. 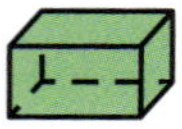

9. Write how many sides and corners this shape has.

_____ sides

_____ corners

10. Draw lines to show how to make this shape with 4 .

11. Bella has a solid shape. She can trace her shape to make a circle. Which shape does Bella have?

A. 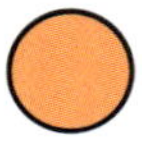
B. 
C. 

12. Write how many sides and corners this shape has.

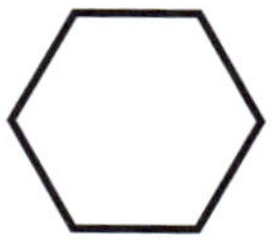

_____ sides

_____ corners

CHAPTER 13
Performance Assessment

Name ____

1. Use some of the shapes to design a stained glass window.

2. Fill in the table. Write how many of each shape you used in your design. Write the number of corners and sides for all of the shapes in the table.

Stained Glass Window Shapes			
	Number of Each	**Number of corners**	**Number of Sides**

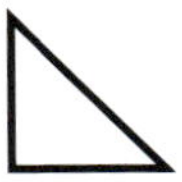			

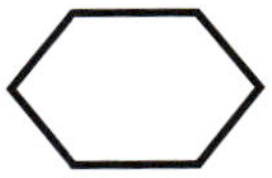			
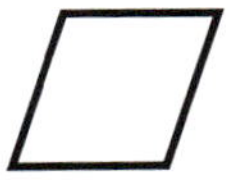			

Name ______________________________

Find the correct answer.

1. Which TWO shapes have 6 sides and 6 corners?

   A. 

   B. 

   C. 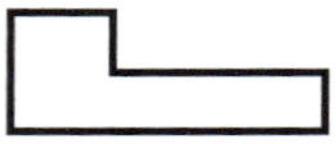

2. Ian has a solid shape. He can trace the shape to make a square. Which shape does Ian have?

   A. 

   B. 

   C. 

3. Subtract.

   $19 - 9 = ?$

   A. 9
   B. 10
   C. 11
   D. 12

4. Which TWO pairs of numbers have a sum of 18?

   A. 9 and 9
   B. 10 and 7
   C. 12 and 6
   D. 6 and 13

5. Subtract.

   $19 - 4 = ?$

   A. 15
   B. 16
   C. 17
   D. 18

6. Add.

   $8 + 8 = ?$

   A. 16
   B. 17
   C. 18
   D. 19

Equal Shares

CHAPTER 14

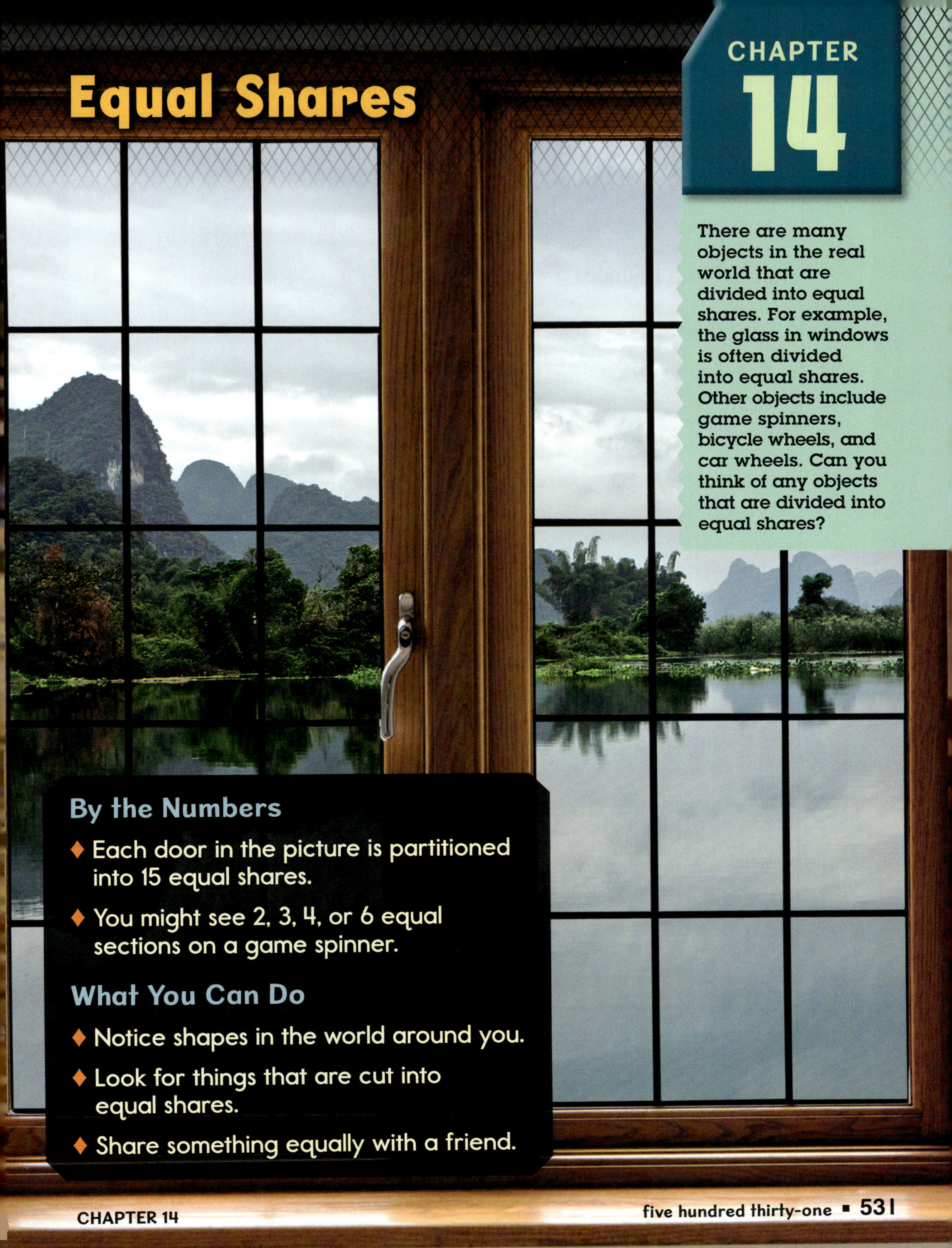

There are many objects in the real world that are divided into equal shares. For example, the glass in windows is often divided into equal shares. Other objects include game spinners, bicycle wheels, and car wheels. Can you think of any objects that are divided into equal shares?

By the Numbers

- Each door in the picture is partitioned into 15 equal shares.
- You might see 2, 3, 4, or 6 equal sections on a game spinner.

What You Can Do

- Notice shapes in the world around you.
- Look for things that are cut into equal shares.
- Share something equally with a friend.

Dear Family,

In this chapter, we will be learning about equal shares.

Here are the Key **Math Words** for this chapter:

equal shares	**fourths**
halves	**fourth**
half	**quarter**

You can use the glossary to check out the definition of each word and help your child make flash cards to study each day we work on the lessons for this chapter.

During this chapter about equal shares, we will also be making STEAM connections about everyday objects. We will explore how windows are divided into equal shares. Read the opening to the chapter together and discuss the **By the Numbers** and **What You Can Do** statements.

Keep Your Skills Sharp

Here is a **Keep Your Skills Sharp** activity to do at home to prepare for this chapter.

Show your child some everyday objects that are circular, rectangular, or square. Ask your child how they can show each object as having 2 equal shares and 4 equal shares.

Name ____________________

Objective

- Identify and show equal shares.

Math Word

equal share

Equal Shares

Vincent draws a rectangle with 4 equal parts. Each part is an equal share of the rectangle. Which shows Vincent's rectangle?

4 shares: same size

4 shares: not the same size

Equal means the same as.

Equal shares are the same size.

The first rectangle is the one that Vincent draws.

PRACTICE

Circle the shape with equal shares.
Then write how many equal shares.

1. 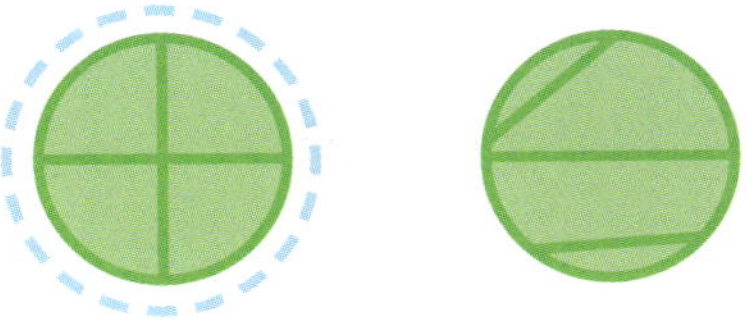

4 equal shares

2. 

____ equal shares

3. 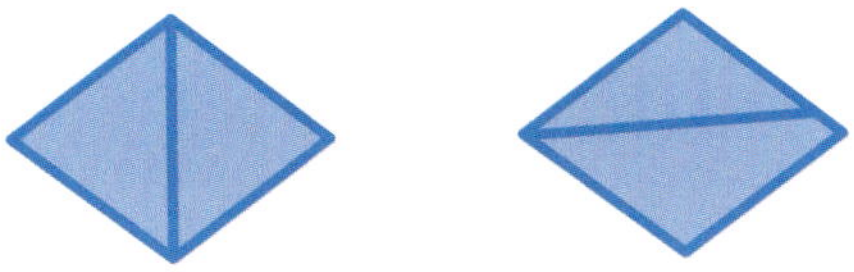

____ equal shares

4. 

____ equal shares

PRACTICE

Circle the shape with equal shares.
Then write how many equal shares.

5. 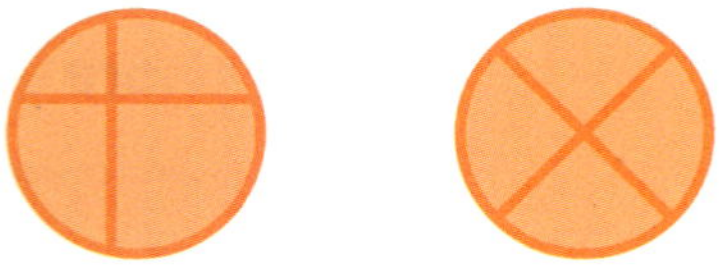

_____ equal shares

6. 

_____ equal shares

Problem Solving

7. Aaron wants to share his sandwich equally with his friend Eric. Show how he can do this.

8. How can you draw a square with 4 equal shares? Is there more than one way? Show how you know.

____

Write About It

9. Explain how you know when a shape has equal shares.

____

____

Name ______________________________

Equal Shares

Equal shares are the same size.

4 shares: same size

These are 4 equal shares.

4 shares: not the same size

These are not 4 equal shares.

MORE PRACTICE

Circle the shape with equal shares. Then write how many equal shares.

1. 

_____ equal shares

2. 

_____ equal shares

3. 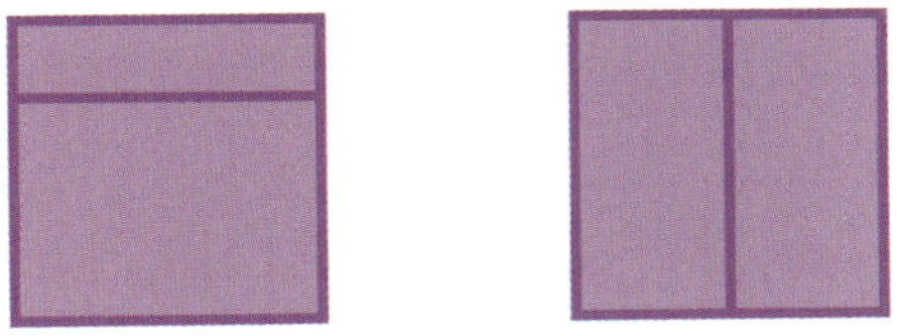

_____ equal shares

4. 

_____ equal shares

HOMEWORK

Circle the shape with equal shares. Then write how many equal shares.

1. 

_____ equal shares

2. 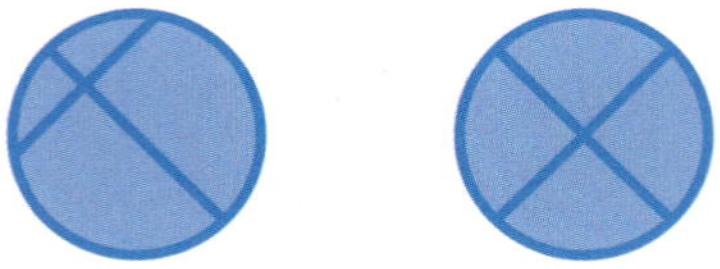

_____ equal shares

Problem Solving

3. Paul's garden is shaped like a rectangle. It is cut into 4 equal shares. Show how the garden can have 4 equal shares.

4. Lucy and Katie are coloring a circle together. Lucy colors more of the circle than Katie. Do they color equal shares of the circle? Tell how you know.

____

____

Write About It

5. Is there only one way to draw 2 equal shares on a circle? Explain.

____

____

Name ____________________

Objective
- Partition shapes into halves.

Math Words
whole
halves
half

Make Halves

Two friends eat equal shares of a watermelon slice. How much of the slice does each friend eat?

Draw a circle. Show 2 equal shares, or halves.

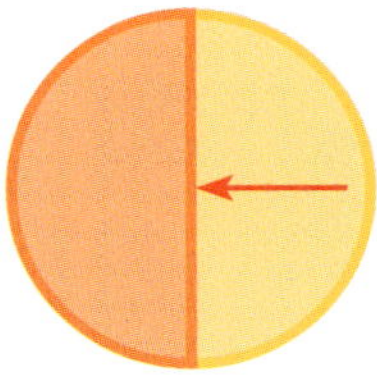

This is one half.

2 halves make a whole.

Each friend eats half of the watermelon slice.

PRACTICE

Circle the shapes that show halves. ✗ the shapes that do not show halves.

1. 

2. 

3. 

4. 

5. 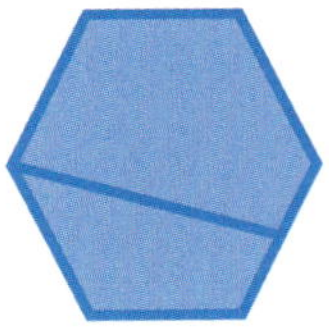

6. 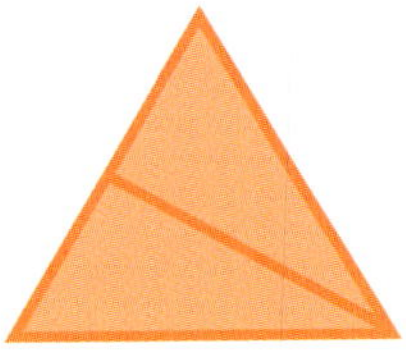

PRACTICE

Make halves. Color one half.

7. 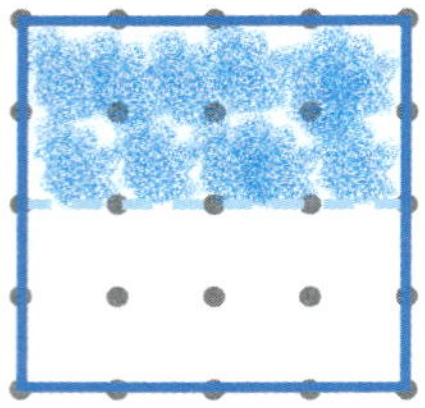

8. 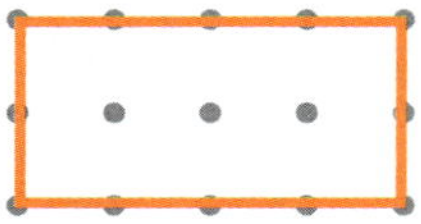

9. 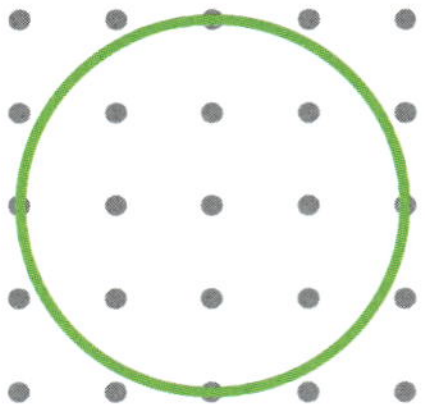

Problem Solving

10. Blake cuts a piece of paper in half. Circle the picture that shows half of Blake's paper.

Half of Blake's paper is 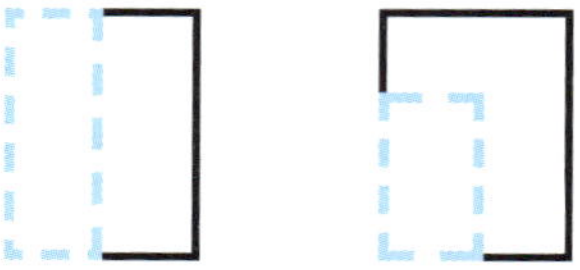

11. Kaylee and Leah each eat half of a square slice of cheese. What shapes can each of their halves be?

The shapes of their halves can be ______________

or ______________.

Write About It

12. Can one half of a shape be larger than the other half? Explain.

____

____

Name ______________________________

Make Halves

You can draw a shape with 2 equal shares, or halves.

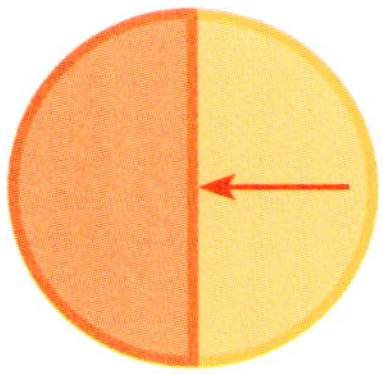

Each side shows one half.

This is one half.

The halves are the same size.

MORE PRACTICE

Circle the shapes that show halves.
✗ the shapes that do not show halves.

1. 

2. 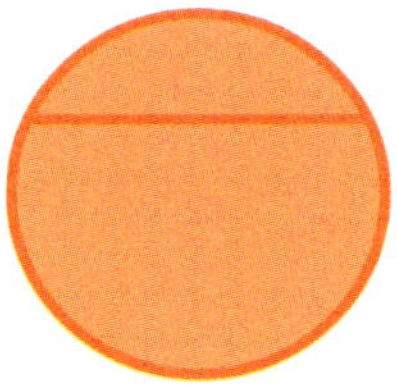

3. 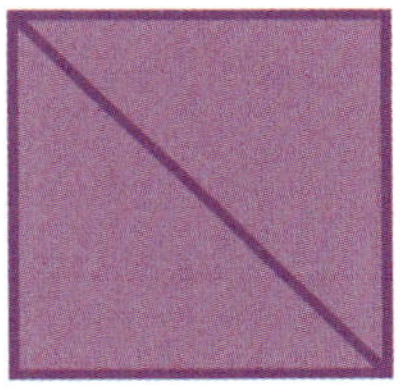

4. 

5. 

6. 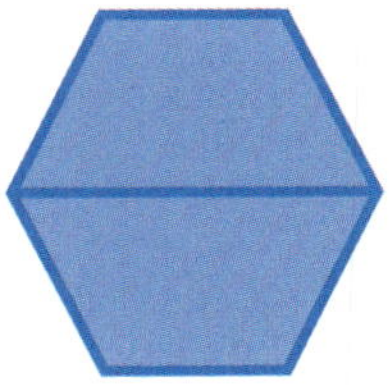

7. 

8. 

9. 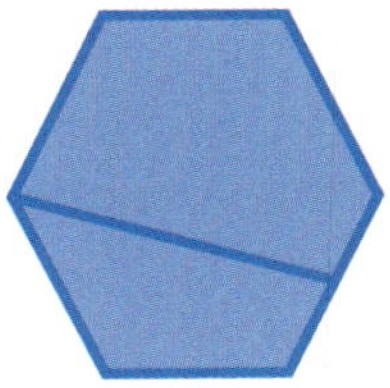

HOMEWORK

Make halves. Color one half.

1. 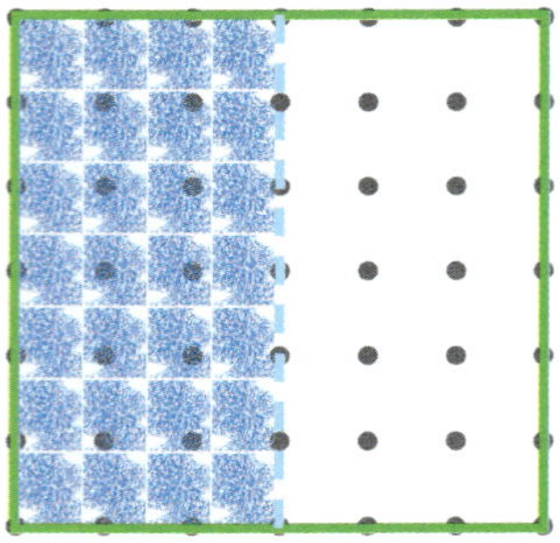

2. 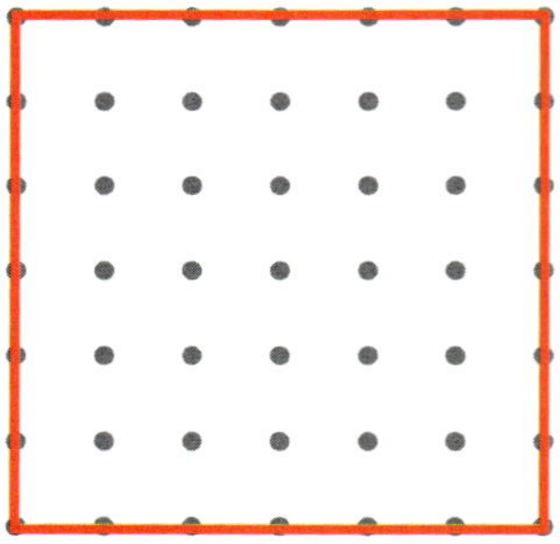

3. 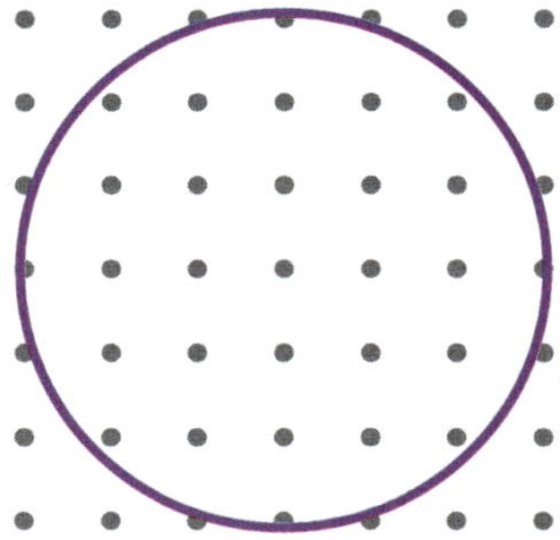

Problem Solving

4. Andrew and Evan are coloring a poster. They each color one half of the poster. Do they color the same amount? Tell how you know.

____

____

____

Write About It

5. How many ways can you draw halves in a circle? Explain.

____

____

____

____

Name ____________________

LESSON 14-3

Objective

- Partition shapes into fourths.

Math Words

fourth
quarter
fourths
quarters
whole

Make Fourths

A sandwich is shared by 4 friends. How much of the sandwich does each friend get?

There are 4 equal shares.

One share of the sandwich is one fourth. A fourth is also called one quarter.

Each friend gets one fourth of the sandwich.

4 fourths or quarters make one whole.

So, four fourths make the whole.

PRACTICE

Circle the shapes that show fourths.
✗ the shapes that do not show fourths.

1. 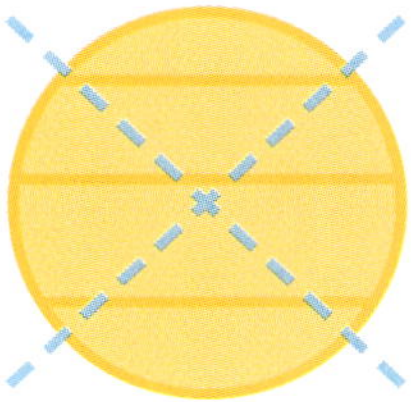

2. 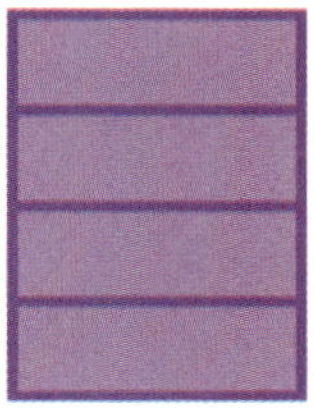

3. 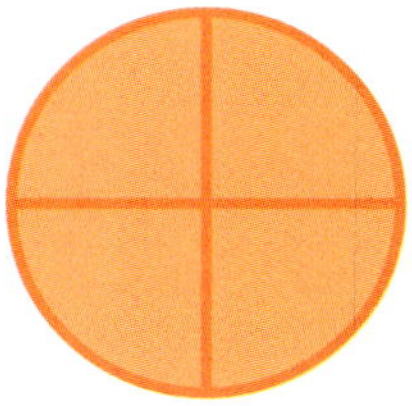

4. 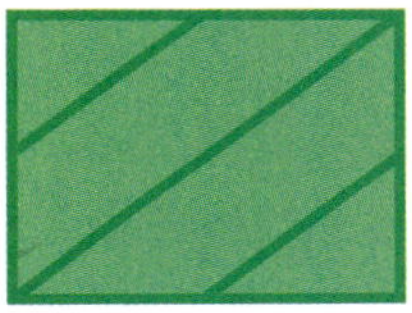

5. 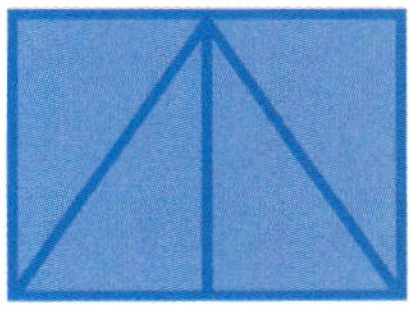

6. 

PRACTICE

Make fourths. Color one fourth.

7. 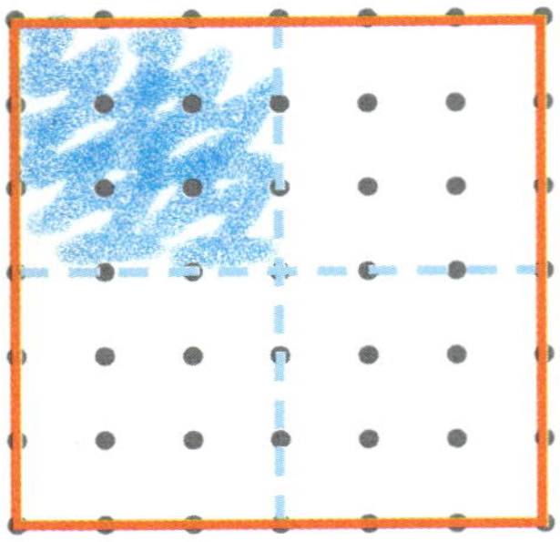

8. 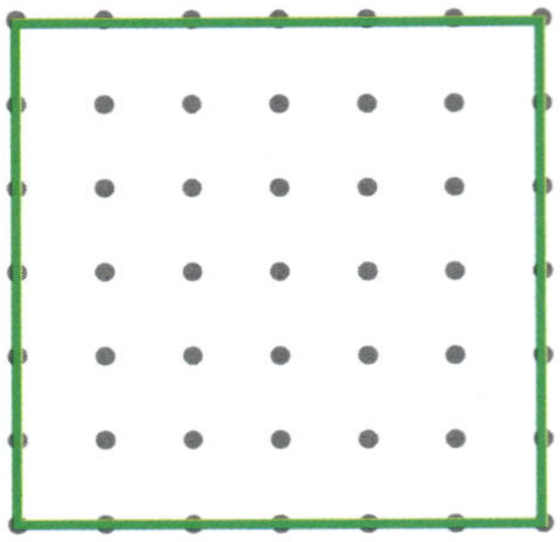

9. 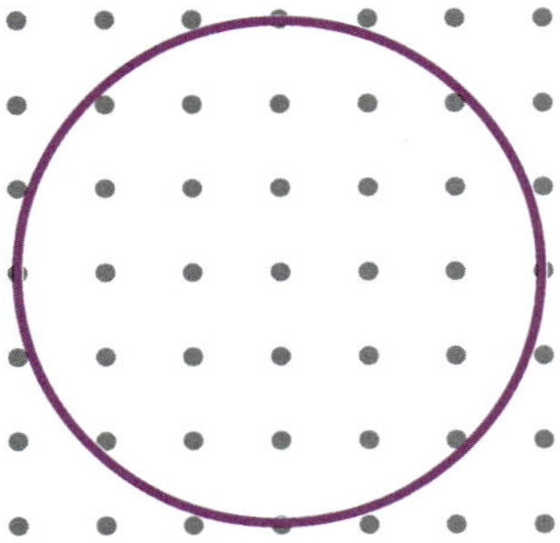

Problem Solving

10. A paper is folded into 4 equal shares. Circle the picture that shows how the paper could be folded.

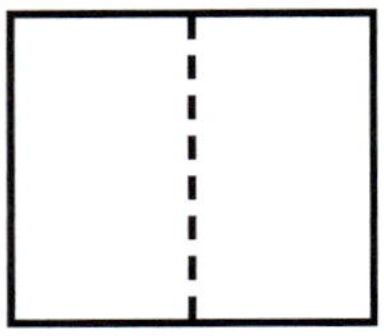 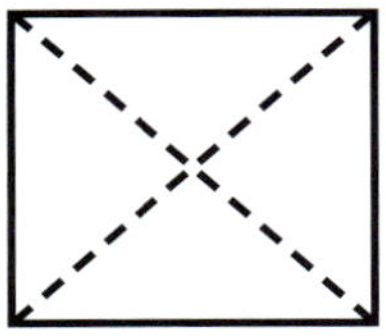

11. Each part of a square garden is one fourth. What shapes could each of the fourths be?

The shapes could be ______________, ______________

or ______________.

Write About It

12. Tell what a shape with 4 equal shares looks like. Draw a picture.

____

____

____

Name ______________________________

Make Fourths

A sandwich is shared by 4 friends.

One share of the sandwich is one fourth.
A fourth is also called one quarter.

4 fourths, or quarters, make one whole.

MORE PRACTICE

Circle the shapes that show fourths.
✗ the shapes that do not show fourths.

1. 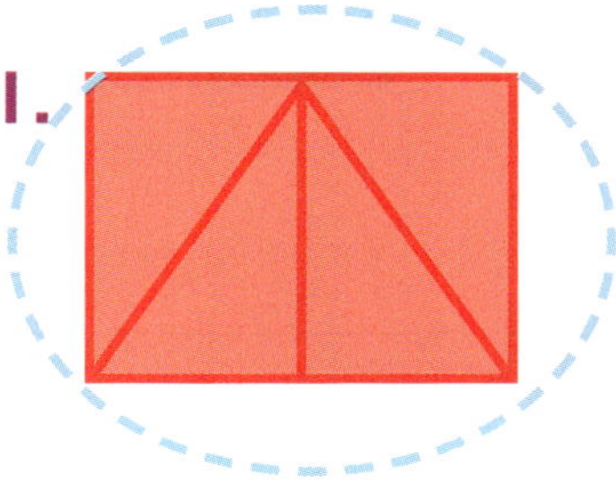

2. 

3. 

4. 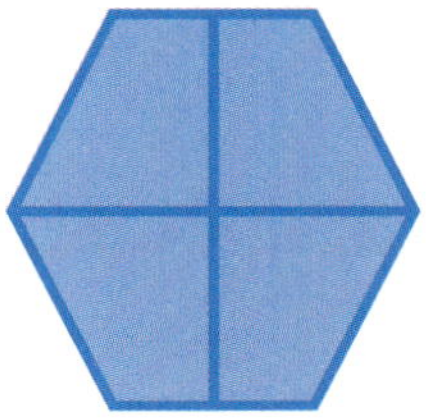

5. 

6. 

7. 

8. 

9. 

HOMEWORK

Make fourths. Color one fourth.

1. 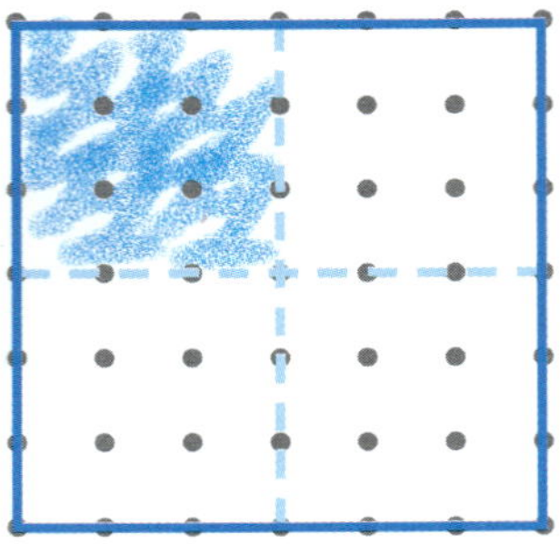

2. 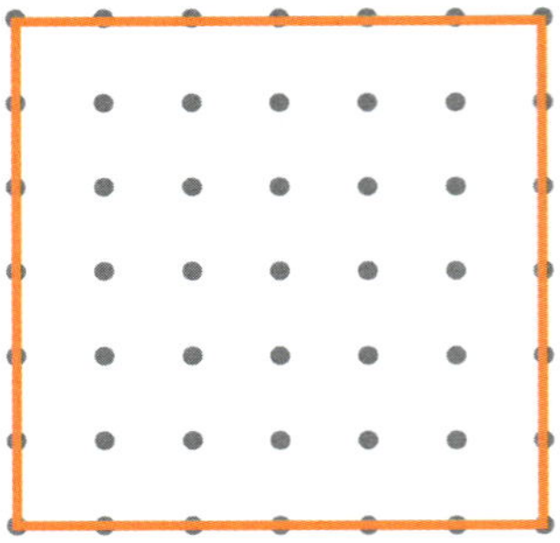

3. 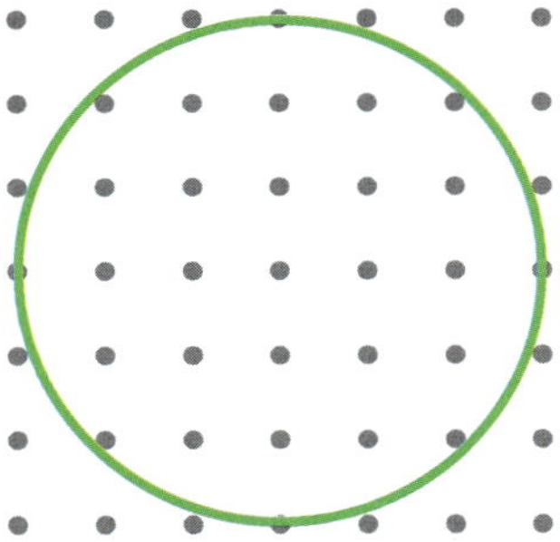

Problem Solving

4. A farmer plants his field in 4 quarters. A different crop is in each fourth. Will each crop have the same amount of space to grow? Tell how you know.

____

____

____

Write About It

5. Is there only one way to draw a rectangle with fourths? Explain. Draw a picture.

____

____

____

____

CHAPTER 14
Check Your Progress

Name ________________________________

Find the correct answer.

1. How many equal shares?

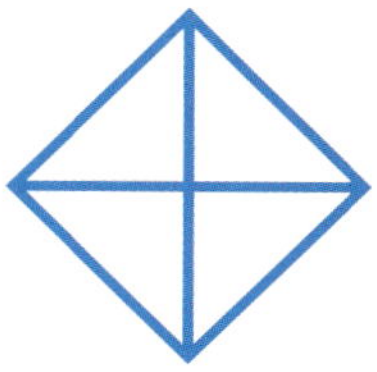

A. 2
B. 3
C. 4

2. How many equal shares?

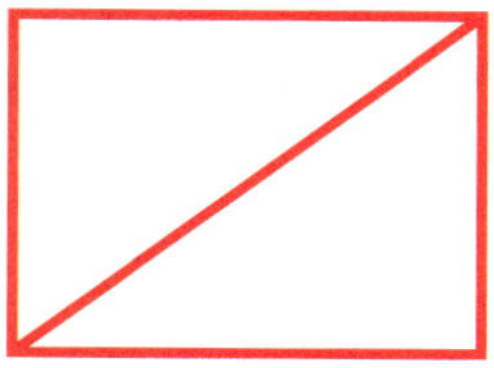

A. 2
B. 3
C. 4

3. Which shows halves?

A. 

B. 

C. 

4. Which shows fourths?

A. 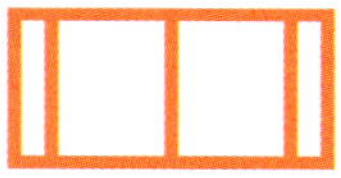

B. 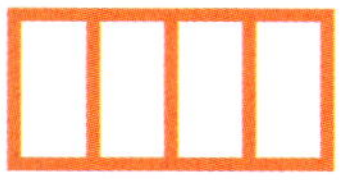

C. 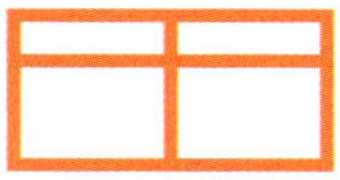

5. Name the equal shares.

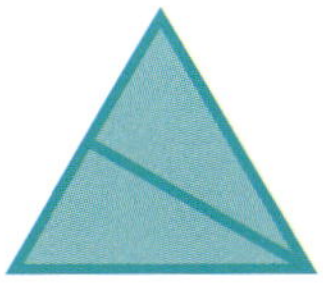

A. halves
B. fourths

6. Name the equal shares.

A. halves
B. fourths

Find the correct answer.

7. How many halves make a whole?

A. 2
B. 3
C. 4

8. How many fourths make a whole?

A. 2
B. 3
C. 4

9. Shelby cut her sandwich into quarters. How many equal shares does she have?

A. 2
B. 3
C. 4

10. Wes and a friend are sharing an apple. They both want the same amount. How many equal shares do they need?

A. 2
B. 3
C. 4

11. Draw a line or lines to show the rectangle with halves.

12. Draw a line or lines to show the circle in fourths.

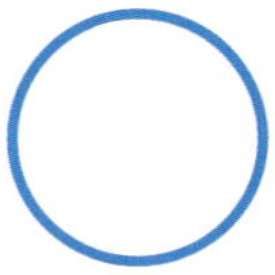

13. Which TWO show equal shares?

A. **B.** **C.** **D.**

Name ______________________________

Halves and Fourths

Objective
- Understand that more equal shares means smaller shares.

Math Words
half
fourth

Two crackers are the same size.
Brooke eats one fourth of her cracker.
Ellie eats one half of her cracker.
Who eats more?

Compare the equal shares.

Brooke's cracker

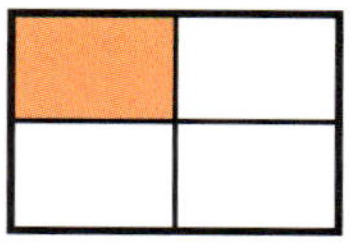

Ellie's cracker

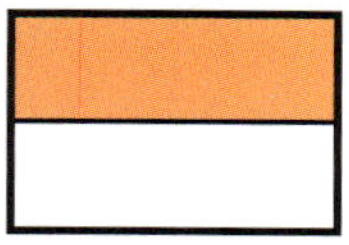

The shaded shares show how much each girl eats.

There are more equal shares in Brooke's cracker.
Each of Brooke's shares is less than Ellie's shares.

Brooke eats less cracker. Ellie eats more cracker.
So, Ellie eats more.

PRACTICE

Color one share in each picture.
Circle the one with the larger shares.

1\. 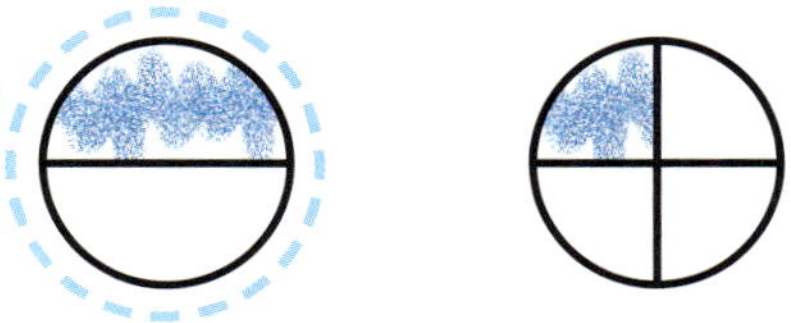

2\. 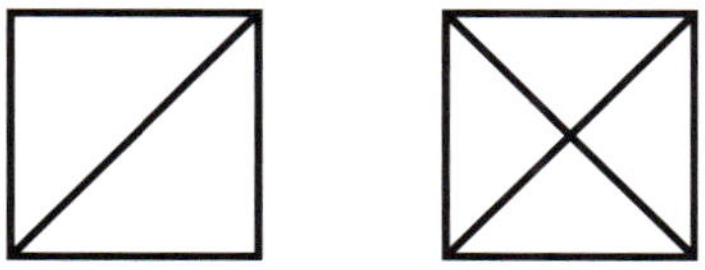

3\. 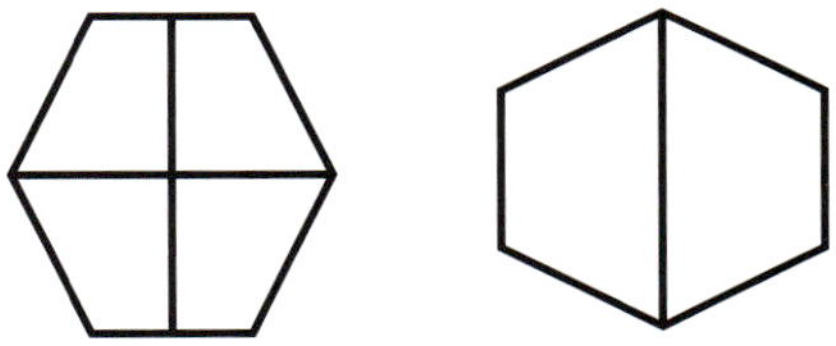

4\. 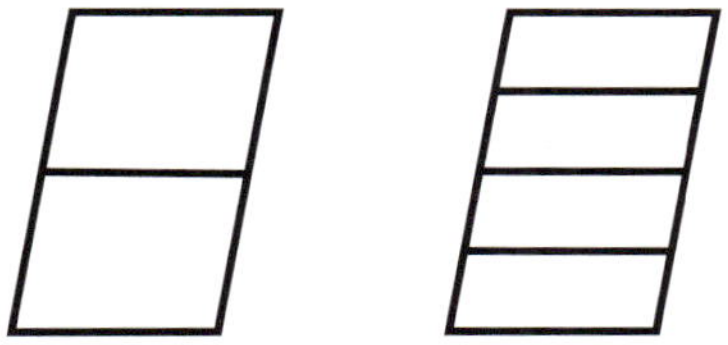

PRACTICE

Show equal shares. Color one share.

5. halves 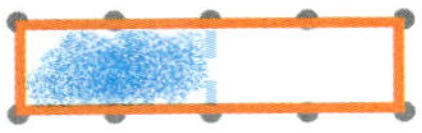

fourths 

6. 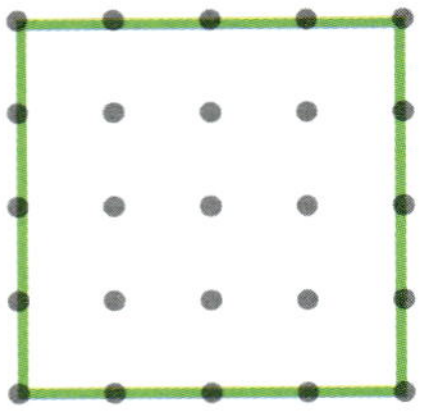 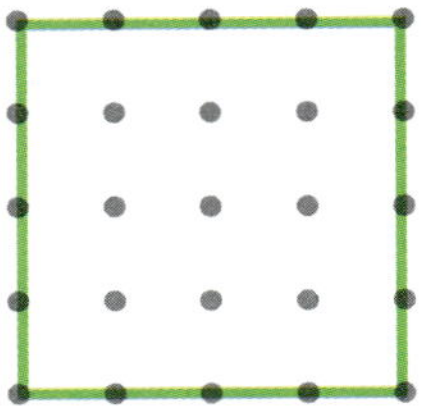

halves fourths

Problem Solving

7. Bea folds a paper in half. She will color one share blue and one share red.

She folds another paper in fourths. She colors one share yellow, one green, one purple, and one orange.

Will Bea color more paper orange or blue?

Bea colors more paper ________.

Folded in half

Folded in fourths

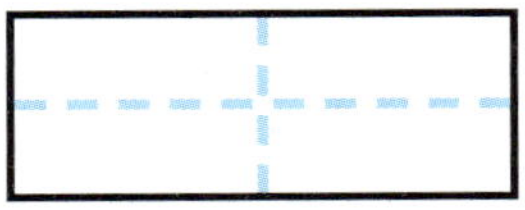

Write About It

8. Kyle and Trey have paper that is the same size. Kyle cuts his paper into 2 equal shares. Trey cuts his paper into 4 equal shares. Trey says his shares are larger since there are more shares. Explain Trey's error.

____

____

____

Name ______________________________

Halves and Fourths

Two same size rectangles show halves and fourths.

Which rectangle has a greater equal share?

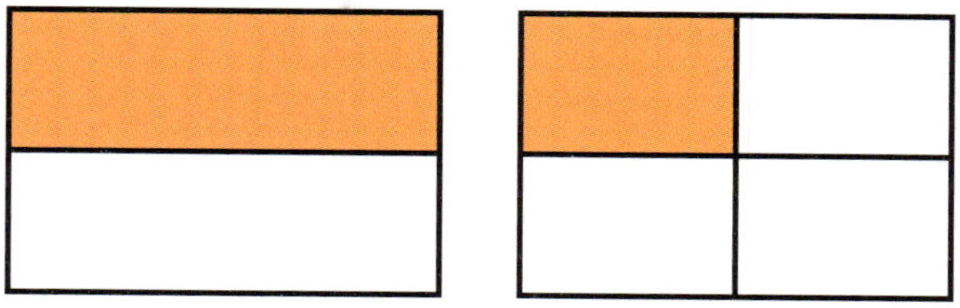

The size of one half is greater than the size of one fourth.

More equal shares means a smaller size share.
Less equal shares means a larger size share.

The rectangle with halves has a greater share.

MORE PRACTICE

Color one share in each picture.
Circle the one with the larger shares.

1. 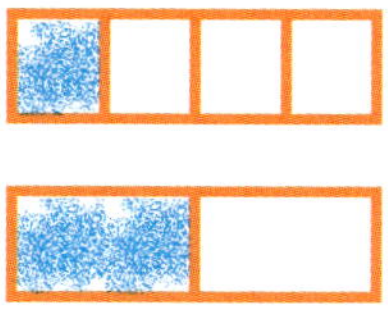

2. 

3. 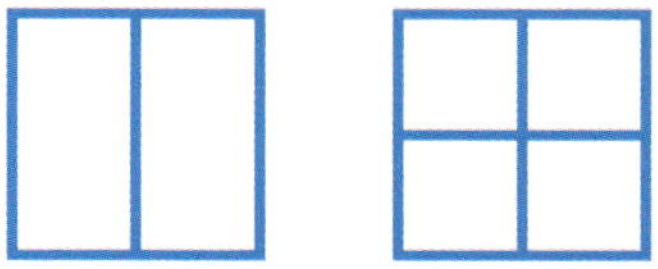

4. 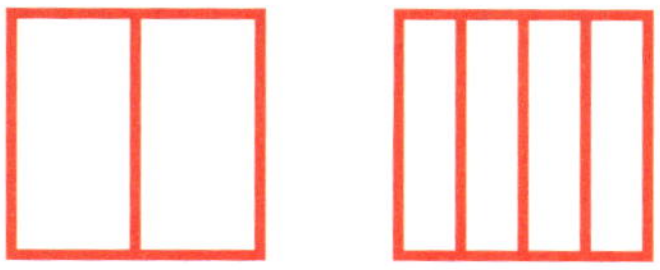

5. 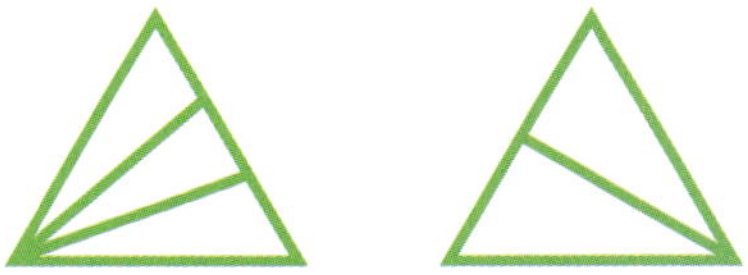

6. 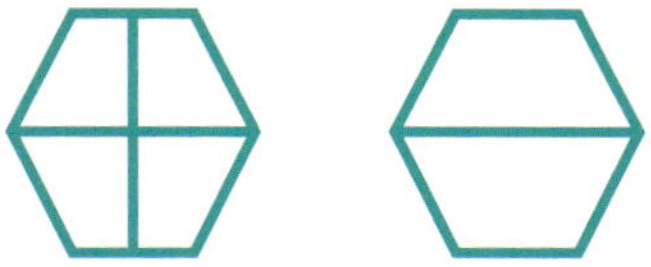

HOMEWORK

Show equal shares. Color one share.
Circle the one with the smaller shares.

1. 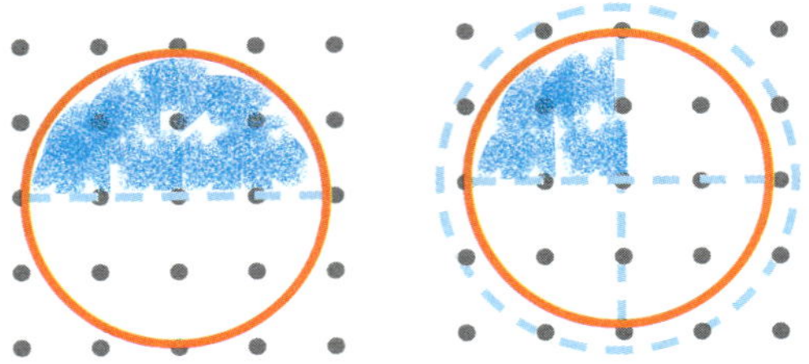

halves fourths

2. 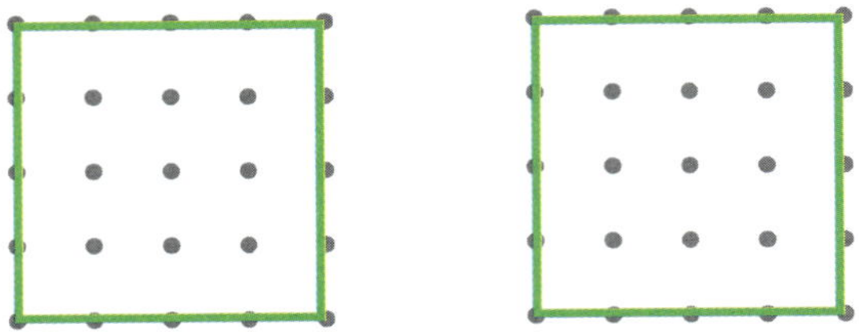

halves fourths

Problem Solving

3. Two rooms in Cara's home are the same size.
She paints half of one room gray.
She paints one fourth of the other room yellow.
Does Cara use more gray or yellow paint?

Cara uses more ______ paint.

4. Jeremy cuts a board into 2 equal pieces.
Levi cuts the same size board into 4 equal pieces.
Circle the words that make the sentence true.

Levi cuts his board into **more / fewer** equal shares,
so his pieces of board are **longer / shorter**.

Write About It

5. Would you rather have a half serving of your favorite food or a fourth? Why?

____

____

Name ____________________

LESSON 14-5

Objective

- Draw a picture to solve problems.

Math Words

half
fourth

Problem Solving

Read › Plan › Solve › Check

Draw a Picture

Tom ate one fourth of a large pizza.
Gene ate one fourth of a small pizza.
Did they eat the same amount of pizza?

Draw two circles, one large and one small.

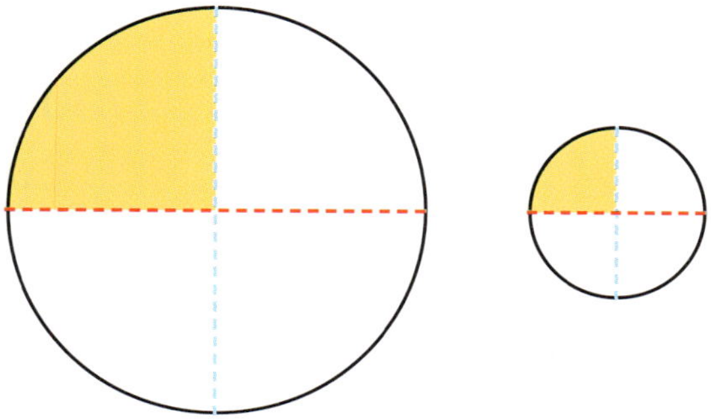

Color one fourth of each circle.
Compare the size of both fourths.

→ Tom ate more pizza than Gene.

Burt ate one fourth of a large pizza.
Did Tom eat more pizza than Burt?

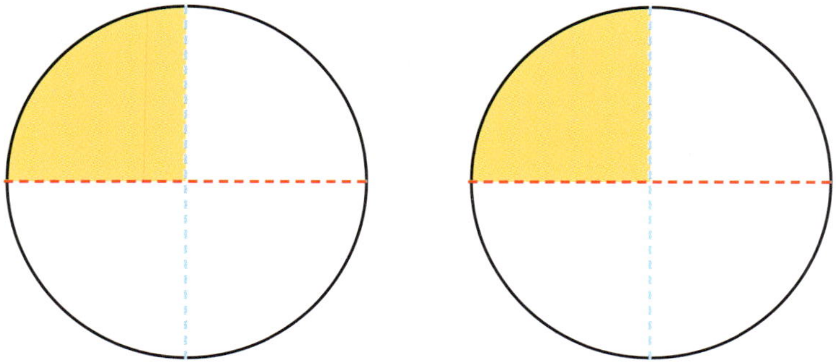

Tom and Burt ate the same amount of pizza.

PRACTICE

Draw a picture. Solve.

1. Landon eats one quarter of a watermelon slice.
   Miguel eats one half of a watermelon slice.
   The slices are the same size.
   Who eats more watermelon?

   __________ eats more watermelon.

2. Mr. Jones and Mr. Tanner have rugs that are the same size. Mr. Jones' rug uses the colors blue and red in equal amounts. Mr. Tanner's rug uses blue, green, yellow, and black in equal amounts. Whose rug uses more blue? Explain how you know.

   ____________ rug uses more blue.

   ____

   ____

Write About It

3. Can two halves ever be different sizes?
   Draw a picture to show the sizes.

   ____

   ____

Name ________________

Problem Solving
Draw a Picture

Pam ate one fourth of a large pizza.
Gina ate one fourth of a small pizza.
Did they eat the same amount of pizza?

Draw two circles, one large and one small.

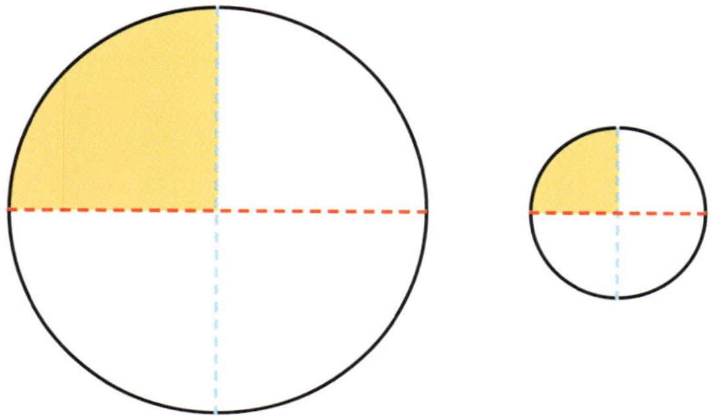

Color and compare the sizes of the shares.

The pizzas were not the same size, so Pam ate more pizza.

MORE PRACTICE

Draw a picture. Solve.

1. Naomi makes two paper circles that are the same size. She cuts one circle into 2 equal shares. She cuts the other circle into 4 equal shares. Which circle has smaller shares?

   The circle she cut into _____ equal shares has smaller shares.

MORE PRACTICE

Draw a picture. Solve.

2. Shawn eats half of a vegetable pie.
Zachary eats a fourth of a vegetable pie.
Both pies are the same size.
Which friend eats less vegetable pie?
Explain how you know.

_________ eats less vegetable pie.

____

____

____

3. Mia colors half of a paper plate.
Lauren colors a fourth of the same paper plate.
Who colors more of the paper plate?

_________ colors more of the paper plate.

4. Mr. Peters and Mr. Lucas have the same size bulletin boards in their rooms.
Mr. Peters covers half of his board with art.
Mr. Lucas covers a quarter of his board with art.
Who covers more of his board with art?

_________ covers more of his board with art.

Name ______________________

HOMEWORK

Draw a picture. Solve.

1. Nate draws shapes on a sheet of paper. A triangle covers about half of the paper. A circle covers about a quarter of the paper. Does the triangle or the circle take up more room on the paper?

   The __________ takes up more room on the paper.

2. Ryan draws a flag using halves and colors each half a different color. Jorge draws a flag using fourths and colors each fourth a different color. Which flag has more colors?

   __________ flag has more colors.

3. Layla and Jada are making scarves. They each have the same size cloth. Layla uses a fourth of her cloth. Jada uses a half of her cloth. Who has more cloth left over?

   __________ has more cloth left over because she uses less.

HOMEWORK

Draw a picture. Solve.

4. Isaac makes a blue circle and a yellow circle. They are the same size. He cuts them so one circle has 4 equal shares and the other has 2. The blue circle has more equal shares than the yellow circle. Does Isaac divide the blue circle into halves or fourths?

   Isaac divides the blue circle into ________.

5. Half of a window is made with colored glass. The other half is made with clear glass. Does the window have more, less, or the same amount of colored glass as clear glass?

   The window has ________________ of colored glass as clear glass.

Write About It

6. Write a problem that you could solve using the picture. Then solve the problem.

____

____

____

____

Name ______________________________

Find the correct answer.

1. Draw a line or lines in the circle to make halves.

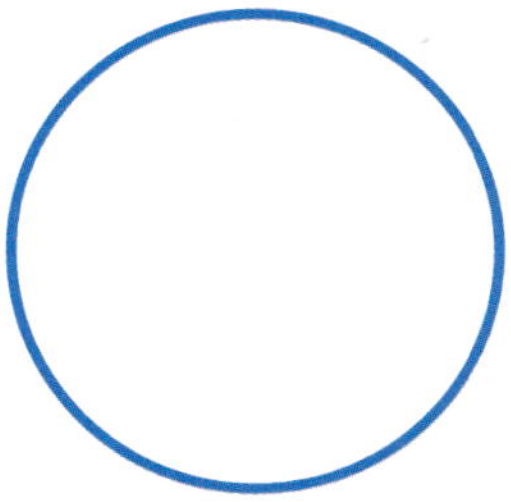

2. Draw a line or lines in the rectangle to make fourths.

3. How many equal shares?

A. 1
B. 2
C. 3
D. 4

4. How many equal shares?

A. 1
B. 2
C. 3
D. 4

5. Name the kind of shares.

A. halves
B. fourths

6. Name the kind of shares.

A. halves
B. fourths

7. How many equal shares are in halves?

A. 1
B. 2
C. 3
D. 4

8. How many equal shares are in fourths?

A. 1
B. 2
C. 3
D. 4

9. Rebecca paints half of a rectangle poster. Mackenzie paints a fourth of a poster that is the same size. Who paints more?

____

10. Rob reads a quarter of a page in a book. Mario reads half of the same page. Who reads less of the page?

____

11. Which shape shows halves?

A. 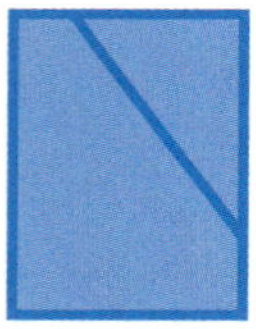

B. 

C. 

12. Which TWO words describe the equal shares?

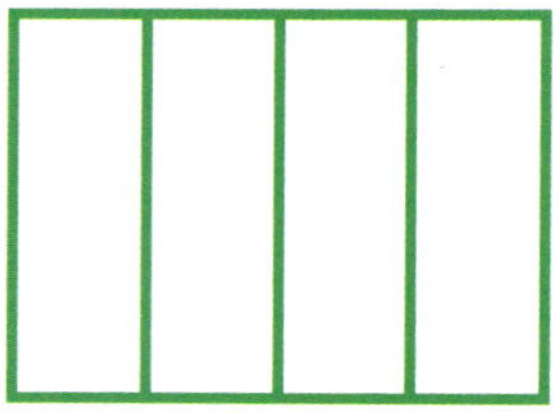

A. fourths
B. halves
C. quarters
D. squares

CHAPTER 14 Performance Assessment

Name ______________________________

1. Does the window in the picture show equal shares? Tell how you know.

The window __________ show equal shares.

____

____

____

____

2. Design two windows.
One should show halves.
The other should show fourths.
Then name the shares in each window.

______________________ ______________________

Name ____________________

Find the correct answer.

1. Which shape shows halves?

A.

B.

C.

2. Find the missing addend.

$18 = ? + 7$

A. 6
B. 7
C. 10
D. 11

3. Which TWO sets of numbers have a sum of 15?

A. 6 and 10
B. 7 and 8
C. 8 and 5
D. 9 and 6

4. Which number is 10 less than 85?

A. 35
B. 55
C. 75
D. 95

5. Subtract.

$$\begin{array}{r} 80 \\ -\,60 \\ \hline \end{array}$$

6. Add.

$$\begin{array}{r} 4 \\ 6 \\ +\,5 \\ \hline \end{array}$$

Time

CHAPTER
15

There are many different types of clocks in the world. One famous clock is called "Big Ben." Big Ben is a clock tower in London, England.

By the Numbers

- The hour hand of Big Ben is 9 feet long!
- Big Ben weighs more than 13 tons; that's as much as a small elephant!

What You Can Do

- Practice reading the time on clocks, watches, and cell phones.

Dear Family,

In this chapter, we will be learning about time.

Here are the Key **Math Words** for this chapter:

minute hand	**one half hour**
hour hand	**day**
half past	**night**
one hour	**pattern**

You can use the glossary to check out the definition of each word and help your child make flash cards to study each day we work on the lessons for this chapter.

During this chapter about time, we will also be making STEAM connections about clocks. Read the opening to the chapter together and discuss the **By the Numbers** and **What You Can Do** statements. If possible, do an Internet search for other famous clocks and compare them to Big Ben.

Keep Your Skills Sharp

Here is a **Keep Your Skills Sharp** activity to do at home to prepare for this chapter.

Encourage your child to identify devices they use to tell time. They may find watches, cell phones, computers, ovens, or microwaves. Ask your child how these clocks are the same or different. Have them use the clocks to tell time on the hour or half hour.

Name ______________________________

LESSON 15-1

Objective
- Tell and write time to the hour.

Math Words
minute hand
hour hand

Hour

The clock shows Abby's dinner time. What are two ways to write this time?

The minute hand is long. It tells the minutes.

The hour hand is short. It tells the hours.

The minute hand is on 12 when the time is on the hour. The hour hand is on 6. So, the time is 6 o'clock.

Another way to show this time is 6:00.

Abby eats dinner at 6 o'clock, or 6:00.

PRACTICE

Write the time.

1. 

3 o'clock

2. 

_____ o'clock

3. 

_____ o'clock

PRACTICE

Trace the hands on the clock.
Write the time in two ways.

4.

4 o'clock

5.

_____ o'clock

6.

_____ o'clock

Problem Solving

7. Aaron eats lunch on an hour that has the hour and minute hands on the same number. What time does Aaron eat lunch?

Aaron eats lunch at _____ o'clock.

Write About It

8. Where are the minute and hour hands on a clock when it is 11 o'clock?

____

____

Name ______________________________

Hour

You can write the time in hours in two ways.

6 o'clock

The minute hand is long and tells the minutes.

The hour hand is short and tells the hours.

6:00

The : separates the hours and the minutes.

MORE PRACTICE

Write the time.

1. 

7 o'clock

2. 

______ o'clock

3. 

______ o'clock

HOMEWORK

Write the time in two ways.

1.

6 o'clock

2.

_____ o'clock

3.

_____ o'clock

Problem Solving

4. When Alexis leaves for school, the minute hand is on the 12. The hour hand is on the 7. What time does Alexis leave for school?

Alexis leaves for school at _____ o'clock.

Write About It

5. How many hours and minutes are shown on the clock?

____

Name ____________________

LESSON 15-2

Objective
- Tell and write time to the half hour.

Math Words
one hour
one half hour
half past

Half Hour

Cole's school ends at the time shown on the clock.
What time does school end?

To find the time, look at the hands on the clock.

There are 60 minutes in one hour.

There are 30 minutes in one half hour.

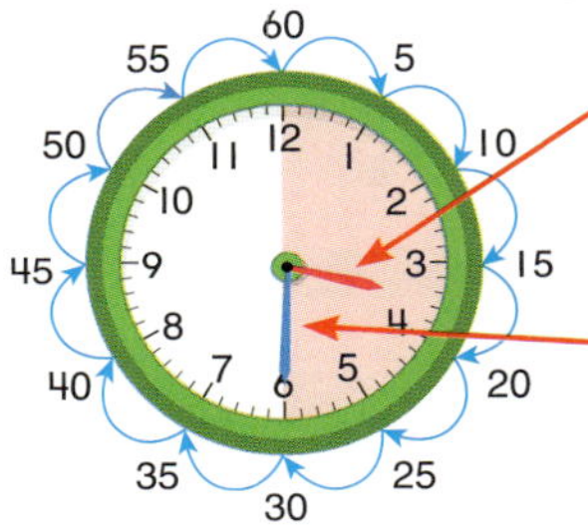

The hour hand is halfway between 3 and 4.

The minute hand is on 6 at half past the hour.

Read this time as:
3 thirty
half past 3
30 minutes after 3

Cole's school day ends at 3:30.

PRACTICE

Write the time.

1.

____ thirty

2.

____ minutes

after ____

3.

half past ____

PRACTICE

Trace the hands on the clock.
Write the time in two ways.

4.

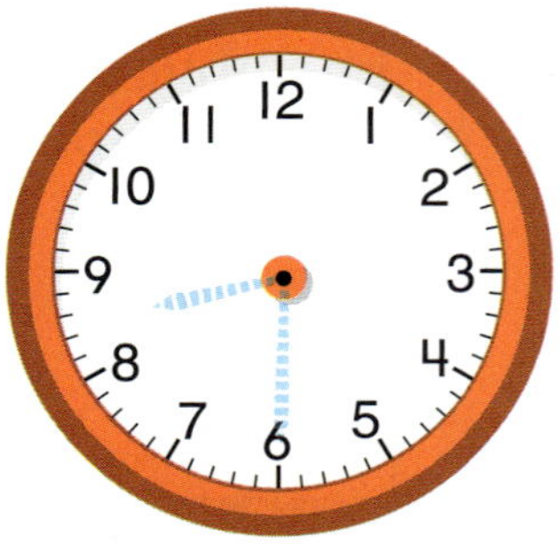

8 thirty

5.

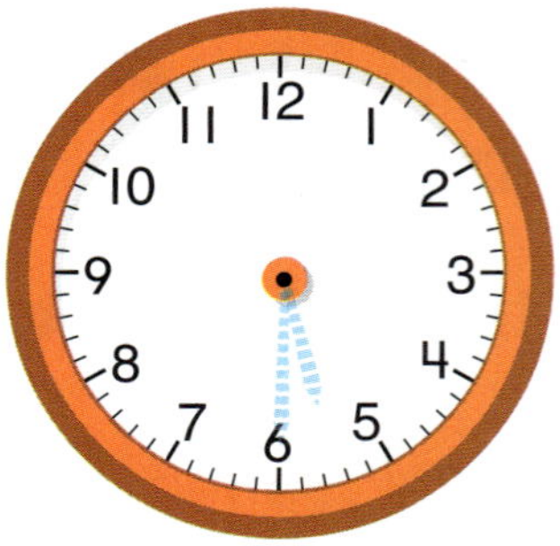

half past ____

6.

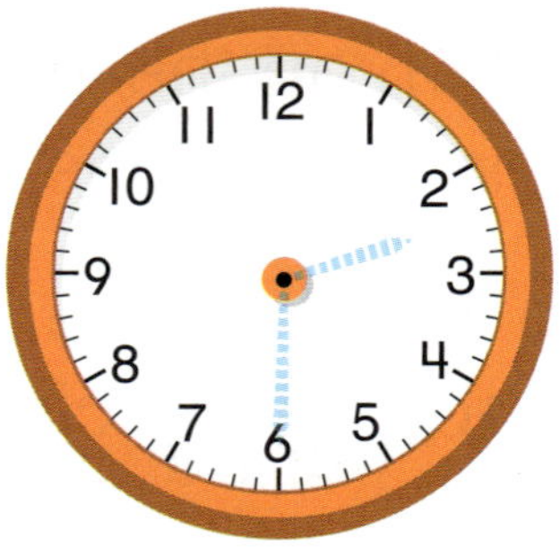

____ thirty

Problem Solving

7. Mr. Nico goes to the gym at half past 4.
What are two other ways to write this time?

____ thirty   ____ minutes after ____

Write About It

8. Are the hour and minute hands both on the same number at 6:30? Tell how you know.

____

____

Name ____

Half Hour

There are 60 minutes in one hour.
There are 30 minutes in one half hour.

Look at the hands on the clock to tell the time.

The hour hand is halfway between 3 and 4.

The minute hand is on 6 at half past the hour.

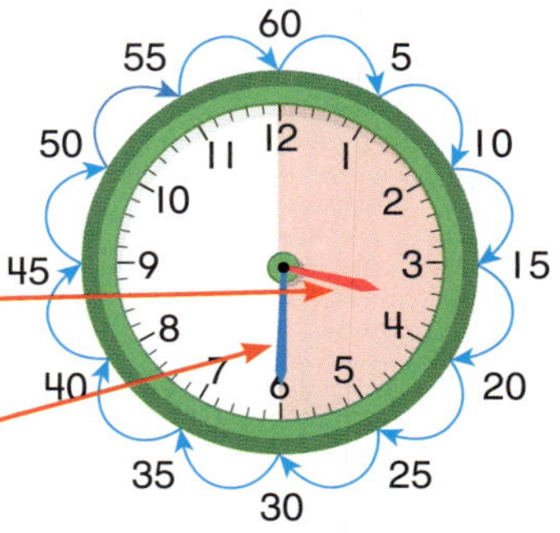

Read this time as:

3 thirty

half past 3

30 minutes after 3

The clocks show 3:30.

MORE PRACTICE

Write the time.

1.

6 thirty

2.

_____ minutes

after _____

3.

half past _____

Write the time in two ways.

1.

10 thirty

2.

half past ____

3.

____ thirty

Problem Solving

4. Delia stops playing at 4 o'clock.
Erin stops playing 30 minutes later.
At what time does Erin stop playing?

____

Write About It

5. Are the hour and minute hands on the same number when it is half past 6?
Tell how you know.

____

____

Name ____________________

Find the correct answer.

1. What time is shown?

A. 3 o'clock
B. 3 thirty
C. 3 sixty

2. What time is shown?

A. half past 2
B. 2 thirty
C. 2 o'clock

3. What time is shown?

A. 9:00
B. 11:00
C. 12:00

4. What time is shown?

A. 6:00
B. 6:30
C. 7:30

5. What time is shown?

A. 4 thirty
B. 4 o'clock
C. 4 sixty

6. What time is shown?

A. half past 3
B. 3 thirty
C. 3 o'clock

Find the correct answer.

7. What time is shown?

A. 7 o'clock
B. 8 o'clock
C. 9 o'clock

8. What time is shown?

A. half past 6
B. 7 o'clock
C. half past 7

9. What time is shown?

A. 10 o'clock
B. 9 thirty
C. 10 thirty

10. What time is shown?

A. half past 5
B. 5 o'clock
C. half past 6

11. Steve takes a nap when the hour and minute hands are on the same number. What time does Steve take a nap?

A. 6 thirty
B. 6 o'clock
C. 12 o'clock

12. Which TWO ways tell the time on the clock?

A. 11 o'clock
B. 11 thirty
C. half past 11

Name ________________________________

LESSON 15-3

Objective
- Describe time patterns.

Math Words
half-hour pattern
hour pattern

Time Patterns

The clocks show times when classes begin. What are the time patterns for the classes?

Dance Classes

Swim Classes

Look at the times to find a pattern.

Dance classes start every half hour. 12:30, 1:00, 1:30

Swim classes start every hour. 12 o'clock, 1 o'clock, 2 o'clock

The times for dance classes show a half-hour pattern. The times for swim classes show an hour pattern.

PRACTICE

Match each time pattern to the type of pattern.

1. 

a. half hour

2. 

b. hour

PRACTICE

Complete each time pattern. Circle to show the type of pattern.

3. 

_____ o'clock   _____ o'clock   _____ o'clock

half hour

hour

4. 

_____ o'clock   _____ thirty   _____ o'clock

half hour

hour

Problem Solving

5. Hailey has art class at 9:00. She has history class at 10:00. If the pattern continues, when is Hailey's next class?

Hailey's next class is at _____.

Write About It

6. How is a half-hour pattern different than an hour pattern?

____

____

____

Name ______________________________

Time Patterns

Look at the times on the clocks to find a pattern.

What are the time patterns?

12:30	1:00	1:30

These clocks show a half-hour pattern.

These clocks show an hour pattern.

MORE PRACTICE

Match each time pattern to the type of pattern.

1. 

2. | 8:00 | 8:30 | 9:00 |
   |---|---|---|

a. half hour

b. hour

Complete the time pattern.

3. | 3:00 | 3: | :00 |
   |---|---|---|

HOMEWORK

Complete each time pattern.
Circle the type of pattern.

1.   

9 o'clock   9 thirty   10 o'clock

half hour

hour

2. 

_____ thirty   half past _____   _____ thirty

half hour

hour

Problem Solving

3. Ella paints a picture every half hour. Jillian paints a picture every hour. Who spends more time painting 3 pictures? Tell how you know.

_______________ spends more time painting.

____

____

Write About It

4. Tell how the minutes are different in a half hour and an hour pattern.

____

Name ______________________________

Day and Night

Objective
- Understand day and night.

Math Words
day
night

Jason starts school at 8:00.
He has soccer practice at 3:00.
After dinner he does his homework at 7:00.

Which things happen during the day?
Which things happen at night?

To decide, think about each activity.

Day Night

Jason starts school at 8:00 in the morning.

He starts soccer practice at 3:00 in the afternoon.

He does his homework at 7:00 in the evening.

- Jason starts school and starts soccer practice during the day.
- He does his homework at night.

PRACTICE

Tell when the activity happens.
Circle day or night.

1. see stars

day night

2. eat lunch

day night

3. go to class

day night

4. go to sleep

day night

Problem Solving

5. Mason goes to the library at half past 12.
Does Mason go to the library during the day or at night?

Mason goes to the library ______________.

Write About It

6. Explain the difference between day and night.

____

____

____

Name ______________________________

Day and Night

Jason starts school at 8:00.
He has soccer practice at 3:00.
After dinner he does his homework at 7:00.

Which things happen during the day?
Which things happen at night?

Day Night

Jason starts school and has soccer practice during the day.

He does his homework at night.

MORE PRACTICE

Tell when the activity happens.
Circle day or night.

1. go to library

day night

2. use a flashlight

day night

HOMEWORK

Tell when the activity happens.
Circle day or night.

1. recess

day night

2. sleep

day night

Problem Solving

3. Jade says she ate breakfast on Saturday at 9:00. She ate dinner on Saturday at 6:00. How can Jade eat breakfast at 9:00 and eat dinner at 6:00? Tell how you know.

____

____

Write About It

4. Can some things happen during the day and also happen at night? Give an example to explain.

____

____

____

Name ______________________________

LESSON 15-5

Objective
- Use logical reasoning to solve problems.

Math Word
half hour

Problem Solving
Read › Plan › Solve › Check

Use Logical Reasoning

Nolan has a skating lesson at 11:00.
Micah has a lesson a half hour before Nolan.
Eli has a lesson a half hour after Nolan.
Who has a skating lesson at 11:30?

Look at the clocks.

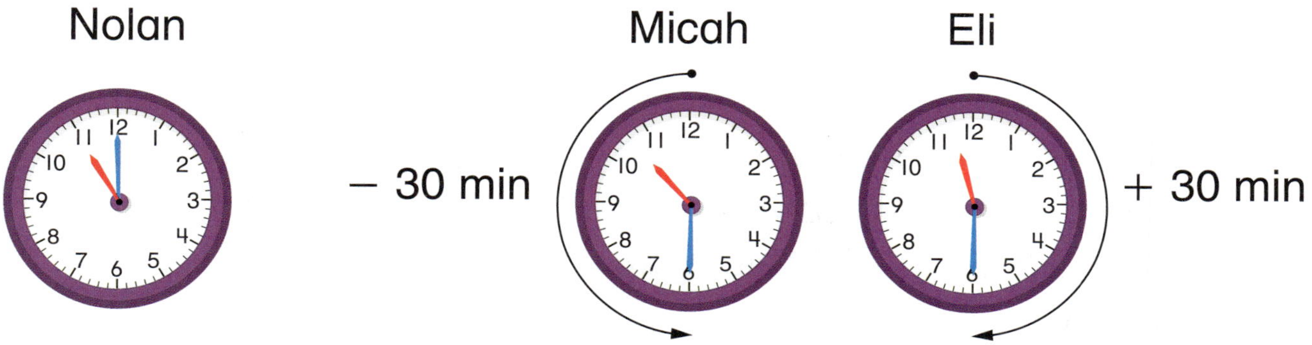

Read the problem.

Nolan has his skating lesson at 11:00.

Micah has his skating lesson a half hour before 11:00.

Eli has his skating lesson a half hour after 11:00.

Make a chart.

When	Who
10:30	Micah
11:00	Nolan
11:30	Eli

Read the problem again.
Check that the times are in the correct order.

Use the chart to find the answer.

Eli has a skating lesson at 11:30.

PRACTICE

Solve. Use logical reasoning. Put the name of each person next to the time in the table.

1. Kelsey finishes her chores at 4:30. Kate finishes her chores at 5:00. Jasmine finishes her chores at 4:00. Who finishes her chores last?

   Kate finishes her chores last.

When	Who
4:00	
4:30	Kelsey
5:00	

2. Emma goes to the playground at 2:00. Sandra goes to the playground one hour after Emma. Brooke goes to the playground one hour before Emma. Who goes to the playground at 1:00?

   ______________ goes to the playground at 1:00.

When	Who
1:00	
2:00	
3:00	

Write About It

3. How does reasoning help you solve a problem about time?

____

____

____

Name ______________________

Problem Solving
Use Logical Reasoning

Nolan has a skating lesson at 11:00.
Micah has a lesson a half hour before Nolan.
Eli has a lesson a half hour after Nolan.
Who has a skating lesson at 11:30?

Read the problem.

Nolan's lesson is at 11:00.

Micah's lesson is a half hour before 11:00.

Eli's lesson is a half hour after 11:00.

Make a chart.

When	Who
10:30	Micah
11:00	Nolan
11:30	Eli

Read the problem again.
Check that the times are in the correct order.
Use the chart to find the answer.

Eli has a skating lesson at 11:30.

MORE PRACTICE

Use logical reasoning to solve. Fill in the chart.

1. Caleb makes a craft at 6:30. Ashton makes his craft a half hour before Caleb. When does Ashton make his craft?

When	Who
6:30	Caleb

MORE PRACTICE

Solve. Fill in the chart to help.

2. Debbie goes to bed at 9:00. Ashley goes to bed an hour later. Danielle goes to bed an hour earlier.

   Who goes to bed at 10:00?

   ______________ goes to bed at 10:00.

When	Who

3. Alan eats lunch at 12:00. Diego eats lunch an hour after Alan. Jason eats lunch a half hour before Alan.

   Who eats lunch at 11:30?

   ______________ eats lunch at 11:30.

When	Who

4. Faith has recess at 2:30. Ellie has recess at 2:00. Karen has recess at 3:00.

   Who has recess first?

   ______________ has recess first.

When	Who

5. Levi feeds his cat at 4:00. Jeremy feeds his cat at 5:00. Oliver feeds his cat at 3:00.

   Who feeds his cat first?

   ______________ feeds his cat first.

When	Who

Name ______________________________

HOMEWORK

Solve. Fill in the chart to help.

1. Lindsey goes fishing at 4:00.
Makenzie goes fishing an hour later.
Sofia goes fishing an hour before.

Who goes fishing at 3:00?

__________ goes fishing at 3:00.

When	Who

2. Raymond goes to bed at 8:30.
Seth goes to bed a half hour after Raymond. Yoshi goes to bed a half hour before Raymond.

Who goes to bed the earliest?

__________ goes to bed the earliest.

When	Who

3. Sadie finishes her homework at 4:30.
Kylie finishes her homework at 4:00.
Victoria finishes her homework at 5:00.

Who finishes her homework first?

__________ finishes her homework first.

When	Who

HOMEWORK

Solve. Fill in the chart to help.

4. The clocks show the times Vanessa, Miranda, and Rita finish a race.

Who finishes the race first?
What time does the winner finish?

_______________ finishes the race first.

She finishes at _____.

When	Who

5. Roger plays in a game at 3:00.
Owen plays in a game at 4:00.
Malachi plays in a game at 5:00.

Who plays in a game last?

_______________ plays in a game last.

When	Who

Write About It

6. How does making a chart help you use reasoning to solve time problems?

____

____

____

Name ______________________

Find the correct answer.

1. What time is shown?

A. 6:00
B. 6:30
C. 12:00
D. 12:30

2. What time is shown?

A. 4:00
B. 4:30
C. 6:00
D. 6:30

3. What are TWO other ways to write the time?

A. half past 8
B. half past 9
C. 8 thirty
D. 8 o'clock

4. What is the next time in the pattern?

A. 10:30
B. 11:00
C. 11:30
D. 12:00

5. Write the time shown on the clock.

_____ o'clock

6. What is the next time in the pattern?

A. 5:30
B. 6:00
C. 6:30
D. 7:00

7. Dean ate lunch at the time shown.

Did Dean eat lunch during the day or at night? Circle the answer.

day night

8. Which does Kylie do during the day?

A. go to bed
B. go to school
C. look at the moon
D. look at the stars

9. Caleb has a piano lesson at 2:00. Shaun has a piano lesson before Caleb. Hal has a piano lesson after Caleb. Who has a piano lesson first?

A. Caleb
B. Shaun
C. Stan

10. Beth plays soccer at 4:00. Lisa plays soccer an hour after Beth. Sue plays soccer a half hour before Lisa. Who plays soccer at 5:00?

A. Beth
B. Lisa
C. Sue

11. Xavier goes to bed an hour before Kyle. Kyle goes to bed at 9:00. Sam goes to bed a half hour after Xavier. Who goes to bed at 8:30?

A. Xavier
B. Kyle
C. Sam

Name ____________________

CHAPTER 15 Performance Assessment

Mr. Robins runs a tennis club. People can use the outdoor courts to play tennis.

1. Mr. Robins wants to use a half-hour pattern to let people use the courts on Monday. The club opens at 9:00. It closes at 4:30. People can use the courts during these times.

   Write times on the clocks to show when people can use the courts.

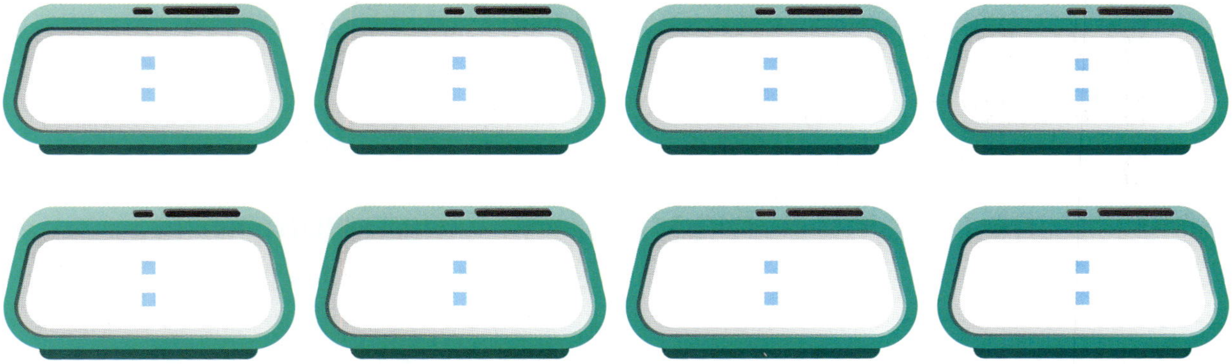

2. Suppose Mr. Robins uses an hour pattern for people to play tennis on Saturday. When could he start and stop court times to make sure that there are at least ten playing times?

   ____

   ____

   ____

Name ______________________________

Find the correct answer.

1. What time is shown?

A. 10:00
B. 10:30
C. 12:00
D. 12:30

2. Which is NOT a way to write this time?

A. thirty minutes after 4
B. half past 4
C. 4 o'clock
D. 4 thirty

3. Find the missing number.

110, ______, 112, 113, 114

A. 11
B. 101
C. 111
D. 110

4. Which number is 10 less than 55?

A. 35
B. 45
C. 65
D. 75

5. Subtract.

60 − 20 = ______

6. Add.

3 + 7 + 2 = ______

Money

CHAPTER 16

Have you ever wondered where our coins are made? The United States Mint makes coins. The Mint makes pennies, nickels, dimes, and quarters. It also makes half-dollar and one-dollar coins.

By the Numbers

- Individual coins do not weigh very much. About 80 quarters equal 1 pound.
- Most coins can last for about 25 years.

What You Can Do

- Collect coins and add the total.
- Order different coins by size or value.

Dear Family,

In this chapter, we will be learning about money.

Here are the Key **Math Words** for this chapter:

penny	**cent (¢)**	**work backward**
nickel	**dime**	**total amount**
quarter	**dollar**	**dollar sign ($)**

You can use the glossary to check out the definition of each word and help your child make flash cards to study each day we work on the lessons for this chapter.

During this chapter about money, we will also be making STEAM connections about different types of coins made by the United States Mint. Read the opening to the chapter together, and discuss the **By the Numbers** and **What You Can Do** statements. Talk about the importance of making new coins when older ones wear out.

Keep Your Skills Sharp

Here are **Keep Your Skills Sharp** activities to do at home to prepare for this chapter.

Put several coins in a bag. Use different coin types if possible. Have your child take three coins from the bag. Work together to find the total amount. Repeat several times.

Name ______________________________

Pennies and Nickels

Otto says a penny has a greater value than a nickel. Kai says a nickel has a greater value than a penny. Who is right?

I **penny** has a value of I **cent (¢)**.

I cent = I¢

heads tails

I **nickel** has a value of 5 cents.

5 cents = 5¢

heads tails

5 pennies = I nickel

I¢ + I¢ + I¢ + I¢ + I¢ = 5¢

Kai is right. A nickel has a greater value than a penny.

Objective

- Identify the value of pennies and nickels, and know their comparative value.

Math Words

penny
nickel
cent (¢)

PRACTICE

Write the value.

I. 

___¢ + ___¢ + ___¢ + ___¢ + ___¢ = ___¢

___¢

PRACTICE

Write the value.

2. 

____ ¢ + ____ ¢ + ____ ¢ = ____ ¢

3. 

____ ¢ + ____ ¢ + ____ ¢ + ____ ¢ = ____ ¢

Problem Solving

4. Jon has 4 pennies. Tim has 2 nickels.
How much money does each person have?

________________ has ____ ¢

________________ has ____ ¢

Write About It

5. How many pennies have the same value as 2 nickels? Tell how you know.

______ pennies = 2 nickels

____

____

____

Name ____________________

Pennies and Nickels

1 penny has a value of 1 cent.

1 cent = 1¢

heads tails

1 nickel has a value of 5 cents.

5 cents = 5¢

heads tails

5 pennies = 1 nickel

1¢ + 1¢ + 1¢ + 1¢ + 1¢ = 5¢

MORE PRACTICE

Write the value.

1. 

1¢ + 1¢ + 1¢ + 1¢ = 4¢

2. 

___¢ + ___¢ + ___¢ + ___¢ = ___¢

HOMEWORK

Write the value.

1. 

___ ¢ + ___ ¢ + ___ ¢ + ___ ¢ + ___ ¢ = ___ ¢

2. 

___ ¢ + ___ ¢ + ___ ¢ + ___ ¢ + ___ ¢ = ___ ¢

Problem Solving

3. Jack has 3 pennies. Kyle has 3 nickels.
Who can buy a sticker for 12 cents?

Jack: ___ ¢ + ___ ¢ + ___ ¢ = ___ ¢

Kyle: ___ ¢ + ___ ¢ + ___ ¢ = ___ ¢

______________ can buy the sticker.

Write About It

4. Would you rather have 2 pennies or 2 nickels?
Explain.

____

____

Name ______________________________

LESSON 16-2

Objective

- Identify the value of dimes and quarters, and know their comparative value.

Math Words

dime
quarter
cent (¢)

Dimes and Quarters

Mike has one dime and one quarter.
He needs 25 cents for the snack machine.
What coin does Mike need for the machine?

1 dime has a value of 10 cents.

10 cents = 10¢

heads tails

1 quarter has a value of 25 cents.

25 cents = 25¢

heads tails

Mike can use 1 quarter for the snack machine.

PRACTICE

Write the value.

1.

____¢ + ____¢ = ____¢

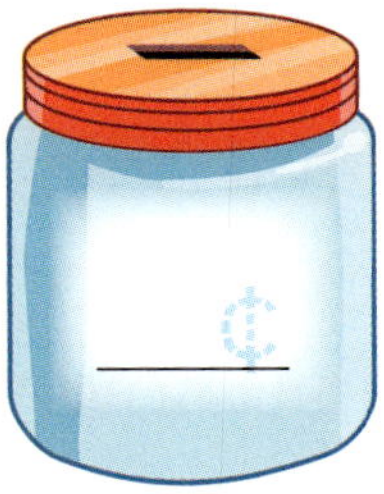

2.

____¢ + ____¢ + ____¢ = ____¢

PRACTICE

Write the value.

3. 

___¢ + ___¢ + ___¢ = ___¢

4. 

___¢ + ___¢ + ___¢ = ___¢

Problem Solving

5. Bill has 1 quarter. Syd has 2 dimes.
Who has more money?

Bill has ___¢. Syd has ___¢. ________ has more money.

Write About It

6. Joni says 2 nickels is more than 2 dimes.
Eve disagrees. Who is right?
Tell how you know.

______________ is right.

____

____

____

Name ____________________

Dimes and Quarters

1 dime has a value of 10 cents.

10 cents = 10¢

heads tails

1 quarter has a value of 25 cents.

25 cents = 25¢

heads tails

MORE PRACTICE

Write the value.

1. 

10¢ + 10¢ + 10¢ = 30¢

2. 

25¢ + 10¢ + 10¢ = 45¢

3. 

___¢ + ___¢ = ___¢

HOMEWORK

Write the value.

1. 

___¢ + ___¢ + ___¢ = ___¢

___¢

2. 

___¢ + ___¢ + ___¢ = ___¢

___¢

Problem Solving

3. Todd has 2 dimes. Circle the stamp that Todd can buy. Then tell why he can only buy this stamp.

____

____

Write About It

4. Would you rather have 1 quarter or 2 dimes? Why?

____

____

____

Name ______________________________

Count On by Dimes and Pennies

Objective
- Find the value of combinations of dimes and pennies by counting on.

Math Word
total amount

Tyler has 2 dimes and 3 pennies.
Andy has 3 dimes and 2 pennies.
How much money does each person have?

Count on to find the total amount.

Count on by 10s for dimes.

Count on by 1s for pennies.

Tyler

10¢, 20¢, 21¢, 22¢, 23¢

Andy

10¢, 20¢, 30¢, 31¢, 32¢

Tyler has 23¢. Andy has 32¢.

PRACTICE

Count on. Write the total amount.

1.

___¢, ___¢, ___¢, ___¢, ___¢, ___¢, ___¢

___¢

PRACTICE

Count on. Write the total amount.

2.

10¢, 11¢, 12¢, 13¢

3.

___¢, ___¢, ___¢, ___¢, ___¢, ___¢

Problem Solving

4. Who has between 20¢ and 30¢?

Mary	Jayda	Lea
3 dimes 4 pennies	2 dimes 5 pennies	3 dimes 1 pennies
¢	¢	¢

__________ has between 20¢ and 30¢.

Write About It

5. What are two different ways to make 40 cents with pennies and dimes?

____

____

Name ______________________________

LESSON 16-3

Count on by Dimes and Pennies

Tyler and Andy have some coins.
Count on to find the total amount.

Count on by 10s for dimes.

Count on by 1s for pennies.

Tyler

10¢ , 20¢ , 21¢ , 22¢ , 23¢

Andy

10¢ , 20¢ , 30¢ , 31¢ , 32¢

MORE PRACTICE

Count on. Write the total amount.

1.

10¢, 11¢, 12¢, 13¢, 14¢, 15¢

15¢

2.

___¢, ___¢, ___¢, ___¢

___¢

HOMEWORK

Count on. Write the total amount.

1. 

10¢, 20¢, 30¢, 40¢, 41¢, 42¢

___ ¢

2. 

___ ¢, ___ ¢, ___ ¢, ___ ¢, ___ ¢, ___ ¢

___ ¢

Problem Solving

3. Who has between 30¢ and 40¢?

Rob	Levon	Matt
3 dimes 14 pennies	3 dimes 8 pennies	2 dimes 17 pennies
¢	¢	¢

__________ have between 30¢ and 40¢.

Write About It

4. Alexa has 7 dimes and 6 pennies. How much money does Alexa have? Tell how you know.

____

____

Name ____________________

LESSON 16-4

Count On by Dimes and Nickels

Objective
- Find the value of combinations of dimes and nickels by counting on.

Math Words
dime
nickel

Pat has 4 dimes and 2 nickels.
How much money does Pat have?

Order the coins by value.

Count on to find the total.

10¢, 20¢, 30¢, 40¢, 45¢, 50¢

Count on by 10s for dimes.

Count on by 5s for nickels.

4 dimes and 2 nickels is 50¢. Pat has 50¢.

PRACTICE

Count on. Write the total amount.

1.

10¢, 20¢, 25¢, 30¢, 35¢

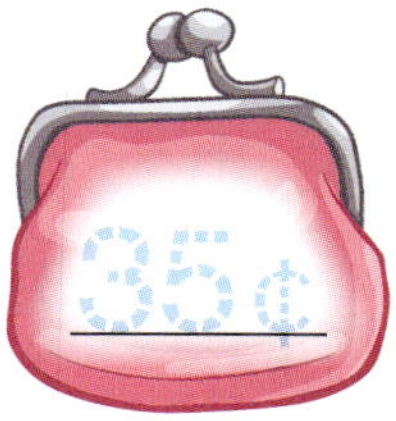

2.

____¢, ____¢, ____¢, ____¢, ____¢

PRACTICE

Count on. Write the total amount.

3. 

____¢, ____¢, ____¢, ____¢, ____¢, ____¢

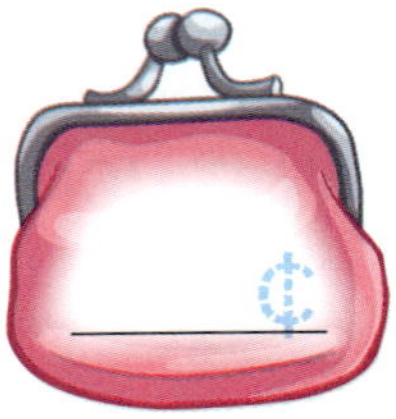

Problem Solving

4. Meg has 4 coins.
She wants to buy some cherries.
How much more money
does Meg need?

Meg needs ____¢ more.

Write About It

5. Anna has a group of coins on her desk. Tell how she can count on to find the total amount.

____

____

____

____

Name ____________________

LESSON 16-4

Count On by Dimes and Nickels

Count on to find the total amount.

Order the coins by value.

Count on to find the total.

10¢ , 20¢ , 30¢ , 40¢ , 45¢ , 50¢

Count on by 10s for dimes.

Count by 5s for nickels.

MORE PRACTICE

Count on. Write the total amount.

1.

10¢, 20¢, 30¢, 35¢, 40¢, 45¢

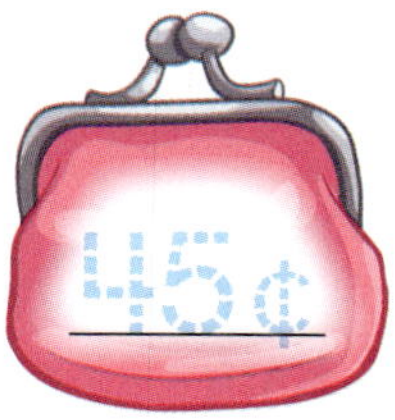

2.

___¢, ___¢, ___¢, ___¢

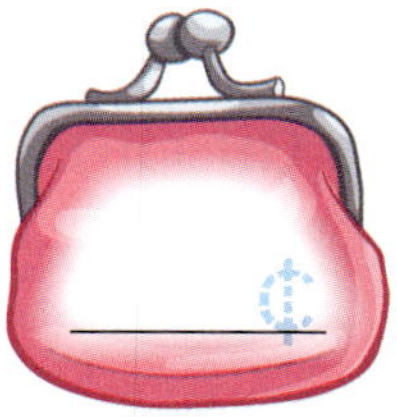

3.

___¢, ___¢, ___¢, ___¢, ___¢, ___¢

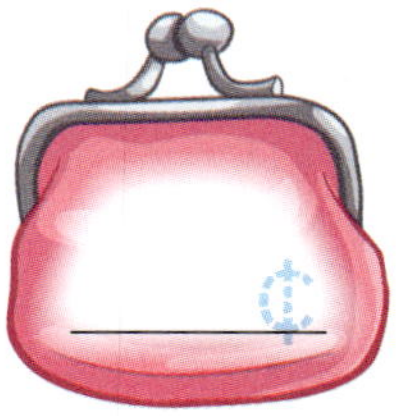

HOMEWORK

Count on. Write the total amount.

1. 

____¢, ____¢, ____¢, ____¢, ____¢

____¢

2. 

____¢, ____¢, ____¢, ____¢, ____¢

____¢

Problem Solving

3. Hal has 4 dimes. Jake has the same amount of dimes and 3 more nickels. How much money does Jake have?

Jake has ____¢.

Write About It

4. Jamal has 6 coins that total 50¢. They are all dimes and nickels. What coins does Jamal have? Tell how you know.

____

____

____

CHAPTER 16 Check Your Progress

Name ____________________

Find the correct answer.

1. Count on to find the total value.

A. 1¢
B. 4¢
C. 8¢

2. Find the total value.

5¢ + 5¢ + 5¢ + 5¢

A. 10¢
B. 20¢
C. 25¢

3. Find the total value.

10¢ + 1¢ + 1¢ + 1¢ + 1¢

A. 14¢
B. 21¢
C. 41¢

4. Count on to find the total value.

A. 4¢
B. 12¢
C. 16¢

5. Count by 10s to find the total value.

A. 15¢
B. 30¢
C. 40¢

6. Find the total value.

10¢ + 5¢ + 5¢

A. 20¢
B. 30¢
C. 40¢

Find the correct answer.

7. Find the total value.

____¢ + ____¢ + ____¢ +

____¢ + ____¢ + ____¢ +

____¢ + ____¢ + ____¢

= ____¢

8. Find the total value.

____¢ + ____¢ + ____¢ +

____¢ + ____¢ + ____¢ +

____¢ + ____¢ + ____¢

= ____¢

9. Count on to find the total value.

____¢

10. Select TWO groups that each have a value of 40¢.

A. 4 nickels

B. 4 dimes

C. 2 nickels, 2 dimes

D. 4 nickels, 2 dimes

11. Jen has 3 dimes and 1 nickel. How much money does she have?

Jen has ____¢.

12. How many nickels have the same value as this coin?

____ nickels

Name ____

One Dollar

Objective

- Identify and combine coins with total values up to one dollar.

Math Words

dollar

dollar sign ($)

Bella puts 4 quarters in her bank.
What is the total value of the 4 coins?

1 quarter = 25¢

2 quarters = 50¢

3 quarters = 75¢

4 quarters = 100¢

One dollar is worth 100 cents.

$1 = 100¢

This is a dollar sign.

4 quarters = 100¢ = $1

The total value of the 4 coins is $1.

PRACTICE

Circle the coins that show the amount.

1. $1

2. 50¢

PRACTICE

Write the value.

3. 

___¢ + ___¢ + ___¢ + ___¢ + ___¢ + ___¢ = ___¢

Problem Solving

4. Who has $1?

Nate

Carlos

Nate: ___¢ + ___¢ + ___¢ + ___¢ = ___¢

Carlos: ___¢ + ___¢ + ___¢ + ___¢ + ___¢ + ___¢

+ ___¢ = ___¢

__________ has $1.

Write About It

5. Denise has 100 pennies. She says she has $1.
Is she correct? Tell how you know.

____

____

Name ______________________________

One Dollar

1 quarter = 25¢

2 quarters = 50¢

3 quarters = 75¢

4 quarters = 100¢

One dollar is worth 100 cents.

$1 = 100¢

This is a dollar sign.

4 quarters = 100¢ = $1

 = 

MORE PRACTICE

Circle the coins that show the amount.

1. 100¢

2. 70¢

HOMEWORK

Write the value.

1. 

25¢ + 25¢ + 25¢ = 75¢

2. 

___¢ + ___¢ + ___¢ + ___¢ + ___¢ = ___¢

Problem Solving

3. Isabelle has 2 quarters and 3 dimes. She wants to buy an apple for 35¢. Does Isabelle have enough money? Tell how you know.

Isabelle __________ have enough money.

____

____

Write About It

4. Would you rather have 3 quarters or 6 dimes? Tell why.

____

____

Name ______________________

Objective

- Solve problems involving money by working backward.

Math Word

work backward

Problem Solving

Read › Plan › Solve › Check

Work Backward

Bob buys an apple for 35¢. He has 10¢ left. How much money did Bob have to start?

You can work backward to solve the problem.

Bob spent 35¢.

He has 10¢ left.

Add to find the total.

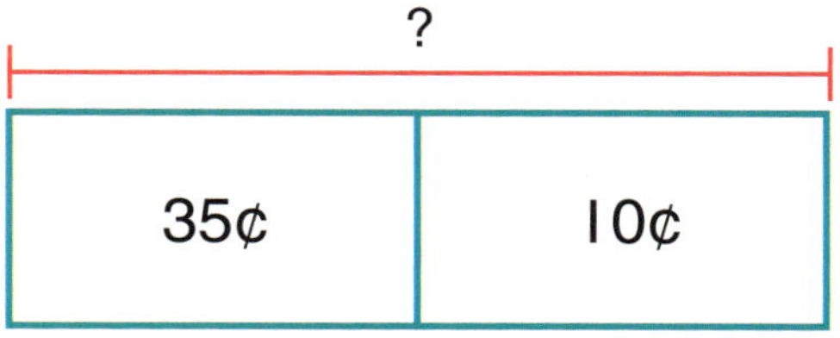

Bob started with 45¢.

35¢ + 10¢ = 45¢

PRACTICE

Work backward to solve the problem.

1. Jill spends 65¢ on pretzels. She has 20¢ left. How much money did Jill have to start?

   Jill had ______¢.

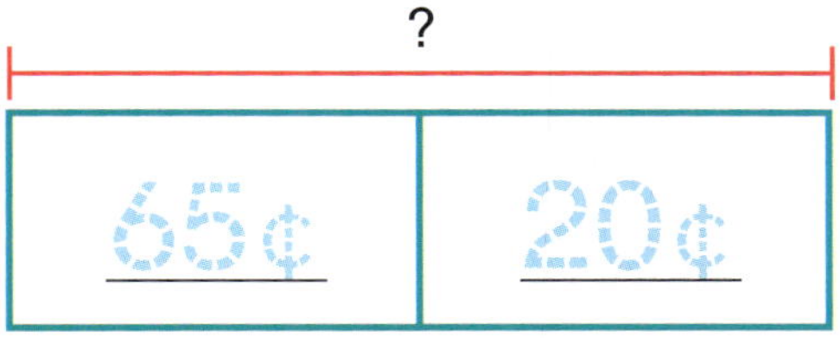

65¢ + 20¢ = ______¢

2. Tim buys some juice for 40¢. He has 25¢ left. How much money did Tim have to start?

   Tim had ______¢.

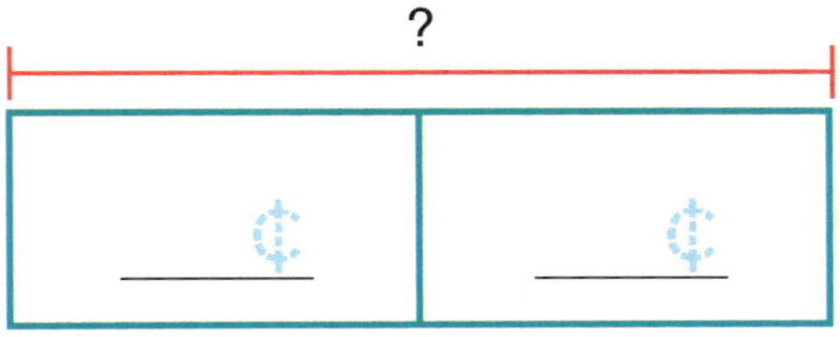

______¢ + ______¢ = ______¢

PRACTICE

Work backward to solve the problem.

3. Jamal buys a pencil for 11¢. He has 28¢ left. How much money did Jamal have to start?

Jamal had _____¢.

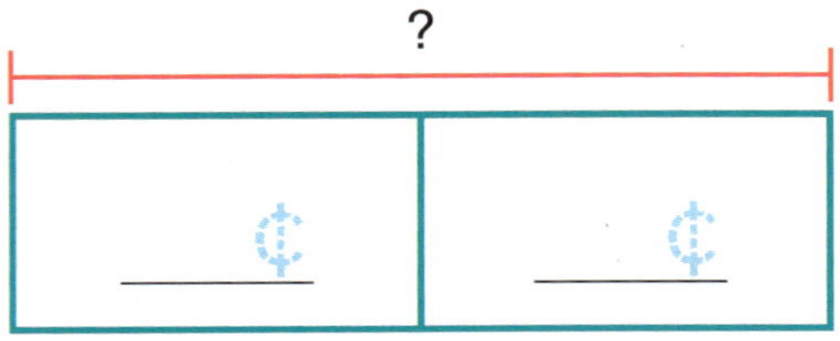

_____¢ + _____¢ = _____¢

4. Quinn buys an eraser for 30¢. He has 18¢ left. How much money did Quinn have to start?

Quinn had _____¢.

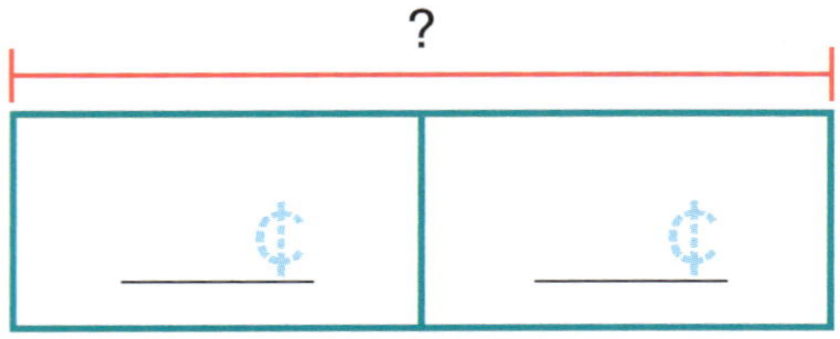

_____¢ + _____¢ = _____¢

5. Ava buys a marker for 50¢. Now she has 40¢. How much money did she have to spend?

Ava had _____¢ to spend.

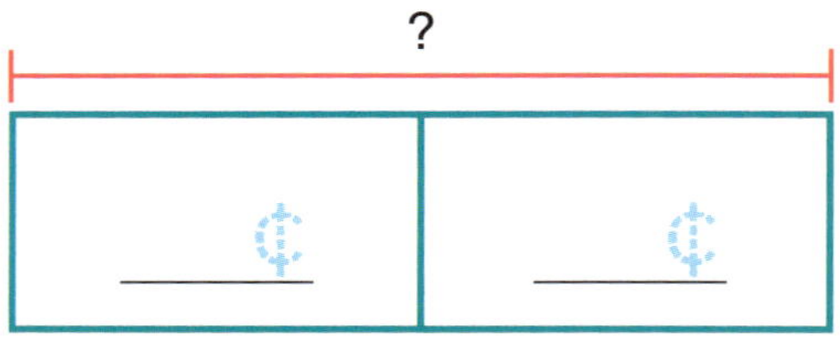

_____¢ + _____¢ = _____¢

Write About It

6. Mary buys crayons for 20¢. She has 50¢ left. How much money did Mary have before she bought the crayons? Tell how you know.

Mary had _____¢.

____

____

Name ______________________________

Problem Solving
Work Backward

Bob buys an apple for 35¢. He has 10¢ left. How much money did Bob have to start?

You can work backward to solve the problem.

Bob spent 35¢.

He has 10¢ left.

Add to find the total.

?	
35¢	10¢

Bob started with 45¢.

35¢ + 10¢ = 45¢

MORE PRACTICE

Work backward to solve the problem.

1. Rick spends 30¢ on grapes. He has 45¢ left. How much money did Rick have to start?

   Rick had ______¢.

?	
30¢	45¢

30¢ + 45¢ = ______¢

2. Lisa buys some carrots for 75¢. She has 20¢ left. How much money did Lisa have to start?

   Lisa had ______¢.

?	
______¢	______¢

______¢ + ______¢ = ______¢

MORE PRACTICE

Work backward to solve the problem.

3. Trisha buys eggs for 85¢. She has 12¢ left. How much money did Trisha have to start?

   Trisha had _____¢.

   ?

   | _____¢ | _____¢ |

   _____¢ + _____¢ = _____¢

4. Jen buys some melon for 61¢. She has 18¢ left. How much money did Jen have to start?

   Jen had _____¢.

   ?

   | _____¢ | _____¢ |

   _____¢ + _____¢ = _____¢

5. Alex had 90¢. He buys a banana. Now he has 60¢. How much does the banana cost?

   The banana costs _____¢.

   90¢

   | ? | _____¢ |

   _____¢ = _____¢ + _____¢

6. Amy had 78¢. She buys a pepper. Now Amy has 4¢. How much does the pepper cost?

   The pepper costs _____¢.

   _____¢

   | ? | _____¢ |

   _____¢ = _____¢ + _____¢

Name ______________________________

HOMEWORK

Work backward to solve the problem.

1. Nisa buys an eraser for 25¢. She has 63¢ left. How much money did Nisa have to start?

   Nisa had ____¢.

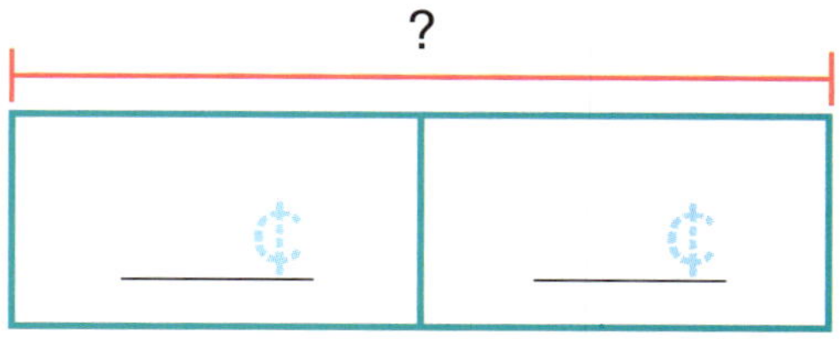

____¢ + ____¢ = ____¢

2. Josh buys some stickers for 62¢. He has 11¢ left. How much money did Josh have to start?

   Josh had ____¢.

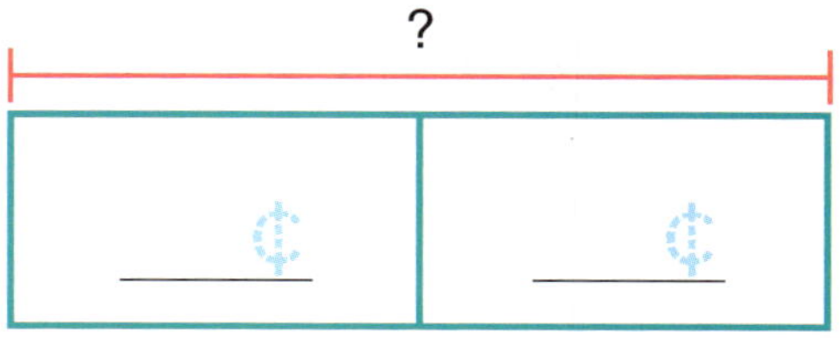

____¢ + ____¢ = ____¢

3. Jess had 98¢. He buys some paint. Now he has 24¢. How much does the paint cost?

   The paint costs ____¢.

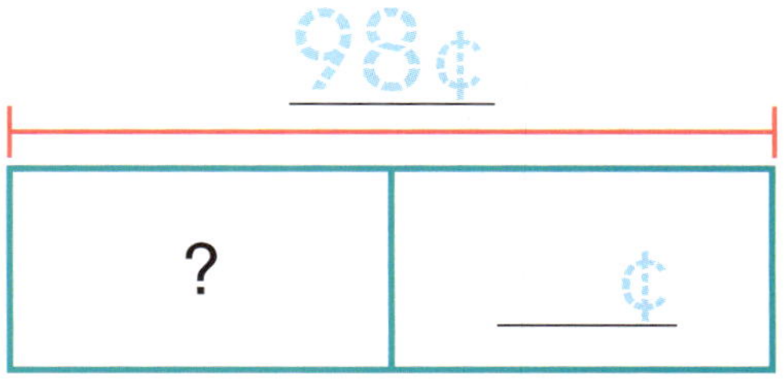

____¢ = ____¢ + ____¢

4. Jared had 75¢. He buys a notebook. Now Jared has 25¢. How much does the notebook cost?

   The notebook costs ____¢.

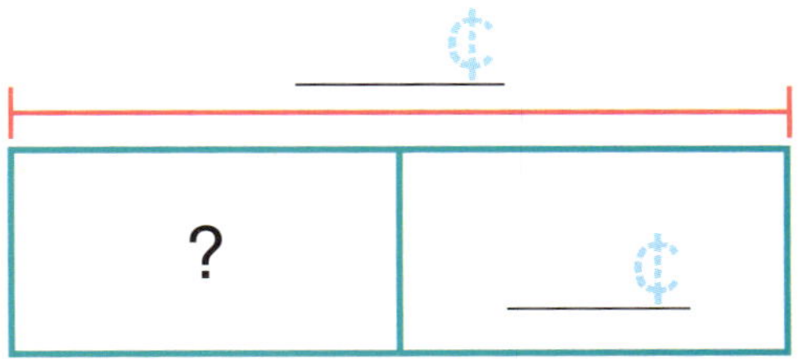

____¢ = ____¢ + ____¢

HOMEWORK

Work backward to solve the problem.

5. Pete buys a glue stick for 50¢. He has 28¢ left. How much money did Pete have to start?

Pete had ______¢.

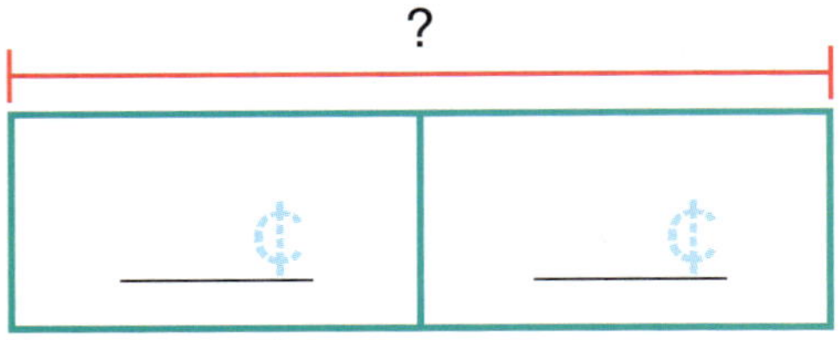

____¢ + ____¢ = ____¢

6. Niki buys a pencil case for 70¢. She has 30¢ left. How much money did Niki have to start?

Niki had ______¢.

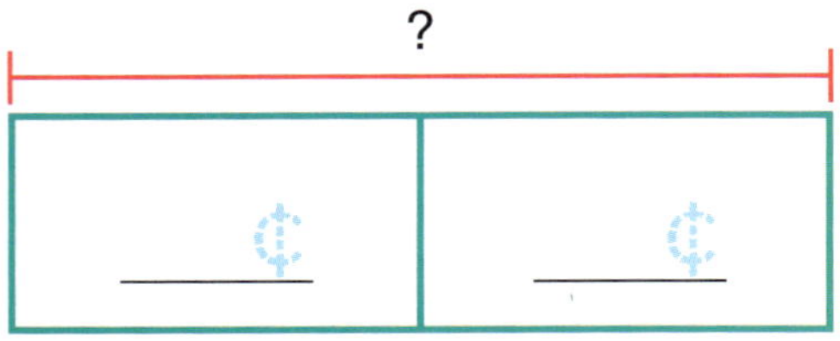

____¢ + ____¢ = ____¢

7. Mary had 85¢. She buys a pen. Now she has 65¢. How much does the pen cost?

The pen costs ______¢.

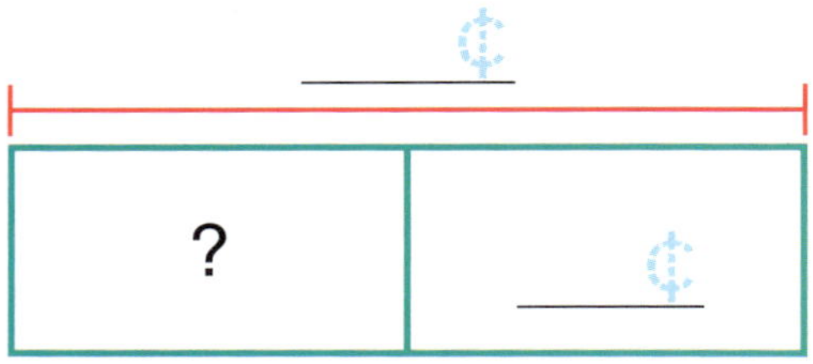

____¢ = ____¢ + ____¢

Write About It

8. Lee buys a bracelet for 22¢. He has 64¢ left. How much money did he have before he bought the bracelet? Tell how you know.

____

____

____

CHAPTER 16

Review

Name ______________________________

Find the correct answer.

1. Find the total.

1¢ + 1¢ + 1¢ + 1¢

A. 1¢
B. 4¢
C. 8¢

2. Find the total.

5¢ + 5¢ + 5¢ + 5¢ + 5¢

A. 10¢
B. 20¢
C. 25¢

3. Find the total.

10¢ + 10¢ + 1¢ + 1¢ + 1¢

A. 23¢
B. 14¢
C. 5¢

4. Find the total.

5¢ + 5¢ + 5¢ + 1¢ + 1¢

A. 5¢
B. 15¢
C. 17¢

5. Count on by 10s to find the total.

A. 25¢
B. 40¢
C. 50¢

6. Count on to find the total.

A. 40¢
B. 35¢
C. 30¢

Find the correct answer.

7. Find the total.

_____ + _____ + _____ + _____

_____ + _____ + _____ + _____

= _____¢

8. Find the total.

_____ + _____ + _____ + _____

+ _____

= _____¢

9. Which amount does NOT equal $1?

A. 4 quarters
B. 10 dimes
C. 2 quarters, 10 nickels
D. 2 nickels, 8 dimes

10. Select TWO groups that each have a value of 50¢.

A. 5 nickels
B. 5 dimes
C. 2 quarters
D. 4 nickels, 1 dime

11. Sam has 2 quarters and 1 nickel. Rowan has 1 dime and 6 nickels. Who has 55¢?

_______________ has 55¢.

12. Select TWO groups that each have a value of $1.

A. 9 dimes, 2 nickels
B. 5 dimes, 1 quarter
C. 3 quarters, 1 dime
D. 2 quarters, 5 dimes

Name ______________________________

1. Stella has saved some coins.
She wants to take $1 to buy things at the school store.

Fill in the table with the number of each coin Stella could take to school.

$1 Total Amount	
	Number of Coins
 Nickels	
 Dimes	
 Quarters	

2. Stella wants to spend all of her $1 at the store.
What can Stella buy?

Eraser Pencil Notebook Crayons Sharpener

____

____

____

CHAPTER 16
Fluency Practice

Name ______________________________

Find the correct answer.

1. Find the total.

_____ + _____ + _____

= _____¢

2. Find the total.

_____ + _____ + _____ + _____

= _____¢

3. Subtract.

18 − 2

A. 16
B. 17
C. 20
D. 21

4. Add.

$$\begin{array}{r} 8 \\ +\,8 \\ \hline \end{array}$$

A. 14
B. 15
C. 16
D. 19

5. Find the missing addend.

5 + ? = 14

A. 9
B. 10
C. 13
D. 14

6. Which TWO pairs of numbers have a difference of 9?

A. 12 and 3
B. 10 and 1
C. 9 and 8
D. 19 and 8

A

add To find how many in all.

2 + 1 = 3

addend A number that is added to another number or numbers.

2 + 4 = 6

addend + addend = sum

addition equation An addition number sentence with an equal sign.

3 + 2 = 5

addition fact An equation of the form part + part = whole.

3 + 4 = 7

part + part = whole

addition strategy A plan or method for solving addition problems.

B

bar model A diagram that uses a series of rectangles to represent the parts and the whole of a problem.

Total number of 🐿 ●●●●●●

🐿 in the tree at first	🐿 that run up the tree
●●●●	?

break apart To put into smaller groups.

Write the addends.	3 + 5	●●●+●●●●●
Break apart 5.	3 + 3 + 2	●●●+●●●+●●

C

cent (¢) 1/100 of a dollar.

circle A perfectly round shape with no sides and no corners.

closed shape A shape with sides that are all connected, so that the shape has no gaps.

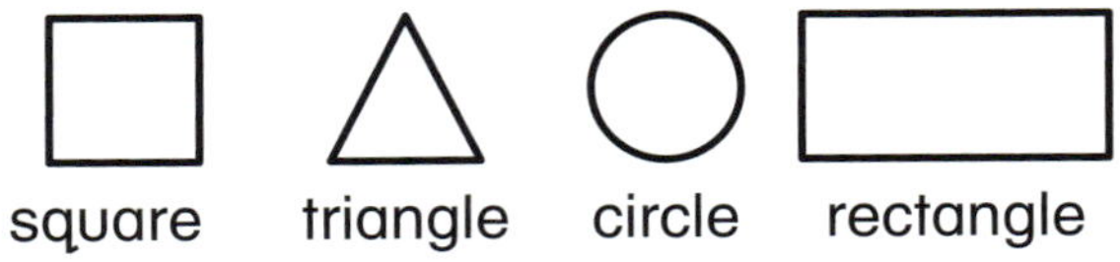

compare To describe a number as greater than (>), less than (<), or equal to (=) another number.

53 and 47.	21 and 25.	34 and 34.
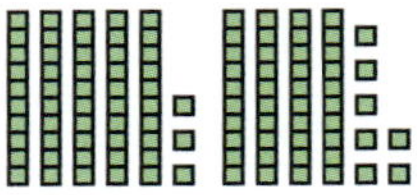	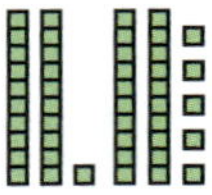	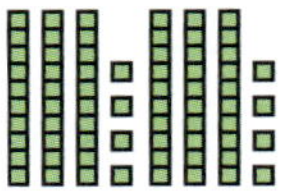
53 is greater than 47.	21 is less than 25.	They are equal.
$53 > 47$	$21 < 25$	$34 = 34$

cone A solid shape with one curved surface and one flat surface shaped like a circle.

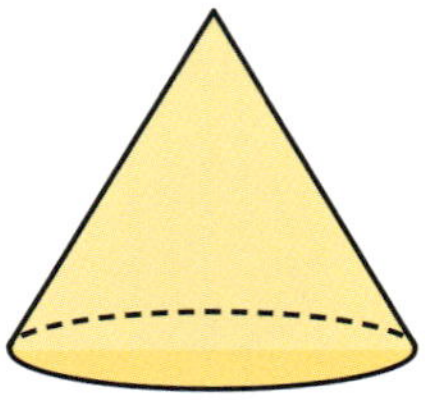

corner The point at which sides of a two-dimensional shape or edges of a three-dimensional shape meet.

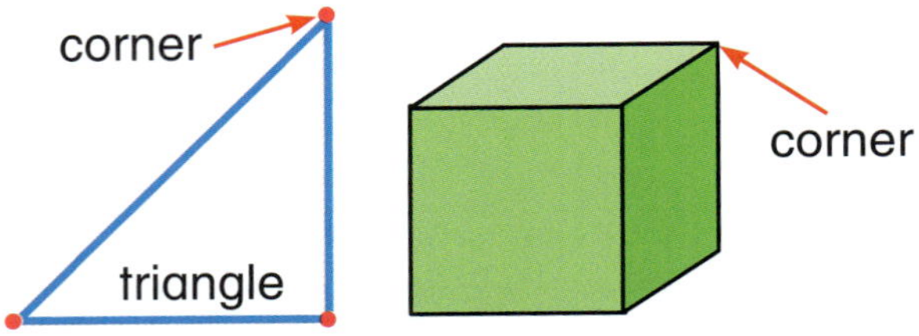

count by 10s To count by adding 10 to the previous number in order to get the next number.

10, 20, 30, 40, 50, 60, 70…

count by 2s To count by adding 2 to the previous number in order to get the next number.

2, 4, 6, 8, 10, 12, 14…

count by 5s To count by adding 5 to the previous number in order to get the next number.

5, 10, 15, 20, 25, 30, 35…

count on To start at a given number and count forward from that number.

7 + 3 = ?

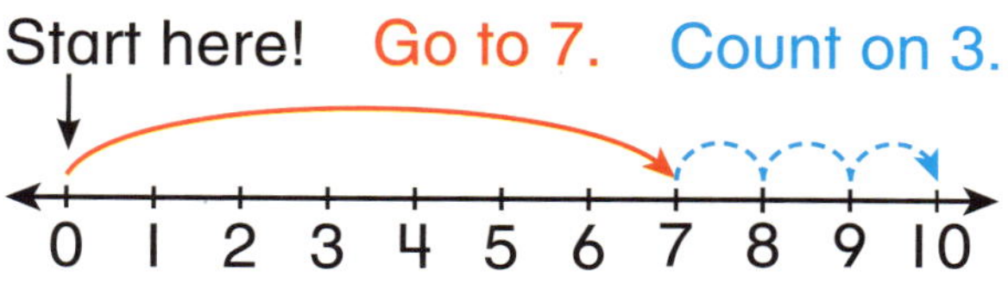

7 + 3 = 10

cube A solid shape with 6 flat surfaces all shaped like squares.

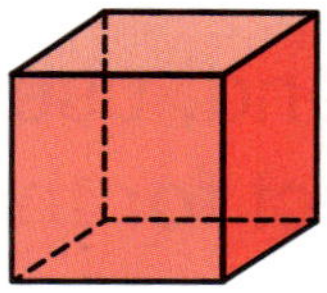

curved Not straight and bending without angles.

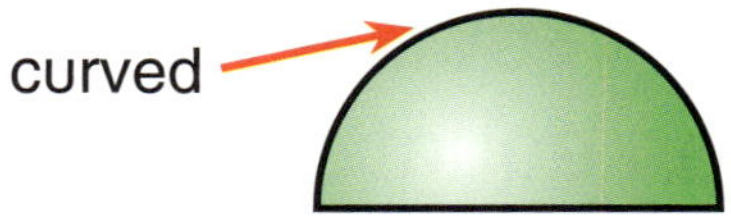

curved surface On a three-dimensional shape, a surface that is not flat.

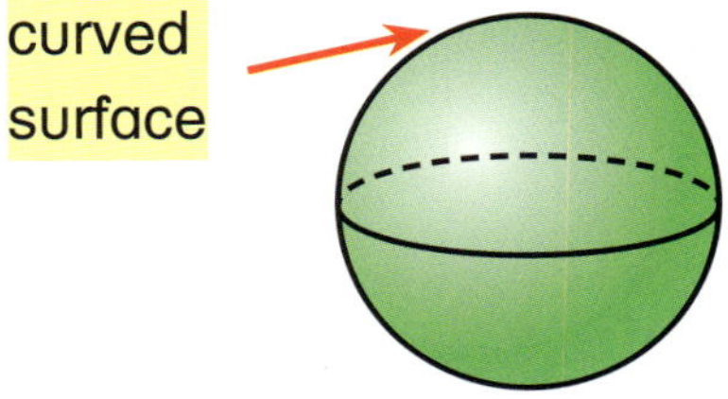

cylinder A solid shape with one curved surface and two flat surfaces shaped like circles.

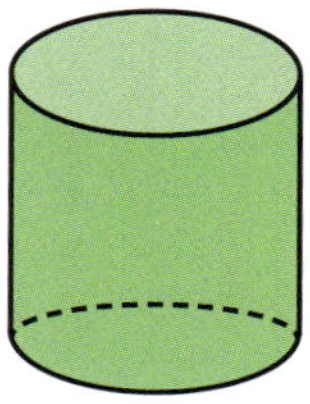

D

data A set of collected values or information.

day The period of light between sunrise and sunset.

Day

decompose To break into smaller parts or groups.

26

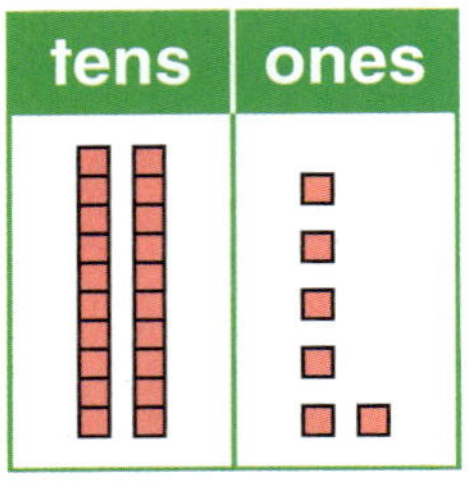

2 tens 6 ones

difference The result of subtracting.

6 − 4 = 2

↑ difference

digit 0, 1, 2, 3, 4, 5, 6, 7, 8, or 9.

47

first digit ↗ ↖ second digit

dime A coin that is worth 10 cents.

dollar ($) An amount equal to 100 cents

doubles + 1 strategy To find a sum where one addend is 1 more than the other addend, use the doubles fact for the lesser addend and add 1.

2 + 3 = 5

doubles fact A two-addend addition equation in which both addends are the same.

2 + 2 = 4

E

edge The line segment where two faces of a three-dimensional figure meet.

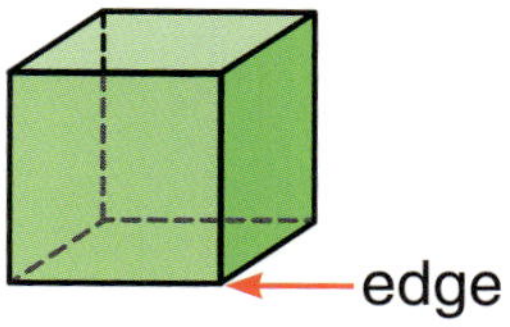

equal shares Pieces of one whole that are the same size.

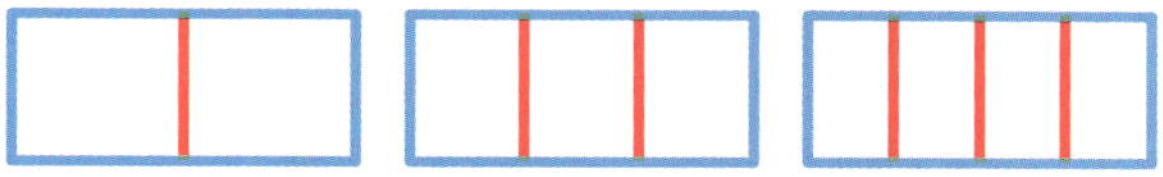

equal sign The symbol =.

$$8 - 1 = 7$$

equation A number sentence with an equal sign (=) that shows the value on the left side is the same as the value on the right side.

$$5 + 2 = 7$$

estimate An approximate answer; to find an answer that is close to the exact answer.

expanded form A form that shows a number written as the sum of the place values of each digit.

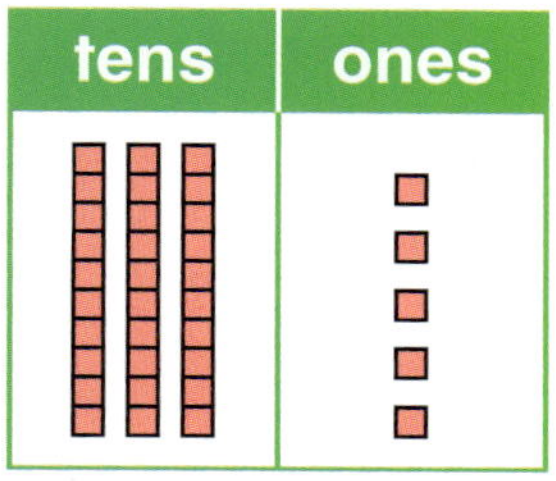

35

30 + 5

F

face A flat surface with straight sides on a three-dimensional shape.

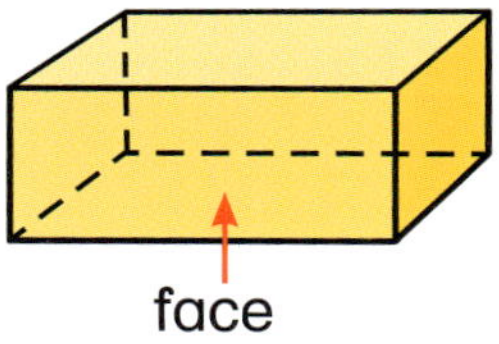

fact family A set of related facts for a given group of numbers.

$4 + 6 = 10$ $6 + 4 = 10$
$10 - 6 = 4$ $10 - 4 = 6$

false Inaccurate; not true.

fewer A lesser number of.

flat surface The face of a three-dimensional shape that does not curve.

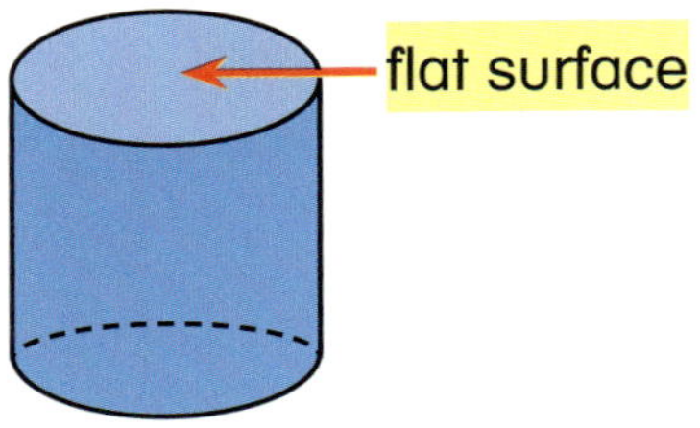

fourth (fourths) One part of a whole that is divided into 4 equal parts.

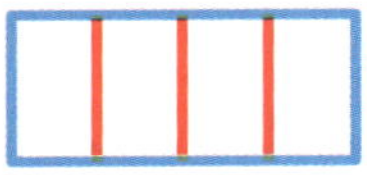

G

greater than (>) More than, having a larger value than.

group To put together.

guess and test A strategy where a guess of the correct answer is made and then tested.

H

half (halves) One part of a whole that is divided into 2 equal parts.

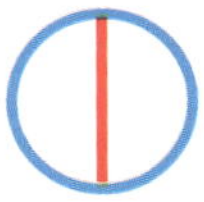

half hour A measure of time equal to 30 minutes.

half past Describes one half hour or 30 minutes past an hour.

half-hour pattern A pattern that shows time by half hours.

hexagon A flat shape with 6 sides and 6 corners.

hour A unit of time that equals 60 minutes.

hour hand The short hand on an analog clock that shows the hour.

hour pattern A pattern that shows time by hours.

hundred 1 hundred = 10 tens = 100 ones.

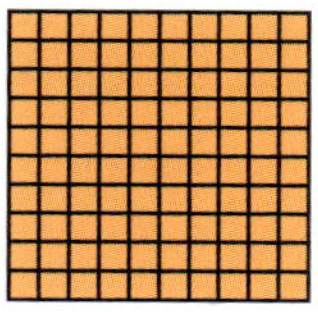

hundred chart A chart that shows the numbers 1 through 100.

1	2	3	4	5	6	7	8	9	10
11	12	13	14	15	16	17	18	19	20
21	22	23	24	25	26	27	28	29	30
31	32	33	34	35	36	37	38	39	40
41	42	43	44	45	46	47	48	49	50
51	52	53	54	55	56	57	58	59	60
61	62	63	64	65	66	67	68	69	70
71	72	73	74	75	76	77	78	79	80
81	82	83	84	85	86	87	88	89	90
91	92	93	94	95	96	97	98	99	100

I

inch (in.) A customary unit of measure to describe length. 12 in. = 1 ft.

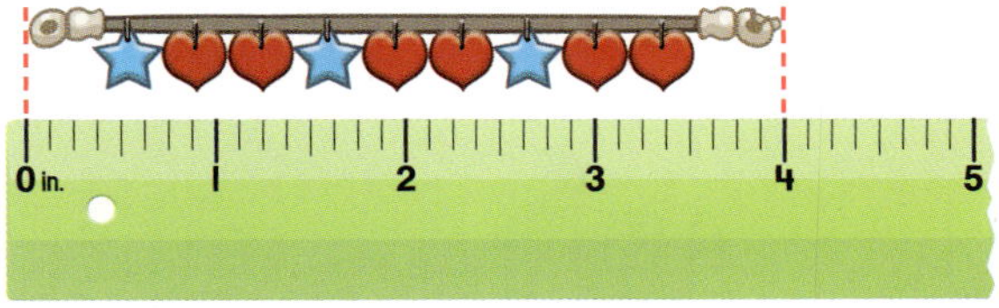

inch ruler A tool used to measure length in inches.

L

length Measurement along a straight line from end to end.

The leaf is 4 [cube] long.

less than (<) Fewer than; having a smaller value than.

logical reasoning Using correct thought processes and steps to solve a problem.

longest Greatest in length.

M

measure To describe an object with a number by using a tool such as a ruler.

minus sign (−) A symbol that means to subtract or take away.

$8 - 2 = 6$

minute hand The long hand on an analog clock that shows the minute.

missing addend An unknown addend in an addition problem.

$5 + ? = 7$

missing addend

model A diagram or picture that represents a problem or helps to solve a problem.

more A greater number or amount of.

N

nickel A coin worth 5 cents.

night The period of darkness between sunset and sunrise.

Night

O

120 chart A chart that shows the numbers 1 through 120.

1	2	3	4	5	6	7	8	9	10
11	12	13	14	15	16	17	18	19	20
21	22	23	24	25	26	27	28	29	30
31	32	33	34	35	36	37	38	39	40
41	42	43	44	45	46	47	48	49	50
51	52	53	54	55	56	57	58	59	60
61	62	63	64	65	66	67	68	69	70
71	72	73	74	75	76	77	78	79	80
81	82	83	84	85	86	87	88	89	90
91	92	93	94	95	96	97	98	99	100
101	102	103	104	105	106	107	108	109	110
111	112	113	114	115	116	117	118	119	120

ones 10 ones = 1 ten

1 ten or 10 ones.

open shape A shape in which not all sides connect.

order property Changing the order of addends does not change the sum.

$$2 + 3 = 5$$
$$3 + 2 = 5$$

P

part Some but not all of something.

partition To divide into parts.

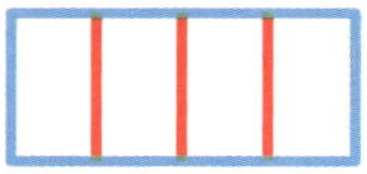

penny A coin worth 1 cent.

picture graph A graph that uses pictures to represent numbers of real-world objects.

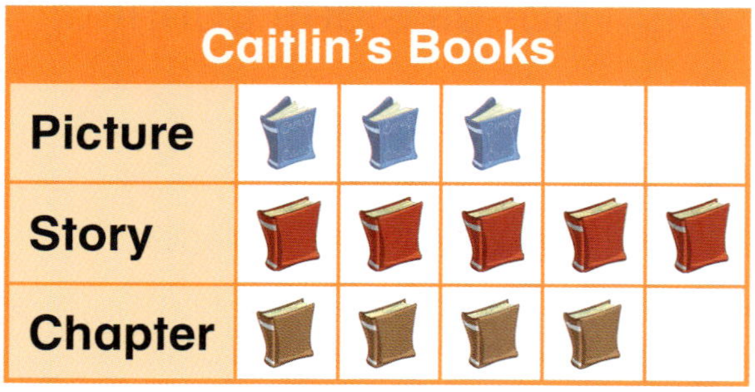

place value The value of a digit depending on its position, or place, in a number.

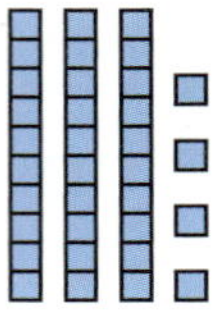

tens	ones
3	4

plane shape A two-dimensional shape. Plane shapes have width and breadth but not thickness. They can be open or closed.

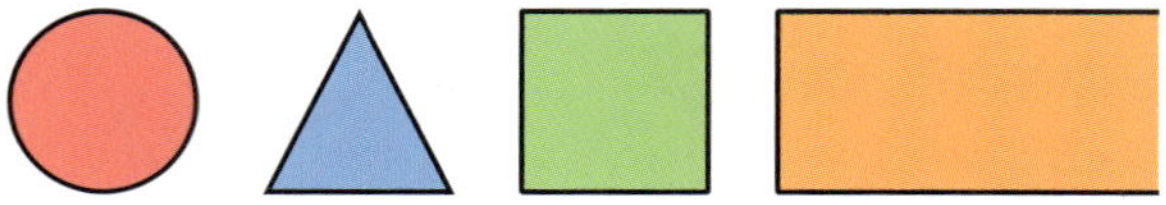

plus sign (+) A symbol that means to add.

$$6 + 2 = 8$$

Q

quarter A coin worth 25 cents.

quarter of One of four equal parts.

R

reasoning The act of forming conclusions from facts or information.

rectangle A shape with 4 sides and 4 corners.

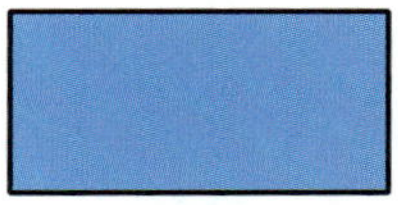

rectangular prism A solid figure with six rectangular faces.

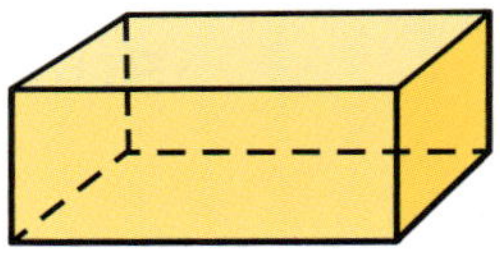

related addition facts Addition facts that use the same numbers.

$$3 + 4 = 7$$
$$4 + 3 = 7$$

related subtraction facts Subtraction facts that use the same numbers.

$$7 - 3 = 4$$
$$7 - 4 = 3$$

rhombus A parallelogram with four sides of equal length.

ruler A tool used to measure length, usually labeled in inches along one edge and centimeters on the opposite edge.

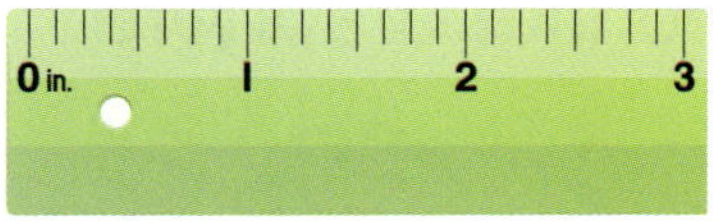

S

shortest Least in length or height.

side A line segment that forms part of a shape.

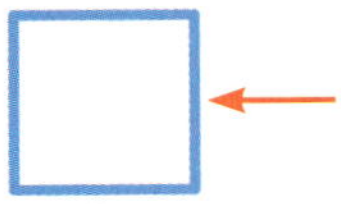

solid shape A shape that is three-dimensional.

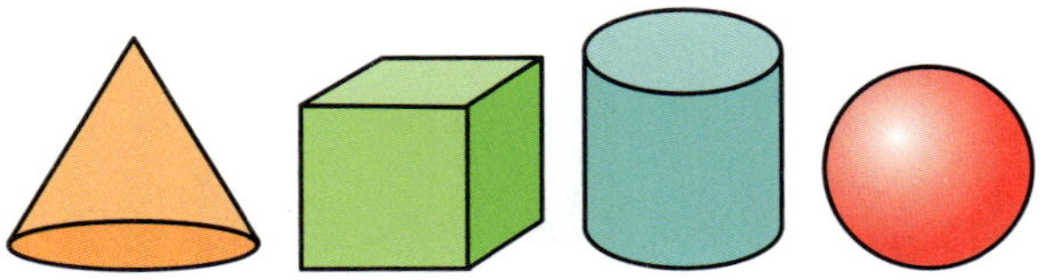

solve To find the correct answer to a problem.

sphere A round three-dimensional figure. For example, a baseball is shaped like a sphere.

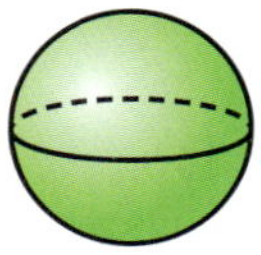

square A shape with 4 sides of equal length and 4 corners.

subtract To take away; to find how many are left.

5 − 1 = ?

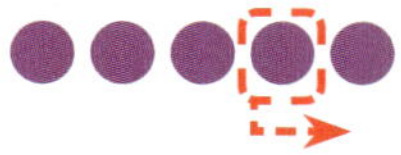

5 ● in all

Take 1 ● from 5 ●.

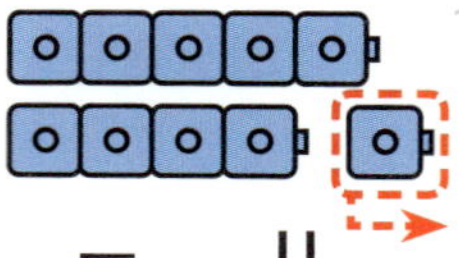

5	−	1	=	4
	minus		equals	difference

subtraction equation A subtraction number sentence with an equal sign.

6 − 1 = 5

subtraction fact An equation of the form whole − part = part.

7	−	4	=	3
whole	−	part	=	part

sum The result of adding.

2 + 4 = 6

↑ sum

T

tally chart A chart that uses tally marks to show numbers of different objects or responses.

Zoo Animals		
Animal	**Tally**	**Total**
Penguin	|||	3
Bear	𝍸 |	6
Seal	𝍸 ||	7

tally mark A mark used in a tally chart to show a count of objects or responses.

ten rod A 10-block made of 10 units in one long rod.

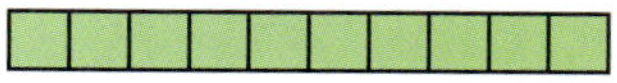

ten-frame A rectangular chart with 2 rows and 5 columns that is used to represent numbers less than or equal to 10.

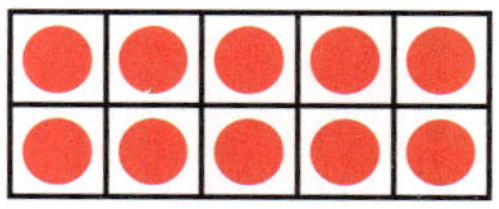

tens number A number with tens and no ones.

50

three-dimensional shape A solid shape that has measurements of length, width, and height.

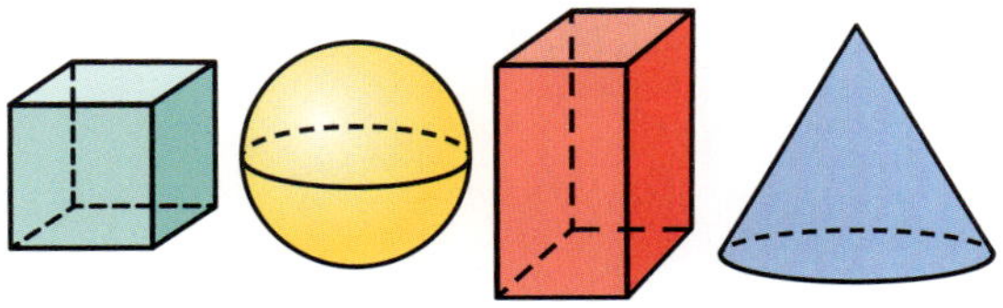

total amount The number of everything counted.

trapezoid A quadrilateral with exactly one pair of parallel sides.

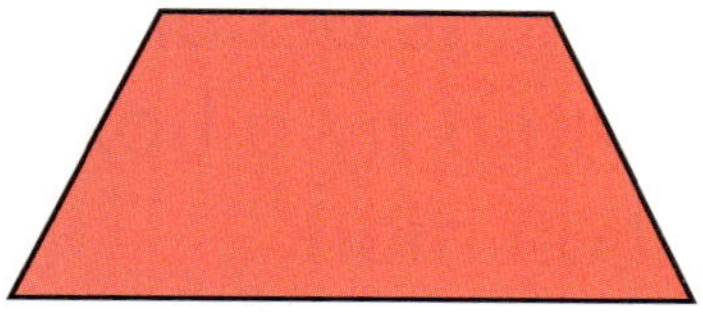

triangle A shape with 3 sides and 3 corners.

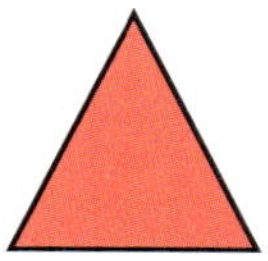

true Accurate; correct.

two-digit number A number consisting of tens and ones.

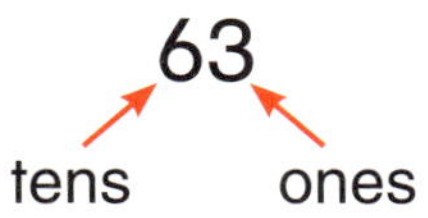

U

unit A particular amount that is used as a standard for counting or measuring.

1 inch is a unit for measuring length.

unknown addend An addend whose value is not known and is usually represented by a box or a question mark.

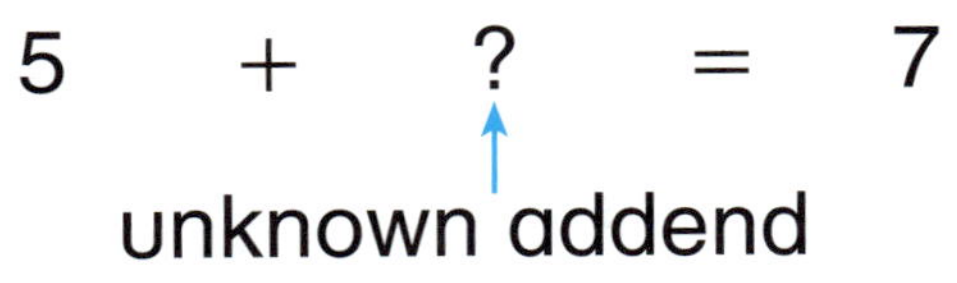

V

vertex (vertices) The point where three edges of a solid shape meet.

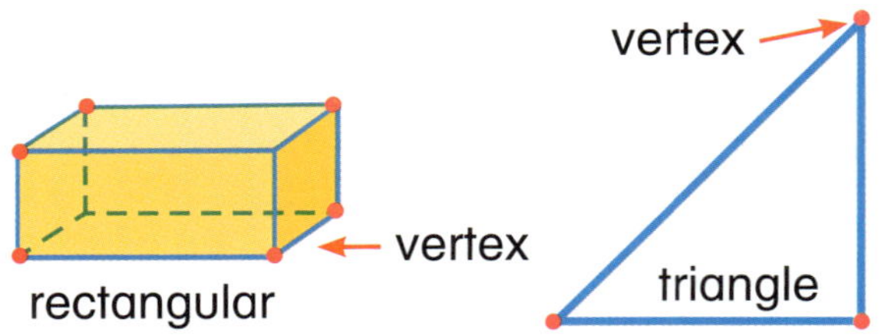

W

whole All of something.

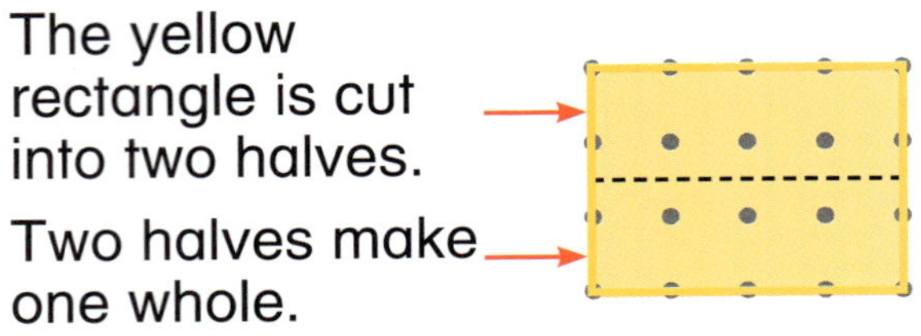

work backward A strategy where the answer is known and the unknown is found by reversing the operations or steps in the problem.

Z

zero The word name for the numeral 0.

There are 0 (zero) muffins in the basket.

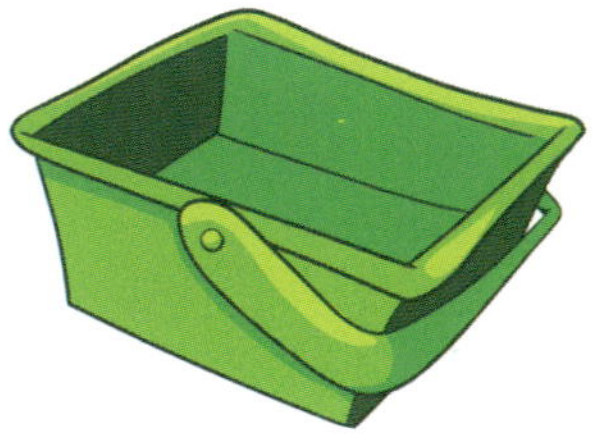

tens	ones

tens	ones

tens	ones

tens	ones

tens	ones

tens	ones

tens	ones

tens	ones

tens	ones

tens	ones

tens	ones

tens	ones

tens	ones

tens	ones

tens	ones

dimes	pennies

dimes	pennies

h	t	o

h	t	o

dimes	pennies

dimes	pennies

h	t	o

h	t	o

Addition and Subtraction Frames

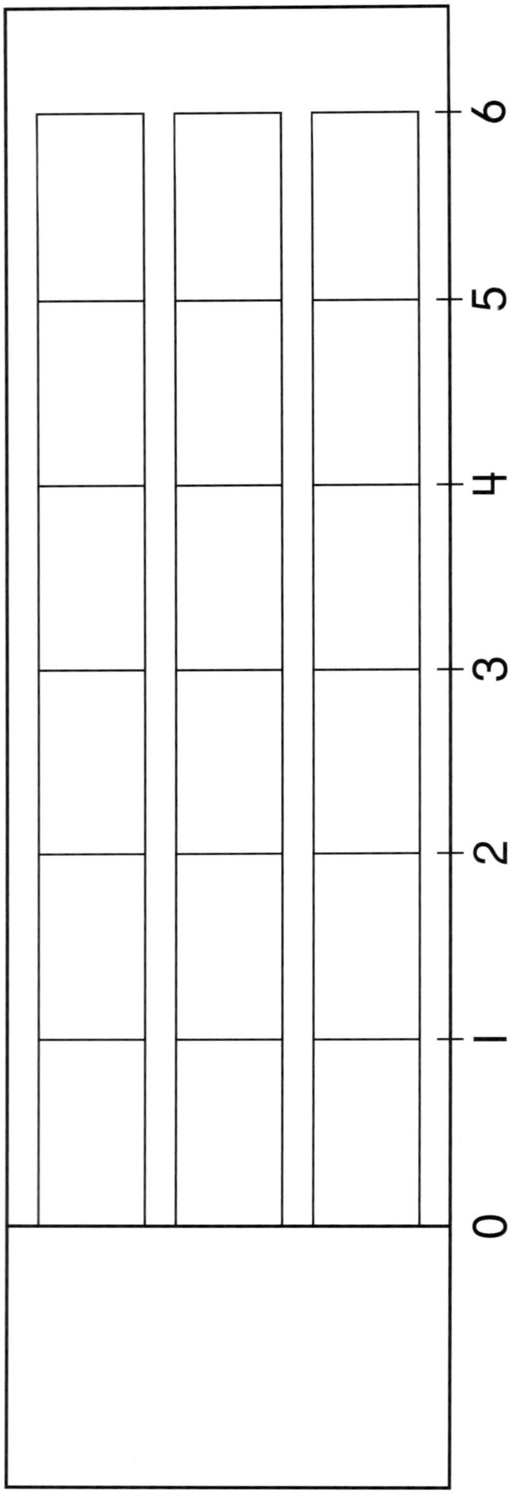

Blank Graphs

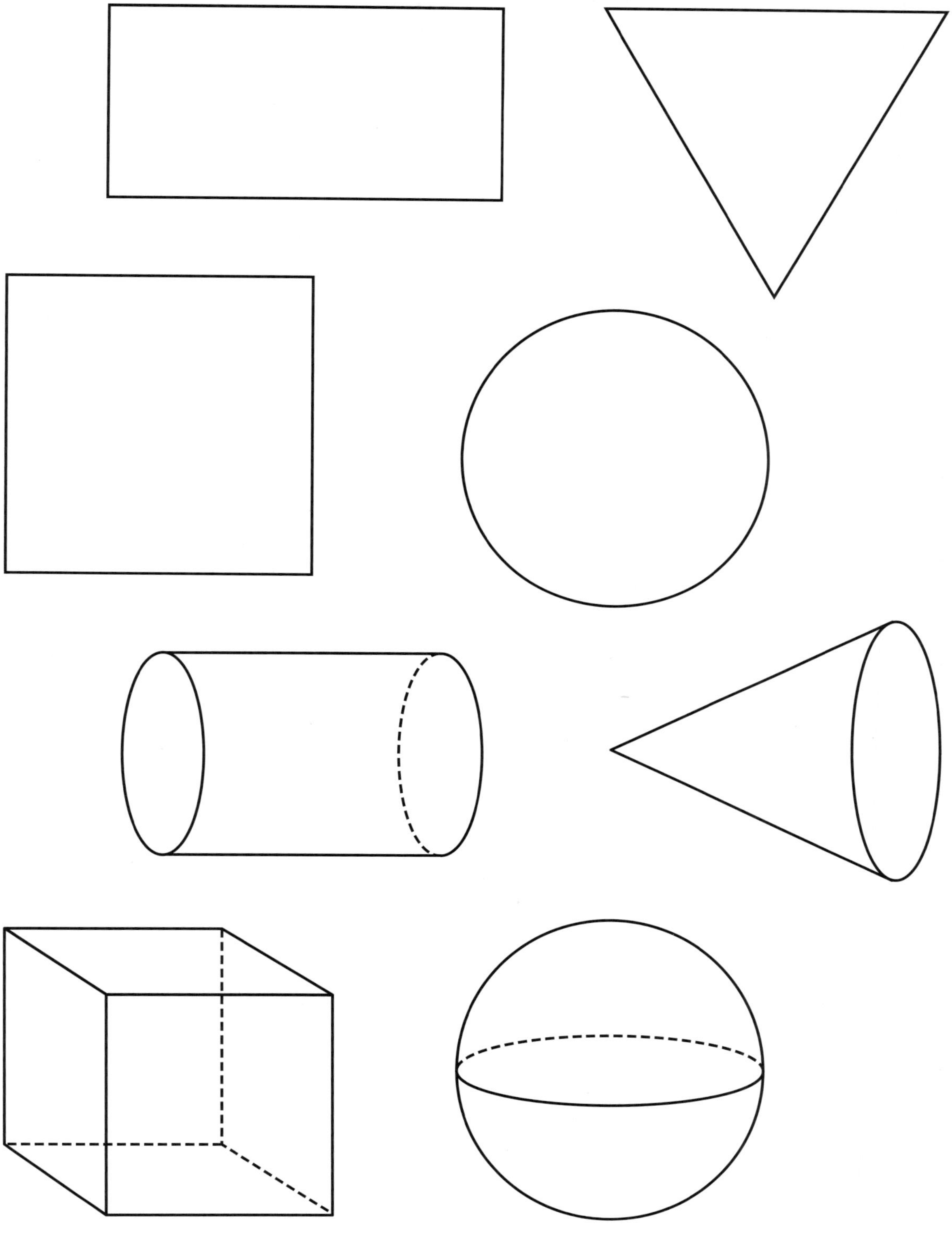

Plane and Solid Figures

Dot Paper

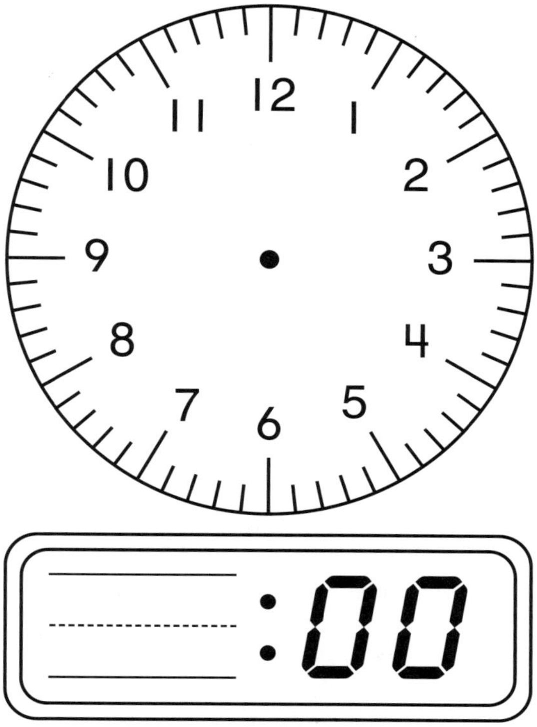
12 1 2 3 4 5 6 7 8 9 10 11
:00
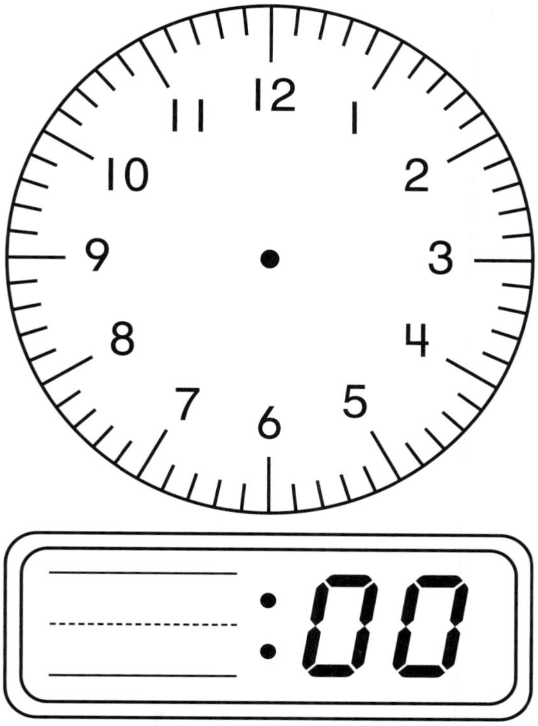
12 1 2 3 4 5 6 7 8 9 10 11
:00
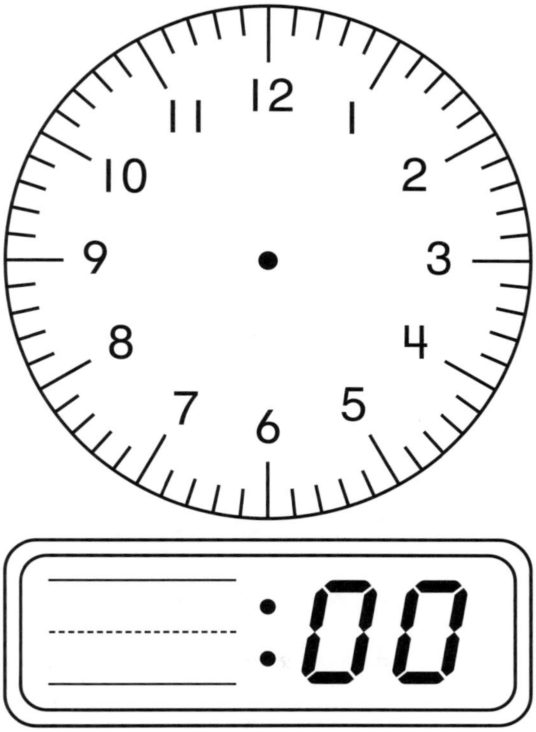
12 1 2 3 4 5 6 7 8 9 10 11
:00
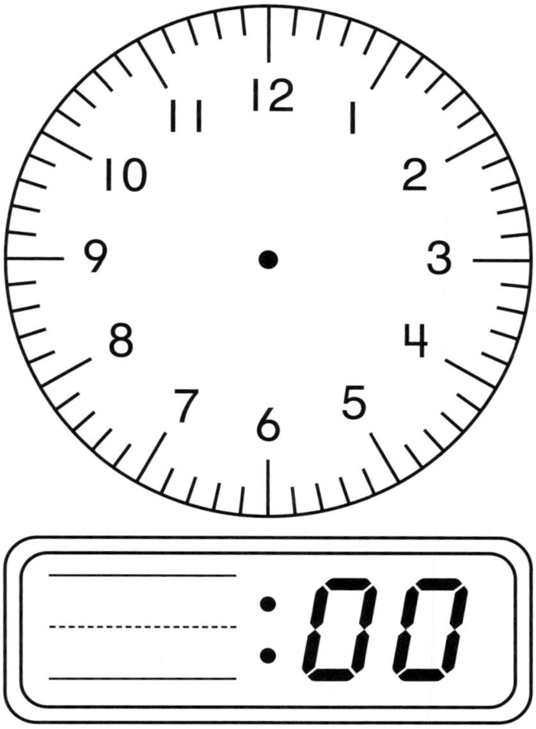
12 1 2 3 4 5 6 7 8 9 10 11
:00

LIBERTY
IN GOD WE TRUST
2016
UNITED STATES OF AMERICA
QUARTER DOLLAR
NEW YORK
1788
GATEWAY TO FREEDOM
2001
E PLURIBUS UNUM
MONTICELLO
FIVE CENTS
ONE CENT
ONE DIME

THE UNITED STATES OF AMERICA
F 05811561 B
ONE DOLLAR

20
EC 14018221 A
TWENTY DOLLARS

5
CF 01336159 C
THE UNITED STATES OF AMERICA
FIVE
DOLLARS

50
AC 63034936 A
THE UNITED STATES OF AMERICA
DOLLARS

10
CB 16425963 C
THE UNITED STATES OF AMERICA
TEN
DOLLARS

100
ONE HUNDRED DOLLARS
FEDERAL RESERVE NOTE
LB 19262752 K
THE UNITED STATES OF AMERICA
FRANKLIN